CONFLICT AT
ROME

Social Order and Hierarchy in Early Christianity

CONFLICT AT ROME

JAMES S. JEFFERS

FORTRESS PRESS   MINNEAPOLIS

CONFLICT AT ROME
Social Order and Hierarchy in Early Christianity

Photo credits:
p. 78 (top): The Basilica of St. Clement, excavations, Christian house of the first century. Sogeman MARZARI S.p.A. Schio; Fotocelere s.r.l. Milan
p. 78 (bottom): Basilica of St. Clement, excavations, a room in the Christian house, first century. Sogema MARZARI S.p.A. Schio; Fotocelere s.r.l. Milan
p. 84: Basilica of St. Clement, excavatins. Temple of Mithras, second century. KINA ITALIA Milano

Interior and cover design: Publishers' WorkGroup

Library of Congress Cataloging-in-Publication Data

Jeffers, James S., 1956-
    Conflict at Rome : social order and hierarchy in early
  Christianity / James S. Jeffers.
        p.   cm.
    Includes bibliographical references and index.
    ISBN 0-8006-2469-6 (alk. paper) :
    1. Rome (Italy)—Church history.   2. Clement I, Pope.   First
  epistle to the Corinthians.   3. Hermas, 2nd cent. Shepherd.
  I. Title.
  BR878.R7J44   1991
  274.5'63201—dc20   90–45965
                                                                          CIP

Manufactured in the U.S.A.   AF 1–2469
95   94   93   92   91   1   2   3   4   5   6   7   8   9   10

CONTENTS

ILLUSTRATIONS

PREFACE

An interdisciplinary work of this nature would not be possible without the active assistance of a number of persons. I wish to thank Richard I. Frank and Lamar M. Hill of the University of California, Irvine, for their helpful contributions. Professor Frank, whom I am proud to call mentor and friend, has provided encouragement and invaluable insights during each phase of this project. The close readings given early versions of this manuscript by Ronald F. Hock of the University of Southern California have helped me strengthen both prose and argument. S. Scott Bartchy of the University of California, Los Angeles, helped direct my thinking during early stages of the research. Bryan R. Wilson helped me understand his sociological model of religious orientations and how it might apply to antiquity. Thanks are also due to the University of California for providing a research grant. I want to thank Fr. Paul Lawlor, resident archaeologist at the Basilica of San Clemente, for helping me better understand the significance of the remains under the basilica, and for his hospitality during my 1985 trip to Rome. Philippe Pergola of the Pontifical Institute of Christian Archaeology provided valuable assistance in my research of the Christian catacombs of Rome, and particularly in my study of the Catacomb of Domitilla. I am grateful to Theodore F. Brunner for assisting my use of the *Thesaurus Linguae Graecae* computer database of ancient Greek literature at the University of California, Irvine. My contact with scholars through the Social History of Early Christianity Study Group and the Social Sciences and the New Testament Section, both part of the Society of Biblical Literature, has stimulated my thinking and forced me to probe deeper into the true nature of early Roman Christianity. In particular, I would like to thank Peter Lampe, Carolyn Osiek, David L. Balch, L. Michael White, and Bruce Malina.

Quotations from ancient authors are rendered in accordance with standard English translations when available, and with the Loeb

Classical Library when possible. At times (and where noted) I have provided my own translation. Unless otherwise indicated, Scripture quotations are from the New International Version. Except where noted, the Greek and English texts of the *Shepherd of Hermas* and *1 Clement* conform to the Loeb Classical Library edition of the Apostolic Fathers. In references to the *Shepherd of Hermas,* I have used the older system (also followed by the Loeb Classical Library), based on the traditional division of the *Shepherd* into *Visions, Mandates,* and *Similitudes.* Some scholars have adopted a system, developed in 1956 by Molly Whittaker, which ignores the traditional three-part division. This new system is used in the *Thesaurus Linguae Graecae*'s text of the *Shepherd of Hermas.* Below is a conversion key for those more familiar with Whittaker's system.

SHEPHERD OF HERMAS NUMBERING SYSTEMS

Old	New	Old	New
Vis. 1.1–4	= 1–4	*Mand.* 10.1–3	= 40–42
Vis. 2.1–4	= 5–8	*Mand.* 11	= 43
Vis. 3.1–13	= 9–21	*Mand.* 12.1–6	= 44–49
Vis. 4.1–3	= 22–24		
Vis. 5	= 25	*Sim.* 1	= 50
		Sim. 2	= 51
Mand. 1	= 26	*Sim.* 3	= 52
Mand. 2	= 27	*Sim.* 4	= 53
Mand. 3	= 28	*Sim.* 5.1–7	= 54–60
Mand. 4.1–4	= 29–32	*Sim.* 6.1–5	= 61–65
Mand. 5.1–2	= 33–34	*Sim.* 7	= 66
Mand. 6.1–2	= 35–36	*Sim.* 8.1–11	= 67–77
Mand. 7	= 37	*Sim.* 9.1–33	= 78–110
Mand. 8	= 38	*Sim.* 10.1–4	= 111–14
Mand. 9	= 39		

I wish to dedicate this work to Bonnie, my partner in life, in appreciation for her helpful ideas and consistent belief in the value of this project.

James S. Jeffers
University of California, Irvine

INTRODUCTION

Early Christianity was an urban phenomenon. Before it spread into the vast rural spaces of the Roman Empire, it took firm root in its cities. The single most significant urban locale for the future of Christianity was the imperial capital, Rome. Its beginnings and early history were humble, to be sure. Rome was overshadowed for many years by the larger and more influential centers of Christianity in the more Christianized East: Antioch, Ephesus, Corinth, and Jerusalem. But Roman Christianity shaped the nature of the church in the West from the earliest period, and it would have unparalleled impact on later world history through the Roman Catholic Church.

Thematic studies of early Christianity, focusing on slavery, women in the church, or Christology, can help us understand better the nature of Christianity in any city of antiquity. But since such studies draw evidence from many places and many times, they can mislead us about the unique nature of a given urban church. This is because the churches in each city of the empire developed independently of those in other cities, often independently even of other congregations in the same city. As a result, the study of Christianity in its specific manifestations in given cities is a necessary corrective to the kinds of overgeneralizations possible in thematic studies.

Such a study is especially necessary and instructive when applied to the city of Rome. Differences between Rome and the other locations of early Christianity caused the Roman congregations to follow significantly different paths of development. By the time of the beginning of Christianity, Rome was considerably larger than any other city of Western antiquity. As the capital, it was home to the wealthiest and most powerful segments of society. It also attracted a smattering of virtually every other ethnic and language group known to the empire. As the center of Italy's slave society, it contained an unequaled number of slaves and descendants of slaves. Its geographic

1

and cultural distance from the centers of Christianity in the Greek East caused Roman Christianity to pursue its own course, even before Roman Christians began to speak Latin.

In the following pages I attempt to show that the unique social challenges facing Roman Christianity caused it to develop in ways that led ultimately to Roman Catholicism and its claims of primacy. Further, this development began long before the congregations of Rome came under the control of Latins; it began among the Jewish and Greek converts of the first century, the first Roman Christians. I will adduce evidence from literary documents, inscriptions, and archaeological remains to suggest that Roman Christianity's unique course resulted in part from the rising authority of Christians enamored with the ideology of the Roman ruling classes. Because these Christians saw no essential conflict between the church and society, they redefined the church's nature in light of Roman concepts of hierarchy. This is not to say that other traditions had no influence on the nature of Roman Christianity. The Roman synagogues, the presence of Paul and Peter, Jewish and Christian texts, and mystery religions all affected the development of the Roman church. They are also explored in the pages that follow. But the unique contribution of this study is its examination of how Roman ideology made its way into the first-century Roman churches and how it affected their self-definitions and attitudes toward the larger society.

1

THE IDENTITIES OF THE FIRST ROMAN CHRISTIANS

The first Roman Christians came from the poorer classes of Rome. They came largely from foreign groups in Rome, especially from the large Jewish community there. They also came from the ranks of those who were slaves or of slave origin. We have only a few hints as to the nature of earliest Roman Christianity from the contemporary literature, so we must use what we know about life among the lower classes of Rome in order to understand what it was like to be one of the first Roman Christians. The generalizations we draw from a study of the Roman lower classes will be tested against the specific evidence we have for the early Christians.

LIFE IN THE CITY OF ROME

No visitor could fail to be impressed by the ever-increasing opulence of the city of Rome during the first century A.D. Wealth on a scale only imagined before, gathered by a growing empire from all parts of the known world, was announced in no uncertain terms. Marble façades graced the massive public buildings of its forums. Ever-larger temples portrayed the greatness of its gods, who had protected Rome and given it victory over its enemies. Hundreds of private mansions dotted the hills of the city. Public baths, theaters, and amphitheaters grew in number and size. Caesar Augustus is supposed to have said of Rome, "I found the city made of brick and left it made of marble."[1] He was only the first in a string of emperors who pursued ambitious building programs designed to make the capital city an appropriate symbol of the power it wielded. Miles of aqueducts brought spring

1. Suetonius, *Augustus* 28.3. For more information on Rome, see John E. Stambaugh, *The Ancient Roman City* (Baltimore: Johns Hopkins University Press, 1988); T. W. Potter, *Roman Italy* (Berkeley: University of California Press, 1987); MacMullen, *Roman Social Relations*; and Carcopino, *Daily Life in Ancient Rome*.

water into the homes of wealthy Romans, and efficient sewers removed the city's waste. Rome's very size announced its greatness: by the first century A.D. it was home to more than one million persons, a population which would not be equaled again by any Western city until the 1800s.

Lower-class residents of urban Rome would not be so impressed by these things. They knew that a majority of Rome's population was composed of slaves and their descendants, and free resident aliens, most of whom had very low formal status. They also were well aware that most Roman citizens, who generally despised and resented all foreigners, were the descendants of farmers who had come to Rome to eke out a living after losing their farms. They resented the fact that because the city's public buildings and private mansions occupied more than one-half of its sixteen-square-mile area the majority of the population was squeezed into a relatively small area. In fact, density levels surpassed those of many modern cities, despite the relative inadequacy or absence of public services.

The majority of Rome's population lived in multiple-story tenement or apartment houses *(insulae)* or in small ground-floor domiciles at the rear of shops *(tabernae)*. The only access to upper levels of an *insula* was by flights of stairs, and the poorer residents, who made up the majority of the population, lived there. A common apartment consisted of one or two rooms which opened onto the street or a central courtyard. The same room often served as sleeping chamber, kitchen, and socializing area. Sometimes several families shared a set of rooms with each family having a private bedroom connected to a common room. Windows were covered with wooden shutters to keep out the cold. Because window glass was terribly expensive, the typical Roman often had to choose between light and warmth. There were no chimneys, and the only source of heat was a charcoal brazier located near the window. Thus, the rooms were small, damp, dark, and cold, except in the summer when they were hot and stuffy. Privacy was virtually unattainable, and the noises of the city made a sound sleep hard to achieve. Although the wealthy had running water, a poor resident of Rome had to get water at a public fountain and carry it up the stairs or hoist it up in a net. Public toilets were available near public baths; chamber pots were often located under stairs.

Life in the *taberna* was no better, except that there were no stairs to climb. It should come as no surprise that the poorer Romans spent many of their waking hours in the streets.

The typical nonslave husband and wife left home around sunrise, accompanied by their children, and headed for the small shop in which they worked. Since private mansions and tenement houses often existed side by side, they could not help but observe the great disparity of wealth in Rome. They might cross paths with an aristocrat, whose slaves would announce his titles and warn people to make way. The nobleman might be accompanied by a large contingent of slaves and free clients, since the size of the entourage proclaimed his importance.

The Roman merchant family probably was inured to the various sights and sounds that would bombard their senses as they traveled through the city. The wife might try to distinguish the sound of a conversation from competing voices speaking in Latin, Greek, and other languages and amidst the sounds of construction. The husband might identify the smell of baking bread among the aromas of various foods and the stench of sewage, urine, smoke, and the sweat of the crowded streets. They would stay on the raised sidewalks where possible to avoid the mud and refuse in the streets, but at times they would have to walk around piles of trash or waste thrown onto the sidewalk from an apartment above. Many of Rome's streets were narrow and hemmed in by towering *insulae*. This might make our family feel claustrophobic, but in the summer they would appreciate the shade.

Arriving at the shop, the wooden folding door or grill would be opened, announcing that the shop was open for business. Roman shops were located on the ground floor of *insulae* or were even built into the sides of the private homes of the wealthy. Merchants specialized in one area such as baked goods, seafood, books, or pottery production. Those who sold food often set up booths in the streets. Itinerant peddlers wandered the streets selling clothing or food. Shops with similar products or services congregated as a form of mutual advertisement of their location and so that the shop owners could support one another. A system of honor and status based upon but separate from the official Roman system existed among these shopkeepers who accepted Rome's official class system but recognized that they had no real identity under it. This social system of the lower classes was the basis for how the first Roman Christians thought of themselves and how they organized their churches.

Typical shopkeepers closed their shops between noon and 2 P.M. in order to eat the main meal and escape the heat of the day. They might return to their *insulae* to a meal cooked on the brazier. Unlike the rich, their diet rarely included red meat. They might eat fish or chicken with the beans and peas that were dietary staples. If they could afford to, they would eat fresh fruit or vegetables obtained at the local food booths. An alternative to eating at home was eating in a local full-service restaurant *(caupona)* or, more likely, in a simpler *popina* where wine and some hot food were available. In a *taberna* one usually ate a cold meal while standing at a counter.

Men who were considered by Roman law to be clients of a wealthy Roman patron often were expected to attend to the patron while he made public appearances or received visitors. They would have to close their shops or leave their families to tend them. Some clients had no means of consistent support beyond the small gift *(sportula)* they received at the end of the day from the patron.

Roman businesses typically stayed open until sundown. Our couple probably would try to get home before dark, since in the absence of streetlights Rome was full of dark hiding places for robbers. The rich went out at night only in the company of bodyguards. The poor received little help from the token 350 soldiers who patrolled the city at night but were concerned with protecting the property of the rich and with preventing riots. If a poor man were beaten or robbed, he was responsible for capturing and bringing to trial his assailant.

Our couple may have been Roman citizens or freeborn foreigners. If they were citizens, even though poor, their legal standing and social status would be well above that of foreigners, no matter whether they were slave or free. The state would investigate the murder of a citizen, but not that of a noncitizen. A citizen could not be beaten without the benefit of a trial and was not subject to the more tortuous forms of execution such as crucifixion. Marriage among noncitizens was not recognized by Roman law. Our couple may have been, like many thousands of others in Rome, freed slaves or the descendants of freed slaves, since the slaves of Roman citizens received Roman citizenship when they were freed. In that case, they would be of non-Roman stock, and their status was inferior to that of freeborn Romans but above that of most freeborn resident aliens *(peregrinni)*. As noted earlier, most of the first Roman Christians were freeborn aliens, slaves, or citizens of slave origin. Thus, if any social elite existed among the early Christians, it would have come from the last group.

FOREIGNERS IN ROME

The lingua franca of earliest Roman Christianity was Greek. Latin, the official language of Rome and the common language of free-born Romans, did not supplant Greek among the Christian churches of Rome until late in the second century. Roman Christianity's surviving documents were all composed in Greek, and most of the burial inscriptions of its adherents were Greek. This was not the Greek of the educated Roman elite, all of whom learned to speak and write Greek as part of their cultural education. Rather, it was the Greek of the common people who spoke it as their native tongue. We can conclude that the vast majority of early Christians were persons of non-Roman stock with roots in the Hellenized East. As observed above, most foreigners in Rome possessed a low legal position and an uncertain unofficial status. As a result, we can perceive the social identities of the first Roman Christians only if we grasp the position of foreigners in Rome.

From the second century B.C., non-Romans made up a large portion of the city's population. Free persons from the provinces who were able and willing to relocate to Rome were discouraged by the lack of industries that might attract free employees. Those who came voluntarily to Rome from the East generally brought their means of livelihood with them. Most foreigners, however, came to Rome involuntarily. Even before the establishment of the Empire, thousands of war captives from Asia Minor, Syria, Egypt, Greece, Africa, Spain, and elsewhere had been brought as slaves to Rome.[2] Most of Rome's slaves were Greeks and persons from Hellenized parts of the Near East. Since they were often able to gain freedom during their lifetimes, free descendants of slaves made up a consider-

2. La Piana, "Foreign Groups in Rome During the First Centuries of the Empire," 189. This remains the definitive work on this subject. See also Frank, *Economic History of Rome*, and idem., "Race Mixture in the Roman Empire," *American Historical Review* 24 (1916): 689–708.

able portion of the free population of Rome by the first century B.C. Tenney Frank asserts that by this time freedmen and their descendants made up the larger element of the common people. Throughout the late Republic and early Empire, the number of foreigners increased while the number of native Romans declined. This was due to factors such as a decrease in birth rates among native Romans, the exodus of natives to new Roman colonies, and military recruitment of native Romans. By the first century A.D., foreigners and their descendants made up the majority of the common people of the city (the *plebs urbana*), a large population of free resident aliens, and the entire slave class. Mommsen concludes that in the imperial era Rome was no longer an Italian community. It had instead become a mixture of parasitic populations. This meant that Rome could absorb foreign groups only slowly into its culture. Rostovtzeff says that peoples from the East "retained their hellenistic characteristics for many generations."[3]

Free foreigners in ancient Rome sought to live with others of their own nationality during the early stages of their socialization into the new culture. Slaves of foreign origin resided with their masters, and undoubtedly had to live and work in close proximity to slaves of various nationalities. New immigrants from virtually all of the Roman provinces around the Mediterranean and western Europe continued to come to Rome during the first and second centuries A.D., replacing those who left the ethnic groups to join the larger society. Roman tenement buildings were usually the only places open to new immigrants. Persons of the same nationality tended to congregate in the same parts of the city, since new arrivals sought the companionship of established compatriots. The Aventine hill was host to a large group of foreigners from early in the Republic. Here they were close to the Roman port on the Tiber which provided work for many of them. In the first century A.D., the Aventine was still occupied by many of foreign origin. The main body of Egyptians in Rome inhabited the Campus Martius area from the first century A.D. Africans preferred the slopes of the Caelian hill. Such groups were better able to maintain their languages and cultures, and thus they lived as partially autonomous units within the city. Juvenal confirms

---

3. La Piana, "Foreign Groups in Rome," 197; T. Mommsen, *Römische Geschichte,* 5 vols. (Berlin: Weidmann, 1920–22), 4:599; Rostovtzeff, *Social and Economic History of the Roman Empire,* 1:100.

this when he complains about Syrian immigrants who continued to use their native language and follow Syrian customs (*Satires* 3.62–65). Foreigners often worked together as well. Certain trades and crafts in Rome were practiced mainly by skilled foreigners from cities or provinces known to specialize in that profession.

The Greek-speaking foreigners of Rome, though a large portion of the population, found themselves always on the outside looking in. They had to find social worth and belonging among themselves. The first Roman Christians among them likewise could not look to Rome for honor or social identity. Like other non-Romans, they were confronted constantly with the differences between themselves and the Roman elite in terms of language, education, wealth, power, and honor. They avoided contact with native Romans whenever possible. If they were like most other foreigners, they did not reject the dominant society—they resented it, realized they could not compete in it, but reproduced it in modified form within their own organizations.

THE JEWS OF ROME

Due in part to the ministries of Paul and Peter in Rome, most of the earliest Roman Christians were Jewish. The Jews, one of the foreign groups most frequently mentioned in Roman sources, were present in Rome from the second century B.C. Around 139 B.C., a praetor named Gnaeeus Cornelius Hispanus, in order to put an end to an unexplained disturbance, "compelled the Jews" to return to their homes.[4] Pompey added thousands to their numbers in 61 B.C. when he brought back Jewish slaves from his conquest of Judaea. In 59 B.C., Cicero complained about the Roman Jewish community to a court audience: "You know how large a group they are, how unanimously they stick together, how influential they are in politics" (*Pro Flacco* 28). The Jews of Rome enjoyed the special privileges granted to their people for supporting Julius Caesar in his rise to power.

---

4. Valerius Maximus, *Factorum ac dictorum memorabilium* 1.3.2. This passage may refer to a delegation from Judaea, however. Concerning the Jews in Rome, see Leon, *Jews of Ancient Rome*; Wiefel, "Jewish Community in Ancient Rome and the Origins of Roman Christianity"; Hermann Vogelstein, "The Jews in Ancient Rome," Book I in *Rome*, trans. M. Hadas (Philadelphia: Jewish Publication Society of America, 1941); S. Lieberman, "Response to the Introduction by Professor Alexander Marx," in *The Jewish Expression* (New Haven: Yale University Press, 1976), 119–33; and R. Penna, "Les Juifs à Rome au temps de l'apôtre Paul," *New Testament Studies* 28 (1982): 348–64.

These privileges included exemption from military service, permission to collect the Jewish Temple tax, and the ability freely to assemble to worship and perform other rites specific to Judaism.

About forty to fifty thousand Jews lived in the city of Rome by the first century A.D., making up one of the largest foreign groups in the city. A number of sources tell us that Jews were expelled from Rome under Tiberius, about A.D. 19, due probably to proselytizing activities. About four thousand Jews were enlisted in the legion auxiliaries and sent to Sardinia. It is very unlikely that all other Jews were expelled.[5] Roman Jews were expelled from the city a second time sometime around 49 (I discuss this below). Jewish war captives may have been used to build the Flavian Amphitheater in the 70s. Many more came to Rome virtually destitute after the A.D. 70 destruction of Jerusalem by Vespasian. Their religion required them to live apart from gentiles and to follow a strict dietary regimen. This caused them to stand out from other foreign groups, and prevented them from fully assimilating into the larger society.

Like other foreigners, the Jews were not respected by most of the Roman elite. Cicero called Judaism "a barbarous superstition" and its followers a "mob." Juvenal depicts Jews as beggars and fortune-tellers who had no permanent residence. He asserts that the Sabbath rest demonstrates their laziness.[6]

Even more than other foreign groups, the Jews lived together. The oldest and largest settlement of Jews was in Transtiberinum (modern Trastevere), but they also settled in the Subura, on the edge of the Campus Martius, and near the Porta Capena. Of the eleven synagogues for which we have documentary or epigraphic evidence, we can locate nine with some degree of certainty. Seven of these were located in Transtiberinum, one in the Campus Martius, and one in the Subura.[7]

The attitudes of Roman aristocrats seem to confirm what we would expect based on the slave origins of many Jews: most Roman Jews were either destitute or barely able to support themselves. Transtiberinum was one of the more economically depressed areas

---

5. Tacitus, *Annals* 2.85.5; Dio Cassius, *Roman History* 57.18.5a; Josephus, *Antiquities* 18.3.5; and Suetonius, *Tiberius* 36. See E. Mary Smallwood, "Some Notes on the Jews Under Tiberius," *Latomus* 15 (1956): 314–29.

6. Cicero, *Pro Flacco* 69; Juvenal, *Satires* 3.14; 6.542–548; 14.105–106.

7. Vogelstein, "Jews in Ancient Rome," 18; Leon, *Jews of Ancient Rome*, 140–59.

in Rome. Although Juvenal was given to hyperbole, there must have been beggars and fortune-tellers among the Roman Jews. Jewish ex-slaves faced the same problem gentile ex-slaves faced: how to survive once they were free. Some Jews, as freed slaves of Roman citizens, possessed citizenship. But citizenship, while conferring a higher legal and social status, did not guarantee a livelihood. Other Jews came to Rome equipped to ply a trade. Aquila, who will be discussed below, was a tentmaker in Rome who was wealthy enough to travel frequently and perhaps maintain several workshops. Since Roman Jews often bought their compatriots out of slavery, some Jews must have had some wealth. Herod Agrippa, king of Judaea from A.D. 37 to 44, was a longtime resident of Rome and a friend of the Julio-Claudians. But since most Jews were poor, most Jewish converts to Christianity were probably poor as well.

According to the Acts of the Apostles and the letters of Paul, a number of the earliest converts to Christianity in the cities of the Empire were gentiles who had first been attracted to Judaism. This was probably true of Rome as well. Although a number of non-Jews found the teachings and practices of Judaism attractive, few seem to have fully converted. Of the several hundred inscriptions we possess, only four or five refer to proselytes. Eight more refer to "God-fearers," persons who had not fully converted to Judaism.[8] Women found it easier to convert fully than did men, mainly because of the Jewish requirement for circumcision of male converts. Leon reports that of the proselyte inscriptions discovered in Jewish catacombs, five refer to females. Josephus mentions two Roman women who became enamored with Judaism: the convert Fulvia, wife of a senator named Saturninus, and the sympathizer Poppaea, wife of Emperor Nero.[9] Partial converts were attracted to the moral teachings of Judaism and kept the Sabbath. They were taught from the Septuagint, the Greek translation of the Old Testament. But they were deterred from full conversion by Judaism's complicated ritual prescriptions, dietary laws, and social limitations. Although they expected to share with ethnic Jews in God's blessings, they were not an integral part of the synagogue's organization and were looked down upon at times by ethnic Jews. Partial converts usually were not allowed access to Jewish ceme-

8. La Piana, "Foreign Groups in Rome," 390–91.
9. Josephus, *Antiquities* 8.3.5.81–84; 20.8.11.195.

teries, so this group may have been much larger than the epigraphic evidence indicates. The foregoing suggests that "God-fearers," or partial converts, would have found attractive a religion like Christianity, which offered the advantages of Judaism without the disadvantages of joining the religion of a specific people.

THE FIRST ROMAN CHRISTIANS

We do not know at what point Christianity first reached Rome. Some believe that Christianity was brought back to Rome by "visitors from Rome," mentioned in Acts 2:10, who heard the preaching of Jesus' followers.[10] But Acts offers no evidence that any visitors from Rome were converted. The word used here for "visitors" (ἐπιδημέω) can refer to resident aliens (see Acts 17:21). The word in Acts 2:5 for "one who dwells" in Jerusalem (κατοικέω) is a technical term used for resident aliens in a city. Thus, we cannot be sure that these witnesses to early apostolic preaching returned directly to Rome. Christianity probably reached Rome during the decade of the 40s through a Jewish convert to Christianity.

The Edict of Claudius

The circumstances surrounding the Edict of Claudius, an order from the emperor expelling Roman Jews, provide the first direct evidence for the existence of Roman Christians. In his account of the reign of Claudius, Suetonius notes the expulsion of the Roman Jews "because they were persistently rioting at the instigation of Chrestus."[11] This edict was issued during the latter part of Claudius's reign, about 45–49. Orosius, referring to a passage in Josephus which does not appear in our modern Josephus corpus, dates this edict to 49. If "Chrestus" is a reference to Christ, then this passage suggests that a dispute between Jews and Jewish converts to Christianity gave rise to

10. Frend, *Early Church*, 41. Frend appears to consider this the only possibility. See also Judge and Thomas, "The Origin of the Church at Rome," esp. 83.

11. Suetonius, *Claudius* 25.4. On the Edict of Claudius, see Lampe, *Die stadtrömischen Christen in den ersten beiden Jahrhunderten*, 5–7; Frend, *Early Church*, 41; Barnard, "Early Roman Church, Judaism, and Jewish-Christianity," 372; Wiefel, "Jewish Community in Ancient Rome," 109; Bruce, *New Testament History*, 297; and Moreau, "Rome and the New Testament," 36.

the edict.[12] Chrestus was indeed a variant spelling of the name of Christ (Christus), and in both Tacitus and Tertullian we find the terms *Chrestianos* and *Chrestianer* used for Christians.[13] This interpretation of the edict is supported by Acts, in which the Jew Aquila and Priscilla his wife flee Rome for Corinth as a result of this edict (Acts 18:1-3). The context of Acts implies that they were Christians before they met Paul; thus, they may have been Christians before they left. In writing to the Romans in the second half of the 50s, Paul also indicates that Christians were present in Rome by the 40s when he says that he has wanted "for many years" (ἀπὸ πολλῶν ἐτῶν) to visit the Roman Christians (Rom. 15:23).

This edict is evidence that the first Roman Christians were Jewish converts to Christianity who came into conflict with the Roman Jewish community. This conflict may have led to the kind of violence portrayed by Acts in cities visited by the apostle Paul. Because of the constant disturbances, the Roman government ordered the expulsion of all Jews from Rome. But since there were so many Roman Jews, and since some were Roman citizens and some were slaves belonging to citizens, probably not all Jews actually left. Many certainly did leave; but it is possible that the expulsion edict was enforced only against the chief figures in the conflict.

The conflict tells us nothing about the number of Roman Christians in the 40s, since even a few persons could ignite divisions within a group like the Jews of Rome. It does suggest that these first Christians retained contact with their synagogues, perhaps even continuing to worship within them. If these Jewish Christians had left the synagogue and broken all contacts with other Jews, it is unlikely that such disturbances would have occurred.

Roman Christianity before Paul

By 57, when Paul wrote the Epistle to the Romans, Rome was host to a significant community of Christians. His commendation that "your faith is being reported all over the world," although perhaps hyper-

---

12. Frend, *Early Church*, 41; Lampe, *Christen*, 5; Barnard, "Early Roman Church," 372; Wiefel, "Jewish Community in Ancient Rome," 109; Bruce, *NT History*, 297; and Moreau, "Rome and the New Testament," 36.

13. Suetonius, *Claudius* 25.4; Orosius, *Historiae adversum Paganos* vii, 6.15; Tacitus, *Annals* 15.44; Tertullian, *Apologeticus* 3; idem, *Ad Nationes* 1.3.

bolic, suggests that Roman Christians were in contact with Christians in other cities (Rom. 1:8). He addresses the letter to "all in Rome who are loved by God and called to be saints" (Rom. 1:7). No city-wide administration of the Roman churches yet existed, since Paul does not address them as "the church of Rome," as was his practice with other churches.[14] Paul uses "church" (συνεργός) in this letter to describe the church that met in the home of Aquila and Priscilla (Rom. 16:3). The fact that he addresses individual Christians in Romans 16 runs counter to his normal practice when addressing churches, and thus supports the contention that no unified church yet existed in Rome. This indicates that the reputation of early Roman Christianity was thus due more to its location than to its size or organization. Harry Gamble presents a persuasive argument for the integrity of the sixteen chapters of Romans, based on a study of Paul's epistolary practices.[15]

The Epistle to the Romans indicates that gentiles made up a large proportion—if not the majority—of Roman Christians in the 50s. Scholars today generally agree that Paul is addressing both Jewish and gentile Christians in this letter, which, among other things, explains how gentile Christians should live in harmony with Jewish Christians. The first non-Jewish Christians came primarily from the Greek-speaking foreign groups in Rome. This is clear since Paul's letter is written in Greek, and since Greek-speaking gentiles constituted the majority of Rome's resident aliens at this time. In 1:5, Paul identifies his mission: "to call people from among the Gentiles." In 1:14, he says he is obligated to "Greeks and non-Greeks," without mentioning Jews by name. In 11:13, he says, "Now I am speaking to you Gentiles." But he clearly addresses Jews at other times, as in 2:17, so he counts Jews among his readers. Wiefel suggests that the gentile Christians needed to understand the place of the Jews in God's plans, and needed a response to the anti-Jewish sentiments in Rome.[16]

14. Bruce, *NT History*, 384.
15. Gamble, *Textual History of the Letter to the Romans*, esp. 84–95. The present study accepts his view, although modern scholarship is still divided on this point. For a consideration of the issues on both sides, see Donfried, ed., *Romans Debate*. The integrity of Romans 1—16 is defended by Wiefel, "Jewish Community in Ancient Rome"; Jewett, "Romans as an Ambassadorial Letter"; and Brown and Meier, *Antioch and Rome*, 105–9. Against this view, see Willi Marxsen, *Einleitung in das Neue Testament* (Gütersloh: Bertelsmann, 1963), 99; La Piana, "Roman Church at the End of the Second Century," 201–4.
16. Wiefel, "Jewish Community in Ancient Rome," 119.

Romans 9—11, which deals with the place of the nation of Israel in God's plan, can be seen as an apologetic on behalf of Jews to a skeptical gentile audience. Jewish Christians were forced to leave Rome along with the other Jews in 49. In their absence, predominantly gentile congregations apparently arose and flourished. When the Jews, including Jewish Christians who had never fully separated from the Jewish community, returned about 54, gentile Christians were faced with their different interpretation of Christianity. Schaff suggests that Jewish and gentile converts may have formed two distinct congregations.[17]

That Paul calls himself a slave and an apostle in the same breath (1:1) would make sense to residents of a city where "rich and influential slaves comprising the imperial bureaucracy" were proud to call themselves "slaves of Caesar" on their burial inscriptions.[18] Paul identifies himself as an honored servant of the King of kings. He reiterates this when in 13:6 he uses the word for government officials ($\lambda\epsilon\iota\tau\text{oup}\gamma\acute{o}\varsigma$) to refer to himself as an "agent" of God (15:16). All this implies that he is addressing people familiar with and perhaps a part of the imperial bureaucracy.

The portrait of Roman Christianity painted so far indicates that internal dissension was commonplace from the beginning. The arrival of Paul and Peter only exacerbated the situation.

Pauline Influence on
Roman Christianity

When Paul arrived in Rome sometime around the year 60, Roman Christianity lacked central organization. According to Acts 28:15, "the brothers there" in Rome met Paul south of Rome on the Appian Way. The Roman Christians are not presented as official representatives of the Roman church, as are the Ephesian church elders who met with Paul in Acts 20:17. Some see this as Lukan bias— intentionally downplaying an organizational structure not set up by Paul. But this passage fits with the image of a disunited church noted above.

Soon after arriving, Paul calls together "the leaders of the Jews." He presents to them the kind of appeal he has used in the past to

17. Philip Schaff, *History of the Christian Church*, 8 vols. (1910; reprint, Grand Rapids: Wm. B. Eerdmans, 1980), 1:372.
18. Jewett, "Romans as an Ambassadorial Letter," 12–13.

gain support from the Jews where no church yet existed. The Jewish leaders seem to have had no direct knowledge of Christianity, which they called "this sect" (Acts 28:22). This is surprising in light of the conflict which resulted in the Claudian edict only eleven years before. But these leaders may have thought that Paul represented a different sect. "Even larger numbers" of Jews met with Paul on a subsequent day, and listened to his daylong presentation of the gospel. Some converted, but most remained unconvinced. This incident tells us several things. Although there were a number of Christians in Rome in 60, and presumably among them some who knew and had been taught by Paul (such as some of those mentioned in Romans 16), there was no central group of elders with whom he could discuss goals and plans. Also, Paul probably believed that the Christians had not yet persuasively presented the gospel to the local Jewish community.

At least one segment of Roman Christianity took a more aggressive and visible stance under the influence of Paul. Paul tells the Philippians that most of the brothers have been encouraged to greater boldness in their witness through his imprisonment (Phil. 1:14).[19] At least some of this witness must have been directed toward the Jewish community, especially through Jewish Christians. Paul mentions divisions within the Christian community: some preach Christ out of selfish motives, hoping to stir up trouble for Paul while he is imprisoned (Phil. 1:15-17). He probably refers here to dissenters who are trying to take advantage of his immobility to gain power in the Christian community. He also seems to refer to a division in the community when he distinguishes "the brothers who are with me" from "all the saints" (Phil. 4:21-22). That Christianity was visible enough to attract Emperor Nero's attention also suggests an increase in the proselytizing aggressiveness (as well as size) of the Roman Christian congregations. That Paul experienced a divisive Roman Christianity is also indicated in *1 Clement* 5, where Paul's martyrdom is said to have resulted from "jealousy and envy."

The First Roman Persecution

A fire in 64 ravaged most of the center of Rome. Only four of its fourteen regions did not suffer damage. Despite the fact that Nero

---

19. Philippians probably was written from Rome. See Judge and Thomas, "Origin of the Church," 93.

quickly undertook the task of rebuilding and at great expense provided for the immediate needs of the victims, Tacitus says that his efforts could not "banish the sinister rumor and belief" that the fire was intentional. Although Tacitus seems to believe the rumors that Nero ordered the fire, there is no hard evidence for this beyond the fact that Nero was able, as a result of the fire, to build his palace on a far grander scale.[20] At any rate, Nero needed to remove blame from himself in the minds of the angry Roman public. He found appropriate scapegoats, according to Tacitus, in the Christians.

Hundreds of Roman Christians, perhaps several thousand, lost their lives in this persecution. Tacitus says that "an immense multitude" was convicted (*Annals* 15.44). Clement uses a similar phrase when he says that "a great multitude" was put to death at this time (*1 Clem.* 6:1). The unanimous testimony of later Christian tradition is that Peter and Paul were both put to death under Nero. *First Clement* 5:4 refers to "Peter, who because of unrighteous jealousy suffered not one or two but many trials, and having thus given his testimony went to the glorious place which was his due." He then mentions the sufferings of Paul. The context of this passage almost certainly is the persecution by Nero. Clement introduces this chapter as a commentary on "examples of our own generation" who have suffered (*1 Clem.* 5:1). Based on these references and the probable age of the Christian community, we can estimate its mid-first-century size at between one thousand and five thousand persons.

Tacitus's description of the persecution indicates that the members of this new religion were poor noncitizens, for a citizen could not have been put to death in the ways Tacitus describes: dismemberment by wild dogs, crucifixion, and death by fire.

Tacitus implies that the Christians were chosen for this role due to their unpopularity: "a class hated for their abominations" (*Annals* 15.44). There were many reasons for their unpopularity. Christians rejected the Roman gods and followed strange practices. Unlike the Jews, they were a new group in Rome. Their strangeness was compounded by the fact that they acted like a nation but lacked an ethnic unity. In addition, popular Christian eschatology looked for the imminent destruction of the world by fire. Some Christians, then, might have openly welcomed the fire as a sign of the end.[21]

20. Tacitus, *Annals* 15.44. See chap. 4 for a description of Nero's palace complex.
21. Bruce, *NT History*, 400–401.

After Nero

In the absence of direct evidence in our sources we must use contemporary events in the larger society to describe the situation from the death of Nero to the end of the first century. After the destruction of Jerusalem in 70, thousands of Jews were brought as slaves to Rome. These Jews probably contributed new converts to Christianity in the following decade, bringing with them the customs and education of Palestinian Jews. Although the Jews in Rome did not lose their unique privileges as a result of the rebellion in Palestine, they must have fallen even further out of grace with the non-Jewish populace. As a result, one would expect Christians to sever any remaining organic ties to the synagogue. Converting Jews probably would be expected to make a clean break with their former identities as Jews.

The years 70 to 95 are free from any hint of persecution by the state. Although Nero probably dealt the Christian congregations a serious blow, they were able to recover and grow apparently unimpeded for the next twenty-five years. Presumably the congregations kept a low profile during this period, learning how to avoid the attention of the government. Since even in Paul's day they included members of the imperial household, we can assume that this group grew in number and provided Roman Christians with valuable information on how the state normally functioned.

THE SOCIAL IDENTITIES OF THE
FIRST ROMAN CHRISTIANS

As I have noted, early Roman Christianity, while heterogeneous, took its members for the most part from among the city's poorer and less respected foreigners. Most were Jews or non-Jews originally from the Greek-speaking East. Most were either slaves of the Roman Empire or their descendants. Few were Roman citizens, and fewer still enjoyed any measure of status in the larger society. The highest social status among Roman Christians in the first century probably belonged to imperial freedmen.

The Epistle to the Romans

The social status and specific identities of Paul's addressees are suggested in his letter to the Romans. At the end of his letter (chap. 16) Paul sends greetings to a number of Roman Christians. This chapter provides our first glimpse at actual Roman house churches. Unfortunately, we cannot conclude that the names in this list are representative of Roman Christianity as a whole, since Paul was at pains to greet people who knew him and who presumably would make sure that his letter was disseminated. The list mentions twenty-eight persons, twenty-six of whom are named.[22]

Romans 16 suggests a strong connection between Roman Christians and the Hellenized East. Almost three-fourths of the Christians in this list either came from or spent time in the East. Aquila came from Pontus (Acts 18:2), while Epaenetus was from Asia Minor (Rom. 16:5). Prisca, Andronicus, Junius, Urbanus, and Rufus and his mother had been part of Paul's missionary team in the East. Others, called "beloved," probably had met Paul in the East: Ampliatus, Stachy, and Persis. Thus, two of the twenty-six certainly came to Rome from the East, and another nine may have come from the East. Eight of the remaining fifteen persons probably came from the Greek East, since their names appear quite infrequently in the collection of inscriptions from the city of Rome (see the *Corpus Inscriptionum Latinarum* VI: Herodion, Patrobus, Olympus, Asyncritus, Hermas, Phlegon, Philologus, and Apelles). This does not prove that three-fourths of Roman Christians came from the Hellenized East, however, since the letter is more likely to mention people Paul met in the East. Nevertheless, the list confirms that a number of Roman Christians came from the East.

Romans 16 demonstrates the earlier conclusion that the Roman congregations included sizable numbers of Jews and Greeks. Five persons are certainly of Jewish descent or are at least Jewish converts: Prisca and Aquila (see below), and three persons identified as fellow Jews ("kinsmen": συγγενης): Andronicus, Junius, and Herodion.

The list also confirms the earlier conclusion that the first Roman Christians were largely slaves or descendants of slaves. Eleven of the twenty-six names may represent this group. Four Latin names, apparently belonging to Greek-speaking Christians, probably represent former slaves or the descendants of slaves: Ampliatus, Julia, Junias, and Maria. Seven Greek names are common slave names in Rome:

---

22. Lampe, *Christen*, 135–53; Heikki Solin, *Beiträge zur Kenntnis der griechischen Personnennamen in Rom* (Helsinki: Societas Scientarum Fennica, 197); and Brown and Meier, *Antioch and Rome*, 107–10.

Asyncritus, Phlegon, Philologus, Hermes, Nereus, Tryphosa, and Tryphaena. In addition to these eleven, Romans 16 greets the Christian slaves who belong to Aristobulus and Narcissus.

Romans 16 gives us our only glimpse of the social makeup of earliest Roman Christianity. Although the names in this chapter cannot be taken as representative of the Roman churches as a whole, they do prove that the churches were made up of both Jews and Greeks and that many Roman Christians were slaves, freedmen, or descendants of slaves. It is very likely that some of these Christian slaves were part of the large imperial bureaucracy in Rome.

Prisca and Aquila

The New Testament provides further information about Prisca and Aquila, two of the Roman Christians greeted in Romans 16.[23] We learn in Acts 18:3 that, like Paul, they were tentmakers. The fact that Aquila plied his trade in Rome, Corinth, and Ephesus indicates a high degree of mobility. We know of four major trips taken by Aquila (accompanied by Prisca on at least three of them). He had traveled from his native Pontus to Rome before he met Paul, and he left Rome for Corinth where he met Paul. A year and a half later, he accompanied Paul from Corinth to Ephesus, and Romans 16 demonstrates that within five years he was back in Rome. These trips would have cost Aquila more than one thousand sesterces—an amount well beyond the budget of a poor craftsman. On the other hand, these trips do not imply that he was rich. Rather, they mean that he was a successful, average craftsman.

How wealthy were they? They left a business behind in Rome when they came to Corinth. Ollrog believes that they must have had slaves in Rome who ran the business in their absence. This is possible, since they eventually resumed their trade in Rome. But it is also possible that they simply shut down their business when they left and started it up again when they returned. The tools of their trade were very portable, and the average tradesman in Rome only rented his shop. The fact that Aquila and Prisca hosted house churches in Rome (Rom. 16:3) and Ephesus (1 Cor. 16:19) is more significant. In large cities where square footage was at a premium, the fact that they

---

23. Acts 18:2–3, 18, 26; 1 Cor. 16:19. Lampe, *Christen*, 156–62; Wolf-Henning Ollrog, *Paulus und seine Mitarbeiter* (Neukirchen: Neukirchener, 1979), 24–27.

could afford to rent residences capable of seating a dozen or two worshipers shows that they were able to live well above a subsistence level.

Prisca may have had a higher social status than her husband. Of the four times their names are listed together, her name appears first three times, which contradicts the usual practice of naming the husband first. Although we cannot know for certain, Prisca may have been a Roman who met and married Aquila in Rome. Prisca was a common Latin name in Rome (the masculine form is Priscus). If she was a Roman, she would possess Roman citizenship and greater social status than her mate.

Prisca and Aquila represent one type of natural leader in the Roman churches. Their wealth, though modest, exceeded that of most residents of Rome and, therefore, probably that of most other Roman Christians. The fact that a house church met in their home would give them a certain amount of honor. They probably led the worship in their house church as well, since in Ephesus they instructed Apollo, an eloquent Jewish-Christian teacher (Acts 18:24-26). They also may have been honored for their experiences as part of Paul's team of workers. Presumably they assisted Paul in his proselytizing activities in Rome.

Hermas

The *Shepherd of Hermas* was written between A.D. 90 and 135, by Hermas, a Roman Christian. Hermas is a fascinating character. Although possessing only a humble education, little wealth, and no official standing in the Roman Christian community, he spoke out forcefully against the moral compromise he detected in its official leaders.

Scholars in general accept Hermas's self-identification in *Vision* 1.1.1. He was raised by a man who brought him to Rome and sold him to a Roman woman named Rhoda. The sense of this verse, though difficult to translate, is that he had gained his freedom a number of years before he met Rhoda again.[24] In the meantime, he had become "rich" and then lost his wealth (*Vis.* 3.6.7). Hermas had

---

24. Lake, *Apostolic Fathers*, 2:7 n. 1. Joly, *Hermas: Le Pasteur*; Lampe, *Christen*, 182–200; Osiek, *Rich and Poor*; Wilson, "The Career of the Prophet Hermas"; Lake, "The *Shepherd of Hermas* and Christian Life in Rome in the Second Century"; and Turner, "The *Shepherd of Hermas* and the Problem of Its Text."

a wife, and also grown children who had become corrupt through his indulgence (*Vis.* 1.3.1; 2.2.2–3). We cannot be certain that all of these autobiographical elements are authentic. The wisest course, as Lampe suggests, is to consider authentic any details which could have been discredited by the contemporary Roman Christians in his audience.

J. P. Audet posits a Jewish origin for Hermas, but certain factors mitigate against this view. Hermas shows no concern for Judaism or for the distinction between Jew and gentile. He never mentions the Jewish nation. The "twelve tribes" mentioned in *Similitude* 9.17, although a Jewish theme, refers not to Israel but to the human race. Barnard believes that while the author is acquainted with the form and content of Jewish traditions, he need not have been Jewish or even a convert to Judaism to learn them. Reiling thinks only someone raised within Hellenistic traditions could use them as facilely as Hermas does in *Mandate* 11. Since the *Shepherd* provides the only testimony to Hermas's ethnic origin, Osiek properly concludes that "both Hellenistic and Jewish backgrounds are strongly represented, and neither can be proved dominant at the expense of the other." Thus, Hermas arose from a "cultural mix that defies reseparation into distinct categories."[25]

Hermas had only a rudimentary education, causing many to consider him a representative of "ordinary Christians" in Rome.[26] Hermas's limited education makes it certain that he was not an imperial freedman. The *Shepherd* is written in the popular language of the Greek-speaking peoples of Rome. Its style is so awkward that even the scribes of its earliest manuscripts made grammatical corrections in the language. The absence of literary devices from the Old Testament and postbiblical Jewish writings, and the lack of allusions to literature beyond these writings, suggest that he had no formal education. The fact that he does not quote from or refer directly to any books of the New Testament is surprising, since his contemporary, Clement, quoted from a number of New Testament books as well as from the Old Testament. The only source from which Hermas

25. Audet, "Affinités literaires et doctrinales du Manuel de Discipline," 82; Barnard, *Studies in the Apostolic Fathers*, 156–58; Reiling, *Hermas and Christian Prophecy*, 26; Osiek, *Rich and Poor*, 7–8.
26. Barnard, *Studies in the Apostolic Fathers*, 163.

quotes directly is the lost *Book of Eldad and Modad* (*Vis.* 2.3.4). This book is listed among the Old Testament Apocrypha in the *Stichometry* of Nicephorus and in other lists of Jewish works. The names Eldad and Modad may come from Num. 11:26-29.[27]

As a slave, Hermas clearly worked neither as a domestic in the great houses of Rome nor as a skilled artisan, but as a farm laborer. He may have been involved in wine production, since he often alludes to this business. For example, he refers to the hand pump (σίφωνα ὕδατος) used for cleaning and watering vines in Italy.[28] He speaks of stacking wine or oil in a cellar, and comments that if someone pouring wine into vessels only fills them halfway, the wine goes sour more quickly (*Mand.* 11.15; 12.5.3). He points out that a vine left untended within a fence is spoiled, wasted by weeds, and becomes useless (*Sim.* 9.26.4). His parable of the elm and the vine (*Sim.* 2.1) refers to the most popular method of viticulture in central Italy, in which elms are used to support the growing grape vines (αρβυστυμ).[29]

As a freedman, Hermas was a grain farmer who most likely worked on rented land. The Lady in the initial visions promises to appear to him in the field where he is "farming" (χονδριζεις).[30] His farm is located a little over a mile south of Rome along the Via Campania. It seems relatively large: in *Vision* 3.1.3 he chooses a "more remote place" on it to meet the Lady in his visions. Probably the land was not very fertile, or undesirable for some other reason. Otherwise, it would be in the hands of a Roman aristocrat, and would be farmed by a slave gang. On the farm he produced spelt, a grain that was the basis of Roman gruel, the staple of the lower classes in republican Rome. By Hermas's time, most people ate bread instead. Thus, his customers must have been the poorest residents of Rome.

Hermas relates that after gaining his freedom he became a "wealthy" businessman (*Vis.* 3.6.7; *Mand.* 3.5). He was probably

---

27. Snyder, *Shepherd of Hermas*, 6:38. Remnants of the text are preserved in James H. Charlesworth, ed., *The Old Testament Pseudepigrapha*, 2 vols. (New York: Doubleday, 1985).

28. *Mand.* 11.18; Lake, *Apostolic Fathers*, 2:125; K. D. White, *Roman Farming* (Ithaca, N.Y.: Cornell University Press, 1970).

29. Osiek, *Rich and Poor*, 146–53.

30. *Vis.* 3.1.2. This apparently refers to preparing "coarsely crushed grain": Bauer, *Greek-English Lexicon of the New Testament*, 891.

"wealthy" by the standards of the lower classes, producing a surplus beyond the amount necessary to feed and shelter his family.

Hermas lost the wealth he had gained, perhaps as a result of his deceitful business dealings. He was promised that his renewed piety would make his former lies become trustworthy (*Vis.* 3.6.7; *Mand.* 3.3.5). Lake suggests that Hermas now had to try to live up to former extravagant pledges and in this and other ways justify his deceitful statements. Lampe thinks he lost his wealth as a result of being denounced to the state as a Christian.[31] But if such a thing happened in the first or second century, the Christian probably would have lost his life as well. This loss of wealth suggests that, while writing the *Shepherd*, Hermas suffered economic deprivation.

Hermas represents the average Roman Christian. Although not Jewish, he was steeped in postbiblical Jewish traditions and had some knowledge of the Old Testament. He was brought to Rome as a slave and worked in agriculture. Later, he was able to gain his freedom and even a certain amount of wealth. Although he had learned to write, he lacked a formal education. Like many of the poorer Romans, he had suffered economic reversals.

Rhoda

Hermas tells us very little about his former Christian owner, Rhoda. Rhoda clearly was not a member of Rome's ruling elite. The fact that "Rhoda" is Greek and does not have a Latin nomen shows that she was not a Roman citizen and thus not the freedwoman of a citizen. Since she was not a freedwoman of a citizen and also certainly not a slave, she must have been freeborn. Apparently she was a widow or was possibly divorced. Her husband had attained some wealth, and she was left in possession of a farm and wine-making equipment in Rome. Rhoda could not have been very wealthy, since Hermas, who believed that rich Christians are spiritually inferior to poor ones (*Sim.* 2.5), considered her a pious Christian. Hermas says that he met her after a number of years while she bathed unattended in the Tiber (*Vis.* 1.1.1, 2). This incident probably should not be taken

---

31. Lake, *Apostolic Fathers*, 2:77; Lampe, *Christen*, 188.

literally, however. Nevertheless, the picture emerges of a Greek-speaking freeborn resident alien in Rome who had either imparted her Christianity to her slaves or gained it from them.

Flavia Domitilla and
Titus Flavius Clemens

The persons mentioned so far in this chapter are clearly Christians, though their social statuses may have been unclear. This couple are clearly Roman aristocrats, but their adherence to Christianity is uncertain. If they prove to be Christians, they would be our only evidence for the existence of first-century Christianity in the highest level of Roman society.

Christian tradition has held that two Roman aristocrats, Flavia Domitilla and Titus Flavius Clemens, were Christians. Not much is known about the activities of Domitilla and Clemens prior to 95. Their two sons were designated by Domitian as his successors, and were tutored by the famous rhetorician Quintilian. Clemens was consul along with Domitian in 95.[32]

Many of Domitian's activities as emperor were very unpopular with the ruling elite. Unlike his predecessors Vespasian and Titus, Domitian vigorously promoted veneration of himself as the divine Augustus. He insisted on being addressed as *Dominus et Deus* (Lord and God) as early as 85–86.[33] Suetonius asserts that due to anxiety about the possibility of revolution or assassination and because of a cruel streak, Domitian put many senators to death, including his cousin Flavius Sabinus, "on the most trivial of charges" (Suetonius, *Domitian* 10).

In 95, the wrath of Domitian fell on Clemens and his wife, Domitilla. Suetonius relates that the emperor "later suddenly put to death on the merest suspicion and almost in his very consulship his own cousin, Flavius Clemens, a man despised for his lack of ambition

---

32. Suetonius, *Domitian* 17; Dio Cassius, *Roman History* 67.14; Suetonius, *Domitian* 15 (Clemens). Lightfoot, *Apostolic Fathers*, 1:16–21; "Flavius," in *Paulys Real-Encyclopädie der classischen Altertumwissenschaft*, ed. Georg Wissowa (Stuttgart: J. B. Metzlersche, 1909), 6:2525–2739, esp. 2536–39; Lampe, *Christen*, 167–71; Quintilian, *Institutionis Oratoria* iv. Prooem.

33. Barnard, *Studies in the Apostolic Fathers*, 7; Pergola, "La Condamnation des Flaviens 'Chretiens' sous Domitien," 408.

(*inertiae*).["34] Most likely Domitian had only the "merest suspicion" that Clemens was a threat to his throne, and in spite of the man's lack of ambition had him put to death.

The second-century Roman historian, Dio Cassius, records the legal charge upon which Clemens and Domitilla were punished:

> In the same year [95] Domitian slaughtered many others, including the consul, Flavius Clemens, though Clemens was his own cousin, and was married to Flavia Domitilla, who was also a relative of his. Against them both was brought the charge of "atheism," for which also many others were condemned who had drifted into the practices of the Jews. Of these some were put to death, others deprived of their property. Domitilla was only banished to Pandateria. (*Roman History* 67.14)

Dio (writing in Greek) says that Clemens and Domitilla were condemned for αθεοτετος, usually translated "atheism" or "godlessness." This term was used of those who had turned their backs on the Roman gods. Moreover, Dio indicates that this charge had to do with taking up Jewish practices. It is not clear whether Dio has in mind full Jewish converts or those who simply followed certain Jewish practices.

The accounts of Suetonius and Dio Cassius are complementary. Suetonius gives what he considers to be the underlying reason for the action against Clemens and Domitilla: an unfounded suspicion of treason against Domitian. He does not present the legal charge levied against them. Dio, on the other hand, deals with the actual charge: atheism. He does not indicate whether or not this charge reflects the real reason for Domitian's hostility toward them.

But there are difficulties in relating the legal charge of "atheism" to the adoption of Jewish practices. The Jewish religion was a *religio licita*, the recognized religion of an allied state. Even after the destruction of the Jewish state under Titus, Judaism's legal status remained unchanged. Jews could freely practice Judaism. No laws

---

34. Suetonius, *Domitian* 15. "Flauium Clementem patruelem suum, contemptissimae inertiae, cuius filios etiam tum paruulos successores palam destinauerat . . . repente ex tenuissima suspicione tantum non in ipso eius consulatu interemit." Scholars have long debated the significance of the term *inertiae*. It could be translated "lack of energy," "lack of activity," or "lack of reasonable ambition." For a discussion of this, see Milburn, "Persecution of Domitian," 158; cf. Tacitus, *Histories* 3.65; 3.75; Merrill, *Essays in Early Christian History*, 149.

prevented Roman citizens from observing Jewish customs. The state did not care how many gods Romans worshiped, as long as they faithfully demonstrated their loyalty to the state by continuing to fulfill obligations toward the native gods. Under Domitian, this included worship of the deified living emperor.[35]

Clemens may have been a Jewish convert who showed real reluctance to carry out his Roman religiopolitical obligations, or he may have simply been accused on a trumped-up charge. Harry Leon presents another possibility: that Clemens, though stopping short of full conversion or even identification as a godfearer, had some sympathy for Jewish practices. Leon suggests that he was executed not necessarily because these practices interfered with his duties toward the state, but because they provided Domitian with an excuse to have him condemned. He believes that Clemens was a Jewish sympathizer who, like many others, was unwilling to completely convert. He thinks Domitilla may have been a full convert.[36]

Although he could not have been a full convert to either Judaism or Christianity, it would not be too surprising to find that Clemens was a sympathizer with Judaism. A number of sources testify that the Jews were successful proselytizers in Rome. As early as the time of Augustus, Horace jokingly warns a critic that if he does not come around to Horace's way of thinking, he will get a group of men who "like the Jews, will force you to come into our crowd." Horace also refers to a Roman friend, Aristius Fuscus, who used his observance of the Sabbath to beg off a meeting. The first-century philosopher Seneca once complained that the observance of the Sabbath had been "adopted in all lands."[37] Though Judaism was a *religio licita*, the Romans regarded it with suspicion and distrust when they found it taking captive some of their own. Tacitus says that the first lesson learned by proselytes to Judaism was to despise the gods, shed their feelings of patriotism, and consider expendable their parents, children, and brothers (*Histories* 5.5). Leon believes that the occasional

---

35. Merrill, *Essays in Early Christian History*, 154.

36. Milburn, "Persecution of Domitian," 160. He is unsure whether or not to make Clemens a Jewish sympathizer; see also Merrill, *Essays in Early Christian History*, 157; Leon, *Jews of Ancient Rome*, 34.

37. Horace, *Satires* I.4.140–143; I.9.67–72. For Seneca, see Augustine, *De Civitate Dei* 6.II.

repressive measures by the emperors toward Judaism and the fear that Judaism undermined traditional Roman customs testify to the success of Jewish proselytism.[38] It seems clear that, as a result of active proselytism or their own curiosity, a small but noticeable number of Roman aristocrats took up some Jewish practices.

It would have been easier for Clemens's wife, Domitilla, to take up Judaism. Not only was circumcision irrelevant, but she did not share her husband's responsibilities in the Roman religion. Later tradition has more to say about Domitilla's religious faith than Clemens's. It calls her a convert to Christianity rather than to Judaism, however. The first reference to Domitilla as a Christian comes from the fourth century in Eusebius's *Historia Ecclesiastica*. He writes that non-Christian sources mention a Flavia Domitilla, niece of a consul of Rome that year (96) named Flavius Clemens, who was exiled to the island of Pontia as punishment for her faith in Christ.[39] This is Eusebius's only reference to Clemens.

Domitilla probably was a convert to or at least a sympathizer with Christianity. Clemens and Domitilla were considered part of the group of sympathizers with Judaism among the Roman aristocracy. Dio's sources may have confused Judaism and Christianity, or the Roman authorities may have made this error. The worship practices of Christians, especially if they were Jewish Christians, probably looked Jewish to the casual observer. Such confusion helps explain the discrepancies between the accounts of Dio and Eusebius. Whether or not Domitilla was a convert herself, she must have allowed servants within her household to practice Christianity. The very existence of a house church in one of her residences could have brought about the charges against her (see chap. 3).

Thus, we find in Domitilla a possible convert among the Roman aristocracy. We can only speculate about how history might have changed if one of her sons had succeeded Domitian as emperor, as he had once planned. But she is the only aristocrat in first-century Rome who likely was a Christian, according to our sources. We must look for the social elite within Roman Christianity on a lower level.

---

38. Leon, *Jews of Ancient Rome*, 252.
39. Eusebius, *Historia Ecclesiastica* 18.4. This is probably a reference to his pagan source named "Bruttius" in Eusebius's *Chronicles*. Attempts to identify this Bruttius have been unsuccessful. Merrill, *Essays in Early Christian History*, 165.

Claudius Ephebus and
Valerius Vito

During the last decade of the first century, a Roman Christian wrote a lengthy letter to fellow Christians in the city of Corinth. This letter traditionally is called *1 Clement* for its author, Clement of Rome.[40] The letter names only three Christians: "Send back quickly to us our messengers Claudius Ephebus and Valerius Vito, together with Fortunatus . . ." (*1 Clem.* 65.1). The sentence construction suggests that Fortunatus was a mere appendage to the two principal messengers (σὺν καὶ Φορτουνάτῳ). Fortunatus was a common Greek slave name in Rome, and in the mind of Clement, he clearly does not have the status of Ephebus or Vito. He may have been a slave of one or the other. If so, he would be the first known example of a Christian slave belonging to a Christian master in the Roman churches.

Claudius Ephebus and Valerius Vito were sent as Clement's representatives to the Corinthians. These men are without doubt Roman freedmen. Slaves of citizens traditionally added part of their former master's name to their own upon manumission. The names of male Romans consisted of three parts: first came the praenomen, followed by family *(gens)* name, the nomen, and the personal name, the cognomen. Ex-slaves normally took the nomen of their former master as a prefix to their (usually Greek) slave name. For example, the author and former Jewish general Josephus prefixed Flavius to his name to show gratitude for the patronage of the imperial Flavian house. Ephebus and Vito (or Bito) are Greek cognomina, so their bearers were of Eastern origin. The nomen Claudius probably refers to the imperial Claudian household. This indicates that Claudius Ephebus was an imperial freedman, the first one we have thus far encountered among Roman Christians. His companion, Valerius Vito, probably was a freedman of the Valerian household. He may have been a slave of the empress Messalina, a member of the Valerian *gens*, and wife of Claudius until 48. In any case, Vito was a freedman of one of the "great houses" of Rome. Most scholars agree with this identification. Lightfoot, in referring to members of the imperial household, cites a

---

40. Scholars agree that the so-called *2 Clement* was written about 50 years later by someone other than the author of *1 Clement*. Its place of origin is uncertain. Lake, *Apostolic Fathers*, 1:125–27.

number of inscriptions that mention both a Claudius/Claudia and a Valerius/Valeria. He suggests that these men may have been freed together, and together passed as clients of the Claudian dynasty to the Flavian dynasty at the beginning of Vespasian's reign.[41]

The most outstanding examples of rising social status in the early empire are all found in the freedmen of the emperor, the members of the *familia Caesaris*.[42] The *familia Caesaris* consisted of those who maintained the emperor's properties and supervised the revenues of the empire. Those who rose to the top of this latter group achieved a status far above that of most people in Rome. The typical path of civil service, the *cursus honorum*, began when the imperial slave boy underwent training in a school such as that of the *Caput Africae* on the Caelian Hill. In school he was taught the basics necessary for administering a Mediterranean empire: Latin, Greek, and applied mathematics. Upon completing training, the student spent several years in domestic service. At the age of twenty, he entered the civil service and usually occupied a number of minor posts. After receiving freedom around the age of thirty, he could move on to intermediate posts such as record officer, correspondent, accountant, or paymaster. In his forties, he might serve in senior posts such as chief accountant, chief record officer, or chief correspondent. Because of his rising social status, even prior to manumission he could marry a freeborn woman, possess his own slaves, and acquire considerable wealth. His position in the imperial bureaucracy allowed him to exercise power far beyond that of any non-Roman or poor Roman citizen.

In light of the foregoing, it is not surprising that imperial freedmen enjoyed a high level of social status among the Roman lower classes, especially among its foreign groups. For example, in his *Letters* Pliny the Younger calls Claudius Aristion "the leading citizen of Ephesus, popular for his generosity" (6.31.8). Based on studies of the surviving inscriptions, imperial freedmen often dominated the leadership of Rome's private associations (see chap. 2). The social

41. Lampe, *Christen*, 154; Grant and Graham, *First and Second Clement*, 99; Lightfoot, *Apostolic Fathers*, 1.1:27–29, 189.

42. Weaver, *"Familia Caesaris,"* 4; idem, "Social Mobility in the Early Roman Empire"; Finn, "Social Mobility, Imperial Civil Service and the Spread of Early Christianity"; and Keith Hopkins, "Elite Mobility in the Roman Empire," *Past and Present* 32 (1965): 12–26.

status of someone like Valerius Vito, the freedman of a family once related to the emperor, was not far below that of Ephebus.

Clement demonstrates a great deal of respect for Ephebus and Vito. He calls them "faithful and prudent (πιστοὺς καὶ σώφρονας) men, who have lived among us blameless (ἀμέμπτος) from youth to old age, and they shall be witnesses between you and us" (63.3). Clement sends them as the eyes and ears of the Roman Christians. He gives them sole responsibility to observe how the Corinthian Christians follow Clement's advice. These older Christians were undoubtedly leaders of some sort in the Roman congregations, based on their age, general reputation, and Clement's high regard for them. P.R.C. Weaver has shown that imperial slaves often were freed around the age of thirty.[43] If Ephebus had received manumission at thirty, not long before the fall of the Claudian dynasty in 69, he would be old but still active at the time of *1 Clement*'s composition (ca. 96).

Clement of Rome

Information on the identity of Clement goes back to the second century. Hermas describes a Clement as the one charged with addressing other churches on behalf of the Roman Christians (*Vis.* 2.4.3). Scholars in general believe that Hermas refers to the author of *1 Clement*.[44] Irenaeus asserts that this Clement, who had conversed with the apostles (Peter and Paul), was the third to succeed them as bishop of Rome. Eusebius identifies him as the Clement mentioned in Phil. 4:3, and reports that in 92 he became the third bishop of Rome to succeed Peter and Paul, serving until 101 (the third year of Trajan). Jerome also places Clement third in the line of succession at Rome.[45]

While the author's name (Clemens) is Latin, *1 Clement* is written in Greek. He may have been a Roman aristocrat educated in Greek

---

43. Weaver, *"Familia Caesaris,"* 97–100. Osiek, *Rich and Poor,* 107 n. 48, supports this view.

44. Richardson, ed., *Letter of the Church of Rome to the Church of Corinth,* 37; Stuiber, "Clemens Romanus I," 3:189; Jaubert, *Clément de Rome: Épitre aux Corinthiens,* 22; Merrill, *Essays in Early Christian History,* 224; Goodspeed, *History of Early Christian Literature,* 10; and, more cautiously, Hagner, *Use of the Old and New Testaments in Clement of Rome,* 1.

45. For Irenaeus, see Eusebius, *Historia Ecclesiastica* 5.6; for Bishop of Rome, see Eusebius, *Historia Ecclesiastica* 3.4, 15–16, 21, 34; and Jerome, *De Viris Illustribus* 15.

or a Greek-speaking freedman who took a Latin name upon manumission. Most scholars dispute Kleist's view, based on the style of *1 Clement*, that the author was "doubtless an educated Roman and conversant with the requirements of good prose style" who wrote in Greek for the sake of his audience.[46]

Those who could write, such as Clement, must have been very unusual, even in the late first century. This may help explain why Clement wrote to other churches on behalf of the Roman congregations (*Vis.* 2.4.3).[47] His education was much better than average for a Greek-speaking resident in Rome. Stuiber makes a good case for crediting Clement with a grammar-school education. *First Clement* makes what Stuiber considers a moderate use of classic Greek rhetorical style. For example, in *1 Clement* 5.1 and 6.1 we see echoes of the shifting from past to present paradigms present in writers such as Demosthenes. Most current scholars doubt that Clement had training in philosophy, however. Harnack believes the author lacks a "higher philosophical education" and a Roman aesthetic taste.

Someone like Clement, a man living in Rome with a Latin name but whose native tongue was Greek, was almost certainly an ex-slave of a Roman citizen. Freedmen might prefix the praenomen of their master, but customarily they did not take his cognomen. But there was no law to prevent a former slave from using the cognomen of his former master, and we know that discharged non-Roman soldiers did so. Clement must have been some sort of exception to the rule, since the traditions about an early Christian leader named "Clement" are so early and strong. The cognomen Clemens was borne by several members of the Flavian dynasty, which led to a proliferation of this name among new Roman citizens in the late first century. Merrill points out that Clemens was one of the more popular cognomina of the Roman army in the early empire, and suggests that the author of

46. Kleist, *Epistles of St. Clement of Rome and St. Ignatius of Antioch*, 6; Cruttwell, *Literary History of Early Christianity*, 31.

47. Stuiber, "Clemens Romanus I," 3:195. For a comparison between *1 Clement* and the *Letter of Claudius to the Alexandrians*, see Stephan Lösch, "Der Brief des Clemens Romanus," in *Studi dedicati alla memoria Paola Ubaldi* (Milan, 1937), 181–86; *Epistula Claudiana* (Rottenburg: Adolf Bader, 1930), 33–44; Harnack, *Einführung in die Alte Kirchengeschichte*, 51. Van Unnik rejects the suggestion that *1 Clement* reflects a sophisticated knowledge of stoicism in "Is *1 Clement* 20 Purely Stoic?"; and "First Century A.D. Literary Culture and Early Christian History."

1 Clement was of military origin.[48] Virtually all other scholars reject this identification, however.

J. B. Lightfoot, in his monumental work on the Apostolic Fathers, suggested that the author of *1 Clement* was a former slave of the T. Flavius Clemens mentioned above. He based this on the similarity of names, and the belief that Flavius Clemens and Flavia Domitilla were Christians persecuted by Domitian. Many have supported the possibility of Lightfoot's hypothesis, but they rightly point out the lack of hard evidence.[49] The mere coincidence of names offers no proof of a connection between Clement and a particular Roman. Such a connection must rest on more substantial evidence. Such evidence is available, however. In chapter 3 I adduce evidence from archaeology to strengthen the suggestion that Domitilla was at least a Christian sympathizer, while in chapter 4 I attempt to show that the house church of Clement was located on land owned by the Flavians.

Clement's relations with Claudius Ephebus and Valerius Vito lend credence to the idea that Clement was an imperial freedman. Since Clement trusts them and evidences personal knowledge of their lives from young adulthood, the three probably belonged to the same house church. It would be natural for Ephebus to continue as a member of the imperial civil service after the Flavian dynasty came to power. The Flavians would have inherited him as a client, and probably he would have continued in the same or similar posts. Clement, as a Flavian slave or freedman, could easily have come into contact with someone like Ephebus. Based on his comparison of *1 Clement* with the *Letter of Claudius to the Alexandrians*, Lösch asserts that Clement must have been one of the imperial slaves who composed official letters.

The ethnic origin of Clement has been a topic of heated debate. Scholars today have uniformly rejected the idea that he was Roman or Latin by birth. Because Clement demonstrates a knowledge of the Septuagint and postbiblical Jewish literature, Lightfoot and Goppelt

48. Merrill, *Essays in Early Christian History*, 217–18, refers to L. R. Dean, "A Study of the Cognomina of Soldiers in the Roman Legions" (Ph.D. diss., Princeton University, 1916), 20–24.

49. Lightfoot, *Apostolic Fathers*, 1:61; Harnack, *Einführung*, 51; Stuiber, "Clemens Romanus I," 3:189; Hagner, *Use of the Old and New Testaments in Clement of Rome*, 4; Richardson, *Letter of the Church*, 37.

think he was Jewish. Cruttwell and Hagner consider him a Hellenistic Jew. Harnack and Stuiber consider Clement more likely a proselyte to Judaism who later became a Christian. Without further evidence, a firm decision as to Clement's ethnic origin cannot be made.[50]

Early Christian sources disagree about Clement's position in the Roman church. A number of late traditions call Clement "pope." Earlier traditions identify him as a bishop of Rome. Hermas refers to him as a foreign correspondent for the Roman churches. The testimony of Hermas has been used to deny other offices to him, at least at the time Hermas wrote *Vision* 2. But there is nothing to prevent a congregational officeholder from having an additional function such as handling foreign correspondence. As the next chapter shows, Roman Christianity was not ruled by a single bishop before mid-second century. Although monoepiscopacies existed in his day, as the writings of Ignatius (bishop of Antioch) make clear, Clement evidences no knowledge of them in his work. He seems to be cognizant only of a body of leaders of relatively equal authority. But someone with Clement's wisdom, education, and tone of authority must have been at least the leader of a house church. He was probably one of the ruling elders in Rome in addition to his work as a foreign secretary. The second-century bishops of Rome may indeed have descended from those who received apostolic authority from Clement. In other words, Clement's followers may have become in time the dominant group not only of the local church but also of Roman Christianity.

CONCLUSION

Most of the earliest Roman Christians were Jewish. But their temporary expulsion from Rome under the Edict of Claudius allowed for the development of independent gentile congregations in the city. This helped lead to the division between Jewish and gentile Roman Christians that Paul addressed in his letter to the Romans.

50. L. Goppelt, *Christentum und Judentum in ersten und zweiten Jahrhundert* (Gütersloh: Bertelsmann, 1954), 238–41. Cruttwell, *Literary History,* 31. Hagner, *Use of the Old and New Testaments in Clement of Rome,* 8. Harnack, "Klemensbrief," 57–60. See also Ziegler, *Neue Studien zum ersten Klemensbrief,* 134; Knoch, *Eigenart und Bedeutung der Eschatologie im theologischen Aufriss des ersten Clemensbriefes,* 33; and Stuiber, "Clemens Romanus I," 3:189.

Roman Christians, Jews and gentiles alike, came from the non-Latin, noncitizen poor of Rome. With few exceptions, they or their recent ancestors began life in Rome as slaves. When they gained their freedom, some found that they were free to starve. Foreigners were accorded little honor in the larger society. Those who received Roman citizenship when they were freed enjoyed protection under the law, but not much higher status than their noncitizen compatriots. But a fortunate few, the imperial freedmen, saw their social status rise considerably during their lifetimes. Christians among the imperial freedmen could be expected to evaluate the state differently from Christians who suffered humiliation and economic deprivation at each turn.

The first-century Christians identified in our sources represent a broad social spectrum. They include foreign slaves and freedmen, both Jew and gentile. They also include freeborn foreigners. Some were poor; others apparently earned a living well above the subsistence level. One Christian may have been a Roman aristocrat (Domitilla). Imperial freedmen represent the highest social level of Christians in this period of which we can be certain. The following chapters will focus on two of these Christians: Hermas, the author of the *Shepherd of Hermas* and a subsistence-level freedman; and Clement, believed to be the author of *1 Clement* and a house church leader who was probably an imperial freedman.

2

THE SOCIAL ORGANIZATION OF EARLY ROMAN CHRISTIANITY

As we have seen, the first Roman Christians came from the foreign groups in Rome, principally at first from the Jews and the poorer classes. We will now discuss how the early Christians used Roman associations and Jewish synagogues as models for organizing their house churches. These two models led Christians to attempt two different strategies to achieve formal legitimacy. References to Christian house churches, from the New Testament to sixth-century traditions, help us track the development of these influences.

ASSOCIATIONS OF FOREIGNERS IN ROME

As noted in chapter 1, foreigners found little acceptance in the larger Roman society. They were disdained by upper-class Romans and resented by lower-class Romans. It comes as no surprise, therefore, that foreigners sought social acceptance in their own groups and often formed voluntary associations *(collegia)*.[1]

Associations enjoyed a long history in Rome. In the republican period, private associations of any type could be organized. But strict laws regulated them from the end of the Republic to the third century. For example, political associations were forbidden, and the formation of any association had to be approved by the Senate or the emperor. Voluntary associations allowed foreigners to practice their unique religious customs. They made it possible for them to follow a social life better adapted to their tastes and social conditions. They also gave them a way to react against the social exclusion practiced by the larger society.

Since associations tended to be either Latin- or Greek-speaking, foreigners usually joined groups of fellow foreigners. Associations

---

1. The principal source for this section is La Piana, "Foreign Groups in Rome." See also Stambaugh and Balch, *The New Testament in Its Social Environment*, 124–27.

were governed by individual charters. All members were equal, at least in theory, and elected their leaders. The chief officer in Greek-speaking groups was called an archon, or ruler (ἄρχον). Larger groups usually were ruled by a governing board on the model of municipal aristocracies. Many groups included one or more wealthy members who acted as patrons of the association. Some associations were named for a wealthy patron.

An association's income came mainly from monthly dues, fines, and patrons' gifts. Its principal expenses included rental or purchase and maintenance of a meeting place, banquets, funerals, and the purchase of sacrificial animals. An association's meeting place ideally included an open courtyard for meetings, a dining room and kitchen, and a small temple dedicated to the group's patron deity. If a group could not afford its own building, it might meet in the public temple of its patron deity or in a private home. Poor men who pooled their resources in this way were able to put on great banquets in imitation of their social betters. A major concern of all associations among the less wealthy was proper funeral arrangements for deceased members.

Foreigners typically formed four kinds of associations: professional, religious, funerary, and household. Professional associations included people occupied in the same trade, such as bakers, porters, carpenters, and shippers. Of the several hundred professional associations in imperial Rome, a number were composed entirely of foreigners.

Foreigners also formed religious associations (collegia sodalicia). Group meetings centered around the worship of a specific deity. This type of association was quite popular among foreigners, since it gave them a chance to worship freely the god of their homeland. They could follow their ancestral religious practices and provide for their own eventual burial. Freedmen and even slaves often joined the religious associations of foreigners, and in this way maintained contact with free fellow expatriates. Some religious associations owned their own halls. These religious associations were possible because of Rome's normally tolerant attitude toward foreign religions. Romans reasoned that when foreign gods allowed their peoples to be conquered, they submitted themselves to the gods of Rome and recognized Roman sovereignty. So adherents of national religions of allied or conquered nations were allowed to worship their gods openly.

Funerary associations attracted poor non-Romans. They were unique to Rome, where they arose in the first century A.D. in response to the desperate poverty of many inhabitants of the city. At first they were not formal *collegia*, but cooperative societies that bought cemetery ground at common expense. As such, they did not need the state's approval. The poor, including freedmen or slaves without wealthy patrons or owners, wished to avoid the fate of those who could not afford a proper funeral: burial in large common pits. Under the Flavians, these cooperatives gradually were replaced by associations organized by and for poor residents of Rome *(collegia tenuiorum)*. Although they did not need recognition by the Senate or emperor as other associations did, they had to submit a list of members in order to obtain a permit from the city prefect. Members paid a fee to join and a monthly membership fee. When a member died, the other members would honor him with a proper funeral procession and burial. But these groups did more than provide burial insurance. Frequent meetings gave the members a sense of social belonging. Individual associations typically honored a patron deity as well, providing members with religious and cultural identity.

Freedmen and slaves of the same household sometimes formed household associations *(collegia domestica)*. Unlike other associations, their members sometimes came from different ethnic backgrounds, having nothing in common other than their relationship to a common master or patron. Also unlike other associations, they were officially part of their common master's household and met on his property. Greeks and Asians predominated in these associations, according to the inscriptions. Household associations were common in the time of Augustus. Our sources do not make clear whether or not they needed formal approval by the state.

There were also unauthorized associations which existed illegally. If they were not involved in public disorder, however, the government often ignored them, which led some illegal associations not to conceal their existence.

THE SYNAGOGUES OF THE JEWS

The synagogues of the Jews were sanctioned by Rome as official religious associations. But they differed considerably from other religious associations.[2] Individual synagogues, for example, did not need to seek authorization as independent associations, since the right to form them was the general privilege of the Jewish people. A consequence of this, which must have had a significant impact on Christians, is that only Jews could form or even join a synagogue. This consequence is explored below. While most associations served primarily social and religious functions, the synagogues also governed the administrative, educational, and juridical needs of their congregations. Unlike other associations, the Roman synagogues distributed a large portion of donated funds to their poorer members.

The synagogues of Rome were heterogeneous in character. For example, the Synagogue of the Vernaclesians in Transtiberinum probably was founded by and originally consisted of Jews born in Rome. The Synagogue of the Tripolitans was named for a city in Phoenicia or North Africa, from which its members originated. Some synagogues were named for individuals, presumably wealthy and generous patrons. The Synagogue of the Augustesians probably was named after Caesar Augustus. La Piana considers this an example of a household association composed of Jewish slaves and freedmen of the imperial household. The Synagogue of the Agrippesians may have been formed from the Jews in the household of M. Vipsanius Agrippa.[3]

The three known Jewish catacombs confirm that Rome's synagogues differed greatly from one another. Since each catacomb normally was used by only a few synagogues, a comparison of the inscriptions in each catacomb gives us a means of comparing congregations. The Appia catacomb shows a greater percentage of Latin usage than do the others: Latin inscriptions here comprise 36 percent of the total number, but only 20 percent of those at Monteverde and 6 percent of those at Nomentana. By contrast, the Nomentana catacomb shows a preponderance of Greek inscriptions: 92 percent, to 64 percent for Appia and 78 percent for Monteverde. Unlike the Greek inscriptions, which are on stone, all four Latin inscriptions at

2. See La Piana, "Foreign Groups in Rome," 349–55; Leon, *Jews of Ancient Rome*, 142–54; Lampe, *Christen*, 26–28, 367–68; R. Penna, "Les Juifs à Rome au temps de l'Apôtre Paul," *New Testament Studies* 28 (1982): 321–47.

3. On Vernaclesians, see La Piana, "Foreign Groups in Rome," 355; on Tripolitans, see Leon, *Jews of Ancient Rome*, 153–54; on Augustesians, see La Piana, "Foreign Groups in Rome," 355; on Agrippesians, see Leon, *Jews of Ancient Rome*, 141–42.

Nomentana are on marble. This suggests that those who had more fully accepted Roman society also enjoyed a higher social status.

The synagogues were autonomous bodies that associated with each other only loosely. No one individual or group exercised supervision over all Roman Jewry. This is in contrast to Alexandrian Jewry, in which the various synagogues formed a formidable political entity. Each synagogue had its own head over religious activities ("synagogue ruler," ἀρχισυναγόγυς). A council (γερουσία) governed its general affairs, the archon (ἄρχον) handled its nonreligious affairs, and another official was entrusted with financial matters. La Piana concluded that the heterogeneous character of Roman Jewry made a single leader over the Roman synagogues impossible, but he thought these terms referred to a council which governed all of them. The evidence, however, indicates that each synagogue was autonomous. The ways in which the synagogues in Rome provided a model for the early Christian congregations is discussed in the next section.

THE EARLY CHURCH IN THE ROMAN SOCIAL CONTEXT

The first Roman Christians, converts from Judaism, probably resisted leaving the Jewish community. We know that in other places converts from Judaism did not wish to reject their Jewishness, but saw in Christianity the completion of their faith. We have no reason to suspect that this was not true of Jewish Christians in Rome. Jewish Christians found in the synagogues ready audiences for the message that Jesus was the promised Messiah. Jews enjoyed special privileges that Jewish Christians would have to relinquish when they left the synagogue. Jews were exempted from emperor worship, and they could freely organize synagogues and worship their God. Christians enjoyed no such privileges. The commitment of Roman Jewry to provide for the material needs of poor members was a social service not available outside the group. Until the Christians in Rome became organized, wealthy, and numerous enough to duplicate this service, they could not easily separate themselves from Judaism. As a result, synagogue organization provided a convenient and natural model for the organization of Jewish Christian house churches.

Jewish Christians presumably met together in homes even before they left the synagogue. Since Christianity was not recognized by the state, their house churches had to be clandestine. Like the synagogues, each house church would be ruled by elders. The various house churches might have cooperated with each other to some degree, such as in circulating the letter from Paul and other correspondence, but, like the synagogues, undoubtedly they lacked a single ruling council or individual. The arrival of Paul and Peter in Rome did not change this, as I will show.

The presence of significant numbers of non-Latin gentile Christians who had no previous exposure to Judaism had a great influence on the organization of Roman Christianity. Gentile Christians in Rome shared a common Hellenistic cultural context and a common language. Most were slaves or freedmen, and thus had a common low economic and social status. But they came from different ethnic groups in Greece, Asia Minor, and the Near East, so they also represented diverse social, cultural, and religious experiences. Most of them probably were part of an ethnic subculture in Rome prior to their conversion. Such converts would most naturally worship with fellow expatriates, or at least with people who shared their ethnic and cultural heritage.

Since gentile Christians in Rome would be concerned above all to avoid the notice of the government, they probably organized as informal funerary associations. Even Jewish Christians, once separated from the synagogue, probably found this form of association the most convenient. They had only to obtain a permit from the city prefect. As a funerary association, they could have met in the home of a member or patron without arousing suspicion. Since most Christians were poor and probably could not provide for their own burial, the funerary association was the most natural and least conspicuous way for them to organize. In the third century, when Roman Christians began to organize centers for administration and charitable distributions, they would find the funerary association an inappropriate structure. But until that time, it worked quite well.

The First Roman House Churches

The greeting to Roman Christians in Romans 16 provides some important evidence regarding the early house congregations. It mentions at least three house churches. The first is "the church (ἐκκλησία) in the household" of Priscilla and Aquila (16:3-5). Since its leaders were Jewish (see chap. 1), it probably was a Jewish Christian house church. The second is the house church including "Asyncritus, Phlegon, Hermes, Patrobas, Hermas, and the brothers with them" (16:14). All of these names are Greek; none is Jewish. Three were common to the Hellenized East, and three were common slave names in Rome (see chap. 1). The third house church is that of "Philologus and Julia, Nereus and his sister, and Olympas, and all the saints with them" (16:15). Julia is a Latin name, while the rest are Greek. Julia most likely was a Greek slave who took a Latin name upon manumission. Philologus and Nereus were common slave names in Rome. The fact that Nereus knew who his sister was suggests that he and his sister were descendants of freed slaves. Thus, the first of these three congregations was predominantly Jewish, while the other two were composed largely of Greek-speaking gentiles who were slaves or former slaves. Two other house churches may be addressed in verses 10 and 11, which refer to "those who are of the [household of] Aristobulus" and "those of the [household of] Narcissus who are in the Lord." These slaves or freedmen may have formed their own household congregations.

The Roman House Churches and the *Tituli* of Rome

The first two centuries of Christianity have provided us with little other documentary evidence for Rome's house churches. During the early 60s, Paul led a congregation that met in his rented residence (Acts 28:30). A marble inscription confirms that in the second century, the congregation surrounding Valentinian met in a suburban villa on the Via Latina.[4] Also in the second century, the congregation of Justin met in rented lodgings over the Bath of the Myrtinus.[5] Justin records that the Christians in his day met in private dwellings (*Dialogue with Trypho* 47.2). One would expect this, since Christians had to meet clandestinely until the time of Constantine.

Further information about the nature of these house churches comes from later church tradition, which says that the Roman congregations numbered twenty-five in the first century. The earliest evidence for this comes from the chronicler of the sixth-century *Liber Pontificalis*. He states that in the first century Pope Cletus, by

---

4. A. Coppo, "Contributo all'interpretazione de un' epigrafe greca cristiana dei Musei Capitolini," *Revista di Archeologia Cristiana* 46 (1970): 97–138.

5. Lampe, *Christen*, 306.

Two examples from the port town of Ostia of private homes
in imperial Rome.

order of St. Peter, ordained twenty-five presbyters to whom Pope Evaristus, at the beginning of the following century, entrusted the twenty-five title churches (*tituli*) of Rome. He further states that Pope Dionysius (259–68) gave the *tituli* to the presbyters as residences, and that Pope Marcellus (308–9) organized the *tituli* as centers of church administration. No surviving evidence corroborates the accuracy of these statements, and the information on Cletus and Evaristus is particularly doubtful. Nevertheless, as J. P. Kirsch indicates, the tradition is so strong, and unchallenged by any alternate view, that it indicates a pre-Constantinian origin for the *tituli*.[6]

The earliest names preserved for the twenty-five *tituli* are: Aemilianae, Anastasiae, Byzantis, Caeciliae, Callisti, Chrysogoni, Clementis, Crescentianae, Cyriaci, Equitii, Fasciolae, Gai, Lucinae, Marcelli, Nicomedis, Praxedis, Priscae, Pudentis, Sabinae, Tigridae, Apostolorum, Damasi, Eusebii, Marci, and Vestinae. The last five *tituli* clearly originated in the fourth and fifth centuries, but the other twenty are probably pre-Constantinian.

Most of the *tituli* came to be identified with a saint only in the sixth century. Kirsch suggests that the renaming may have resulted from a special occasion, such as the building of the basilica, or from the fact that the annual celebration for a martyr took place at that location. The pre-Constantinian *tituli* may have belonged to a devotee of a particular saint in whose memory the house church was dedicated. It is also possible that later Christians confused the name of the building's donor with that of a saint.[7]

Basilicas exist today on all twenty-five sites (Fig. 1). Archaeological evidence shows that the first basilicas built on the *tituli* sites date only to the fourth century or later. But "almost without exception" the remnants of large tenement buildings or private homes, dating from the second or third century, are incorporated into the walls or preserved below the floors of these basilicas.[8] These buildings, prior

6. L. Duchesne, *Le Liber Pontificalis*, 3 vols. (Paris: Cyrille Vogel, 1886–92), 1:122, 126, 157, 164; Kirsch, *Die römischen Titelkirchen im Altertum*, 117. See also Lampe, *Christen*, 301–7; Filson, "Significance of the Early House Churches"; Krautheimer, *Early Christian and Byzantine Architecture*, 23–24; Peterson, "House-Churches in Rome"; C. Cecchelli, "Roma: Archeologia e Topografia Cristiana," in *Enciclopedia Italiana* 29 (Rome: Instituto della Enciclopedia Italiana, 1949), 607–10; Mâle, *Early Churches of Rome*.

7. Kirsch, *Titelkirchen*, 11, 147.

8. Krautheimer, *Early Christian and Byzantine Architecture*, 29.

to the fourth century, usually were owned by Christians. The church modified them for use as centers of administration and for the storage and distribution of food and clothing to needy Christians. This suggests that the *tituli* were private house churches, like those in Romans 16, which evolved into regional centers and later into basilicas.

Thus, the *titulus* did not originally refer to a basilica. It is a legal term, from which the English term "title," as in property, derived. In the cities of Italy, and especially in Rome, buildings often were named after their builder or present owner, whose name customarily appeared on a marble slab above the entrance. The names of the *tituli*, except those that are clearly of late origin, may have come from these slabs (referring to an earlier owner or the original builder), or may have belonged to the individuals who donated the properties to the church. Thus, the concept of a "title church" must have originated in the early third century at the latest, when the church did not yet possess property of its own.[9]

It appears probable that the twenty *tituli* stand out from the other churches of Rome because they, as the oldest congregations, became the church's administrative and charitable distribution centers. Kirsch suggests that in the second century, while they were still private homes, the *tituli* were used for Christian worship services. The archaeological remains help confirm this. The private buildings at many of the sites were modified either structurally or superficially in the late second and third centuries. This remodeling was done by the church, once it came to possess these buildings, to adapt them for use as centers of the church's organization.[10]

At this point, we can visualize the evolution of house church congregations in Rome. In the first and second centuries, Christians met in small, essentially autonomous house congregations. As with Roman Judaism, little or no central organization existed. Each house church would have to decide whether to meet in absolute secrecy or to declare itself a voluntary association. The synagogue model as well as the association model and the Romans 16 list suggest that each congregation was ruled by several leaders. Local congregations were named very practically after the Christian in whose home the

---

9. Peterson, "House-Churches," 266.
10. Kirsch, *Titelkirchen*, 134.

house church met. New house churches would arise spontaneously as needed, while others periodically would die out. When popular teachers such as Valentinus or Marcion arrived in Rome, they would naturally host a new house church. As Roman Christianity achieved central organization, it began to take over the operation of local house churches needed as administrative centers. Roman Christians, who revered their traditions, would convert the oldest house churches to this purpose whenever possible.

The *Titulus* of Clement

The Roman *tituli* preserve the locations of a number of second-century house churches, and some of them may even date to the first century. Unfortunately, the *Liber Pontificalis* gives us little dependable evidence about the identities or beliefs of their members. However, the name of one *titulus* is the same as the name of a first-century house church leader: Clement (see chap. 1). The *Enciclopedia Italiana* includes it among the five *tituli* it considers clearly pre-Constantinian. Kirsch and Krautheimer agree with this assessment.[11] The *Liber Pontificalis* identifies the *Titulus sancti Clementis* with T. Flavius Clemens, calling him the son of Faustus or Faustinus.[12]

CONCLUSION

Early Roman Christianity had to develop its own organization. In its earliest years, no apostles were present to enforce a single model. Paul and Peter, during their later and brief stays in Rome, could have had only limited influence on existing house churches. But the first Roman Christians did have organizational models: foreigners in Rome, from whom they were descended, often organized in associations. House churches provided a number of the benefits of these associations: a sense of belonging, a personal social identity, a feeling of honor lacking in the larger society, and a way to practice common beliefs. Christians also were influenced by that specialized religious

---

11. Cecchelli, "Roma," 608.
12. Duchesne, *Liber Pontificalis*, 1:123. This information first appears in the third-century texts ascribed to Clement—the Clementine *Homilies* and *Recognitions*. However, these stories are highly suspect. More reliable is the testimony of Jerome, who in 392 wrote that during a visit to Rome he had seen the church which preserved up to his day the memory of the name of Clement of Rome ("Nominus ejus memoriam usque hodie Romae exstructa ecclesia custodit" [Jerome, *De Viris Illustribus* 15]).

association, the synagogue. The autonomous nature of their synagogues helped preserve their differing customs and ways of adapting to Roman society. Like the synagogues, the early house churches were independent. Since significant variations in social identity existed among the synagogues, we should expect significant differences among the house churches of Jewish Christians. After all, they had to meet in smaller groups, since they could not build their own meeting places.

Two basic social groups existed among the early Roman Christians: Jewish converts to Christianity (and perhaps a few gentile proselytes to Judaism who in turn converted to Christianity), and a larger group of gentile Christians. Undoubtedly, a number of variations were represented within each group. Since Roman Christians remained Greek-speaking through most of the second century, the gentile Christian group probably was composed predominantly of free Greek-speaking foreigners at Rome and Greek-speaking slaves and freedmen.

3

THE FIRST
ROMAN CATACOMB

A central thesis of this book is that Clement of Rome, the author of
1 Clement, because of his connection with the imperial family of
Flavius Clemens and Flavia Domitilla, belonged to a social elite in
the Roman churches. No incontestable evidence for this connection
exists, however. The connection would be more plausible if Clemens
and Domitilla were Christians or patronized Christians within their
household. While documentary evidence of Christians within Domitilla's household is too late to be reliable, archaeological evidence
suggests that Domitilla sponsored a congregation of Christians. In
chapter 4 I offer evidence for the presence of this Christian house
church. In this chapter we will see that Domitilla, whether or not she
was a Christian, patronized Christians among her dependents.

The most recent excavations at the Catacomb of Domitilla have
given credence to suggestions of a connection between it and a first-
century Christian aristocrat named Flavia Domitilla (see chap. 1).
There is reason to think that the land on which the catacomb sits
was originally intended in part for first-century Christians within
Domitilla's household. This should, in addition, cause scholars to
rethink some of their basic assumptions about the practice of Christian burial.

THE CATACOMBS OF ROME

In Rome, as in the rest of the Empire, free persons had to provide
for their own burial. Cemeteries were located outside the city gates.
Most Romans were cremated, and their ashes were placed in urns
alongside the ashes of family members. Jews rejected cremation,
however, and buried their dead in underground cemeteries maintained by the various synagogues (see chap. 2). Roman Christians
followed the Jewish pattern of burying their dead unburnt. The cem-

eteries of the Jews and Christians in Rome are called "catacombs" because they are located underground. All known Christian cemeteries in the East, and most of those in the West, are open-air. Catacombs are found only in parts of Italy and North Africa.[1]

Since Christians lacked the financial resources of Roman Judaism in the first century, the earliest Christian burials had to be on private land owned by Christians or by their wealthy pagan patrons. As time progressed, Christians who owned burial land donated it to the Christian community. As a result, the early underground burial chambers, or *hypogea*, became the nuclei of subterranean galleries excavated to hold the ever-increasing number of deceased Christians. The galleries usually were a meter wide and two to three meters high. Niches (*loculi*), just large enough to hold one body, were dug on both sides of the galleries. The opening was closed with large tiles or bricks, or with a marble slab if the family could afford one. Small vases for perfume, placed throughout, helped mask the odor of decomposition. Pottery lamps attached to the walls helped visitors find their loved ones. Wealthier Christians had larger chambers excavated to provide space for the bodies of entire families. The volcanic soil (tufa) into which most of these catacombs are dug proved ideal for the purpose. It is easy to dig, but very stable. Even after nearly two millennia, cave-ins are virtually unknown.

A number of mistaken ideas have been perpetuated about the Roman Christian catacombs. The catacombs never served as regular meeting places for Roman Christians. The chambers were far too small to hold more than a handful of mourners at any one time. The constant stench also would have prohibited their being used for worship. Only burial services were held there, and they were attended only by the family and friends of the deceased. Large halls were erected near the catacombs for this purpose, from the third century on. Moreover, the catacombs were not secret. Their entrances typically fronted on major roads. They were protected from sacrilege by Roman law, which considered any tomb inviolable. Also, Romans feared to violate even the tombs of poor and despised persons lest they be troubled by the departed spirits. Clearly, Christians did not need to keep their tombs secret.

---

1. Kirsch, *Catacombs of Rome*, 1–4. See also DeVisscher, *Le Droit des Tombeaux Romains*; and Krautheimer, *Early Christian and Byzantine Architecture*, 29–36.

Christian catacombs usually were named after the original owner of the property under which they were excavated: Domitilla, Priscilla, Pretaxtatus, and Commodilla. Others were known by their location: "in the hollow," "between the two laurels," or "at the watermelon hill." Later catacombs were named for martyrs and other saints. The Domitilla and Priscilla catacombs probably are the earliest, dating to the end of the first or beginning of the second century. New catacombs were added during the second century: Callistus, Pretextatus, and Calepodius. These catacombs were enlarged and extended many times in the next century. New cemeteries in the third century included Pamphilus, Maximus, Thrason, Jordani, St. Hippolytus, St. Lawrence, "between the two laurels," "in the hollow," and Pontianus. The date of origin cannot yet be ascertained for a number of other catacombs.

The earliest truly public Christian catacomb is that of Calixtus. Around the year 200, the Roman church came into possession of land on the Appian Way, south of Rome. The deacon Calixtus considerably enlarged this cemetery before he assumed the bishopric of Rome. During the third and fourth centuries, the other major Christian catacombs came under the control of the Roman bishop. Once they were donated to the church, the catacombs were administered by the titular churches (see chap. 2).

THE CATACOMB OF DOMITILLA

Of all the Roman catacombs, that of Domitilla provides one of the best opportunities to find hard evidence as to the nature of first- and second-century Roman Christianity.[2] It is one of only two cemeteries that can be dated to this early period and it appears to be named

2. For the history of excavations at this site, see Umberto M. Fasola, *Guide to the Catacomb of Domitilla* (Vatican City: Pontifical Commission of Sacred Archaeology, 1974), 3. See the untitled articles by G. B. De Rossi in the *Bulletino de Archeologia Cristiana* 3 (1865): 33–46, 89–99; 19 (1881): 57–74, 123; Pergola, "Coemeterium Domitillae: le Labyrinthe de la Via Ardeatina"; idem, "La Condamnation des Flaviens 'Chretiens' sous Domitien"; idem, "Il Praedium Domitillae sulla Via Ardeatina"; idem, "La Region Dite du Bon Pasteur dans le Cimetiere de Domitilla sur l'Ardeatina"; idem, "La Région Dite des Flavii Aurelii dans la Catacombe de Domitille." See also Ferrua, "Il Cubicolo dei Mattei nella Catacombe de S. Domitilla"; Ermini, "L'Ipogeo detto dei Flavi in Domitilla I, II." The most significant current work at the Domitilla Catacomb site is being done by Philippe Pergola of the Pontifical Institute of Christian Archaeology.

A third-century gallery in the Catacomb of Domitilla.

after the Flavia Domitilla referred to as a Christian or sympathizer with Christianity in chapter 1.

The Catacomb of Domitilla is one of the Christian burial grounds south of Rome, along the Via Ardeatina. According to tradition, it was named after a member of the imperial Flavian family exiled as a result of her Christian faith by the Emperor Domitian in 96.

Inscriptions Attesting to Ownership

Four first-century inscriptions give evidence for the ownership of this estate. The first inscription is a fragment found not at the Domitilla site but in a vineyard near the cemetery. It is now in the fourth-century basilica on the site. The following is its text with the restorations suggested by Theodor Mommsen, which most scholars accept as probable:

> Tatia Baucylla, nurse to seven great-grandchildren of the deified Vespasian, the children of Flavius Clemens and his wife Flavia Domitilla, the granddaughter of the deified Vespasian. Having

received this place by favor, I have made this burial place for my freedmen and freedwomen and their descendants.[3]

This inscription, written to a pagan freedman named Baucylla, commemorates the gift of space for a sepulcher by Flavia Domitilla, granddaughter of Vespasian (and wife of Flavius Clemens if Mommsen's restorations are correct).

The second inscription fragment also records the donation of a plot of land. Its first half is preserved at the Capitoline Museum in Rome and its second half is at the Basilica of San Clemente in Rome. It is also presented with Mommsen's suggested restorations:

Flavia Domitilla, daughter of Flavia Domitilla, and granddaughter of the Emperor Caesar Vespasian, made this for Glycerae and her husband Onesimus and their descendants, he being in charge of the work and an honorable man.[4]

The owner of the donated land is the daughter of Flavia Domitilla and the granddaughter of another well-known person. Based on the last inscription and the words of Suetonius, Mommsen makes her the granddaughter of Vespasian and identifies her as Flavia Domitilla. This clearly would identify as owner the Flavia Domitilla married to Flavius Clemens.

The third inscription was found on the catacomb site in 1871 in a pagan sepulcher over the catacomb. The inscription is now lost. It apparently was complete, but partly illegible:

Publius Calvisius Philotas assigned, as a burial place for his very dear brother Servius Cornelius Julianus and for his wife Calvisia as well as for himself, a space 35 feet broad and 40 feet long, by kind permission of Flavia Domitilla.[5]

---

3. *Corpus Inscriptionum Latinarum*, VI n. 8942 (hereafter cited *CIL*). Suggested completions of the partially illegible inscription are provided in brackets. "TATIA BAVCYL[la . . . nu]TRIX SEPTEM LIB[erorum pronepotum] DIVI VESPASIAN[i filiorum Fl Clementis et] FLAVIAE DOMITILL[ae uxoris eius, divi] VESPASIANI NEPTIS A[ccepto loco e]IVS BENEFICIO HOC SEPHVLCRV[m feci]MEIS LIBERTIS LIBERTABVS PO[sterisque eorum]." For comments on the inscription, see Styger, "L'origine del cimitero di Domitilla sull'Ardeatina," 90.

4. *CIL*, VI n. 948. "[Flavia Domitilla] FILIA FLAVIAE DOMITILLAE [Imp Caesaris Vespasi]ANI NEPTIS FECIT GLYCERAE L ET [post]ERISQVE EORVM CVRANT[e] ONESIMO CONIVGI BENE MER[enti]."

5. *CIL*, VI n. 16246. "SER CORNELIO IVLIANO FRAT PIISSIMO ET CAL[visi]AE EIVS P CALVISIVS PHILOTAS ET SIBI EX INDVLGENTIA FLAVIAE DOMITILLAE IN FR P XXXV IN AGR P XXXX."

This inscription refers to a third plot of land donated by Flavia Domitilla. The inscription differs from the other two in two ways: it makes no reference to the divine Vespasian, and the size of the plot is spelled out. The names of the beneficiaries indicate that they were once slaves but had gained their freedom by the time of the grant.

The final inscription, a fragment, was discovered in 1770 in the area of the Domitilla site:

For the father of the granddaughter of the deified Vespasian.[6]

In light of the first three inscriptions, most experts accept this as a reference to Flavia Domitilla. Thus, it constitutes a fourth independent grant of burial land in this estate.

The view of Pergola and Styger seems most likely. They maintain that all four inscriptions refer to the same Flavia Domitilla, granddaughter of Vespasian, niece of Domitian, and wife of Flavius Clemens. The first inscription clearly refers to this person. Since we know of only two others named Flavia Domitilla, her mother and grandmother, the second inscription must refer to Clemens's wife or to her mother. If it refers to her mother, no logical completion of the second line is possible since her grandfather was Flavius Sabinus.[7] Thus, this inscription also must refer to Clemens's wife.

We know that Livia, wife of Caesar Augustus, made grants of burial plots to her dependents. So it is not surprising that a wealthy Flavian woman would make the same kind of grants. But for the lengthy passage of time, we might have found many more inscriptions at the Domitilla site, since the dependents of a Flavian household undoubtedly numbered in the hundreds. The land encompassed by the Domitilla estate is large enough to accommodate many such grants. Domitilla could also have made grants to funeral associations established by the poor among her dependents to collect dues for burial expenses (see chap. 2).

The apparent pagan nature of these inscriptions seems to conflict with the suggestion that Domitilla was a Christian. Most scholars consider all four inscriptions to be pagan in nature, made by a pagan landowner to pagan dependents.[8] The maker of the first and fourth

6. *CIL*, VI n. 949. "[D]IVI VESPASIANI NEPTIS PATRI."
7. Pergola, "Condamnation," 416; Styger, "L'origine," 94. See Lightfoot, *Apostolic Fathers*, 1:17.
8. Pergola, "Condamnation," 421; Styger, "L'origine," 42.

inscriptions refers to the "divine" Vespasian, so was certainly pagan. The third was found in place in a pagan sepulcher, so its recipients presumably were pagan. The second makes no Jewish or Christian references, but neither does it make any pagan references.

Domitilla may have granted land to pagans in her household, even though she was a convert to Judaism or Christianity, or she may have made these grants prior to her conversion. These inscriptions, recorded by the recipients, should not be expected to tell us anything about the religious beliefs of the donor. Rather, they provide evidence only that Domitilla did donate burial land to her dependents. Unfortunately, we have no direct evidence that she granted land to Christian dependents. But it is safe to assume that she made many more than four grants and that among those may have been grants to Christian dependents.

Above-Ground Columbarii

Pergola is at pains to point out a fact that many studying the Catacomb of Domitilla have overlooked or slighted: The developments above ground have a direct and significant relationship to those below ground. The wall discovered in 1926 is 70 meters long and 1.5 meters high (Fig. 1), and is near the fourth-century subterranean basilica. Its *opus reticulatum* style indicates that it was built sometime between the reigns of Domitian and Hadrian (ca. 81–135). It surrounds seven columbarii, one of which housed about two hundred and fifty urns. Above-ground funeral rites in this area were not limited to cremation, however. Excavators have also discovered pagan sepulchers, which indicate that the area was used by pagans both before and after the transition among pagans from cremation to interment around the time of Hadrian (117–35). Further evidence of the long period of pagan use includes first-century B.C. inscriptions and a post-Hadrianic pagan tomb. A lamp, dating to the latter half of the second century, was found near this tomb. Thus, pagans used the above-ground region of the Domitilla estate as a cemetery from the time of Julius Caesar until the latter half of the second century.[9]

---

9. Pergola, "Praedium," 321; idem, "Condamnation," 331. Pergola thinks that the columbarii which have yet to be excavated are the oldest. Styger, "L'origine," 95, 321, 324. Cf. Blake, *Roman Construction in Italy From Tiberius Through the Flavians.*

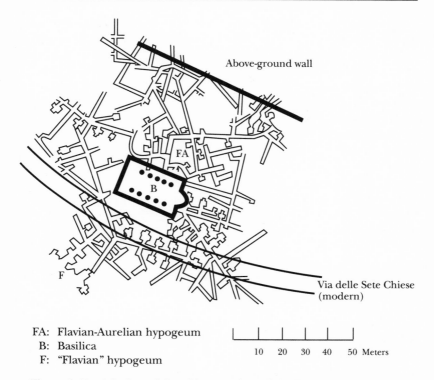

FA: Flavian-Aurelian hypogeum
 B: Basilica
 F: "Flavian" hypogeum

10   20   30   40   50 Meters

Figure 1: Partial plan of the oldest portion of the Domitilla Catacomb.

The "Flavian" Hypogeum

In 1865, De Rossi discovered an opulently decorated underground gallery for sarcophagi (hypogeum). He proclaimed it the "Vestibule of the Flavians" (Fig. 2). Scholars today accept Styger's detailed critique and ultimate rejection of De Rossi's conclusion.[10] No inscriptions here record the names of Flavian aristocrats known to us. It may have been planned by a wealthy Roman *collegium* or designed for a limited number of dependents of a Roman aristocratic household. Based on the style of the original wall painting, the hypogeum was first excavated and used during the latter half of the

10. Styger, "L'origine," 99–111.

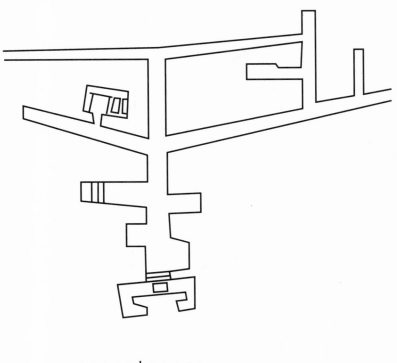

5   10 Meters

Figure 2: The "Flavian" hypogeum.

second century. No fragments of Christian inscriptions or identifiable Christian sarcophagi have been found in the oldest part of the hypogeum. Even more significant is the presence of clearly pagan decorations, for example, bucolic scenes depicting animal sacrifices. However, Ermini considers two pictures securely Christian: "Daniel Between the Lions" and "Noah in the Ark." Although the subject matter is from the Old Testament, the absence of any other evidence of Jewish occupation, the later presence of Christians here, and the fact that the early Christians often painted themes from the Old Testament make it clear that these pictures were not painted by adherents to Judaism. While Fasola dates these pictures to mid-second century, Pergola and Ermini agree that they are more probably from the early third century.[11]

Thus, the original excavators and users of the Domitilla estate were pagans. But sometime in the beginning of the third century, within fifty years of its origin, the "Flavian" hypogeum was taken over by Christians. They extended corridors, added new corridors, and, by the fourth century, joined these corridors with those of other parts of the Christian Domitilla catacomb.

The Flavian-Aurelian Hypogea

The inscriptions found in these hypogea give them their name. Though once considered one hypogeum, this area was later determined to be two autonomous hypogea joined at a relatively early date. In their original state, the two were about forty meters apart (Fig. 3). The hypogea date from the end of the second century. Styger placed the origin of the older of the two, A, at mid-second century. Later excavations exposed more of the main stairway to this hypogeum. Seven bricks with stamps found in place have allowed modern scholars to assign the hypogeum a date no later than near the end of the second century. This is the only certain *in situ* evidence for the date of origin of either hypogeum.[12]

The earliest inscriptions, in Greek, have no overtly Christian messages. Some of the later Greek inscriptions include the Christian *chi-rho* monogram. Over time, probably during the third century, Greek inscriptions gave way to Latin ones.

Most scholars consider these hypogea Christian in origin and thus one of the nuclei of the most ancient Christian catacombs in Rome.[13] Scholars cannot tell for certain whether a number of the earliest decorations are Christian. Only one side-room *(cubicula)* in the earliest part of the hypogea has identifiably Christian decorations, which may be no earlier than mid-third century. Nevertheless, it appears that the Flavian-Aurelian hypogea were dug by Christians near the end of the second century.

11. Ermini, "L'Ipogeo," 160–61; Pergola, "Praedium," 325; Fasola, *Guide*, 24.

12. For the Flavian-Aurelian area, see Styger, "L'origine," 111–26; U. M. Fasola and Pasquale Testini, "I Cimiteri Cristiani," *Atti del IX Congresso Internazionale de Archeologia Cristiana* (Vatican City: Pontifical Institute of Christian Archaeology, 1975), 103–39; and Pergola, "Région," 241.

13. Pergola, "Région," 185.

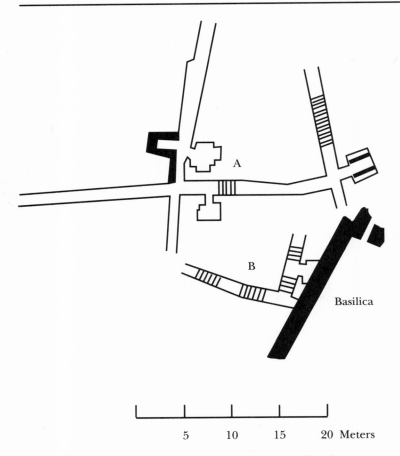

Figure 3: The two sections of the Flavian-Aurelian hypogeum
just prior to their union.

The Reasons for Underground Burial

The discovery of underground pagan hypogea challenged the standard explanation of why Christians constructed their hypogea underground. It has been generally assumed that Christians, as members of an unsanctioned religion, built underground to avoid exposing the cult to public notice. According to this reasoning, burial above ground would have entailed a much greater risk. But this does not explain why pagans decided to take their sepulchers underground. It is more than coincidence that within two generations of the transition from cremation to interment at this site, another transition occurred: from above-ground columbarii to subterranean hypogea. Between the second and fourth centuries, existing cemeteries such as that on the Domitilla estate were converting to farms.[14] This happened in part because many great families of Rome, such as the Flavians, were in decline and had less need for the land. Underground burial allowed the surface land to be farmed, while the land below was used for burial. The farmer need only sacrifice a few square meters here and there for the entrance stairwells. Thus, Pergola concludes that the few pagan users of the land remaining at the end of the second century were forced to go underground as the surface land was converted to agricultural use. It may be that underground Christian cemeteries, at least here, were more a result of economic concerns than of fears of persecution or the Palestinian Jewish precedent.

Inscriptions in the
Domitilla Catacomb

The inscriptions found in the Domitilla hypogea give us additional information about the early users of this site. An inscription from the fourth century demonstrates that Constantinian Christians called this the Catacomb of Domitilla. A fragment of a marble loculus closure slab, 32 cm. high and 45 cm. long, found in the catacomb (but not *in situ*) reads "MVZISO QVIV[xit annis . . .] DEPOSITVS ESTIN[p incoemeterio] DOMITILL[ae]."[15] Thus, Domitilla's name was associated with it while the catacomb was still in use, and before the veneration of early Christian burial sites and the attendant exaggeration of martyrdom stories became strong. Epitaphs that gave the name of the cemetery were quite rare in Rome.[16] The inscription suggests that early Roman Christians associated Domitilla with this site, and perhaps with Christianity.

Two early inscriptions have been discovered among the above-ground columbarii. Both refer to members of the *gens* Cerellia who

14. F. Coarelli, *Dintorni di Roma* (Bari: G. Laterza, 1981), 11–13.
15. A. Ferrua and Silvagni, eds., *Inscriptiones Christianae Urbis Romae*, 4 vols. (Vatican City: Pontifical Institute of Christian Archaeology, 1956), 3:6830. The completion suggested here is not contested by scholars. See, e.g., Ferrua, "Nomi di catacombe nell'iscrizioni in Lucinis," 240.
16. Ferrua, "Nomi di catacombe," 247.

held public office: one at the time of Marc Antony, the other during the reign of Emperor Tiberius. They indicate that this area was used as a necropolis as early as the first century B.C. It may have been in the hands of the Flavian family for most of this time prior to Flavia Domitilla.

Of all the names represented in the underground catacomb inscriptions, the Flavian family names are the most ancient. All appear to be pagan, with the exception of Flavilla and possibly Flavius Sabinus, which appear later in securely Christian contexts. This latter name is interesting, since Flavius Clemens's grandfather, father, and brother all were named T. Flavius Sabinus. This inscription probably refers not to any of those Romans but to a freedman within the Flavian household. Either he or an ancestor, according to common practice, adopted the gentile name of his owner upon receiving his freedom.

The next oldest family names represented in the inscriptions are Aelius and Aurelius. Though most of these inscriptions are pagan, many clearly are Christian. Both pagan and Christian names include the nomen and cognomen. For example, there are pagan names such as Aelia Secunda and Aurelius Callimorphus, and Christian names such as Aelia Calliope and Aurelius Silvanius. They date approximately to the Antonine Age (mid- to late-second century). It seems that they were the names of the last pagans and the first Christians to use the site. Over time, names showing a connection with the imperial household disappear. They are replaced by simple, servile-looking names. Styger concludes from this that the descendants of the imperial dependents who had been given this land by Domitilla gradually converted to Christianity (around the latter half of the second century), and in the third century made their inheritance available to the general Christian community.[17] This fits with the general evolution of catacomb use detailed above.

The Issue of Confiscation

The status of Domitilla's property, following her forced exile from Rome (see chap. 1), is crucial to the origin of the catacomb. Dio reports that of those condemned for drifting into "Jewish ways," some were executed "and the rest were at least deprived of their property.

17. Styger, "L'origine," 133–34, 144.

Domitilla was merely banished to Pandateria."[18] Banishment was usually accompanied by the confiscation of property. In view of Domitian's desperate need for money, the most logical reading of this passage is that Domitilla was not executed but was only banished after her property was confiscated.

If her property was confiscated, was it later restored to her? Dio tells us that Nerva "restored" those banished by Domitian.[19] One would assume that Domitilla thus returned to her property and servants in Rome soon after her banishment. But Domitilla's situation was unique. Suetonius relates that Stephanus, Domitilla's *procurator* (steward), took part in the conspiracy to kill Domitian (*Domitian* 17). The imperial household must have known about the actions of Stephanus and his relationship to Domitilla. She was never implicated formally in the assassination, but soldiers who were after blood would care little for legal formalities. She would have had at least the appearance of responsibility—after her husband's murder, she certainly had a motive to plot against Domitian. Thus, Pergola suggests that the praetorian guard would have compelled Nerva not to restore Domitilla's property. Whether they felt as strongly about Domitian's assassination as did the common soldiers is uncertain, but the captain of the praetorian guard under Domitian continued in that position under Nerva. In addition, land such as the Domitilla cemetery estate was juridically bound to the imperial family and thus not considered entirely private property.[20] Thus, there was less reason for the new emperor to return that property to Domitilla, even if he returned her other properties.

Second-century developments on the Domitilla cemetery land can be understood if the land was never returned. This would explain, for example, the large number of second-century burial land grants to dependents of the imperial household throughout the area of the Domitilla estate.[21] If the land did not remain at the disposal of one person, it could be used by various groups within the imperial household. Pergola suggests that this also explains the sud-

18. Dio Cassius, *Roman History* 67.14.
19. Ibid., 68.1. See also "Patrimonium," in *Paulys Real-Encyclopädie der classischen Altertumwissenschaft*, Supplements 10, ed. Wilhelm Kroll and Karl Mittelhaus (Stuttgart: J. B. Metzlersche, 1965), 493–500.
20. Pergola, "Condamnation," 422.
21. O. Marucchi, *Roma Sotterranea Cristiana* (Rome: Desclee, 1909), 1:24–28.

den appearance of Christians at the end of the second century. He points out that, even though burial land might be confiscated, the *loca religiosa* of earlier donations were legally protected. Those donations could not be given to new recipients.[22] So if Christians within her household had been granted burial space in her cemetery estate, they would not have been able to use it after her banishment. But they would retain the right to the plots, and if circumstances changed, the plots could be claimed by them or their descendants.

CONCLUSION

Flavia Domitilla, wife of Flavius Clemens and granddaughter of Emperor Vespasian, probably patronized the practice of Christianity in her household. Christians in this household congregation, as dependents of an imperial household, had economic and social advantages not normally available to other slaves and freedmen.

Toward the end of the second century, as pagan use of the Domitilla cemetery estate diminished, the Christian descendants of Domitilla's Christian dependents finally could use this land. One might argue that the intervening period of time is too great to make this likely. The first Christians using this land would have to be at least the grandchildren of Domitilla's Christian dependents. But surely a story as dramatic as that of Domitilla, Clemens, and Emperor Domitian would have survived several generations of family storytelling. The memory of a grant of burial land also would have been preserved from parent to child as part of the story.

22. Pergola, "Condamnation," 422.

4

THE HOUSE CHURCH
OF CLEMENT

In chapter 1, we noted that Flavia Domitilla was probably a Christian or was at least a sympathizer with Christianity. The similarity between the name of her husband, Flavius Clemens, and a house church leader active during their time, Clement, has caused many to suppose that Clement was a freedman in their household. But scholars lacked substantive proof of this connection.

A Christian house church almost certainly met under Domitilla's auspices, as we noted in chapter 2. Church tradition for centuries has associated the name of Clement of Rome with one of the *tituli* or parish churches of ancient Rome. If this connection is authentic, and if a relationship between this parish church and the Flavian household can be demonstrated, we may be more certain about the social status of Clement and his congregation.

THE SAN CLEMENTE COMPLEX

We now consider the tradition surrounding the *titulus* of Clement and the archaeological investigation of this monument. Did a first-century house church worship here? Such physical surroundings could have helped shape the development of early Roman Christianity. We also consider the idea that the first-century buildings under San Clemente, the *titulus* of Clement according to tradition, were raised by a part of the Flavian family on land it owned. This information can help us understand more about the social status and social identity of the first Roman Christians.

Historical and Topographical
Contexts

Located in the dip between the Esquiline and Caelian hills of Rome, the San Clemente complex sits less than three hundred meters east of the Flavian Amphitheater (Colosseum). Prior to the rise to power of the Flavian dynasty, this area was dramatically reshaped by Emperor Nero to create the Domus Aurea, his "Golden House."[1] Most studies of the San Clemente remains neglect its historical and topographical setting during the first century of imperial Rome. But such an approach provides valuable insights into the ownership and use of the buildings in this early period. As a result, the following study places the San Clemente remains within time and space contexts.

Nero began construction of the Domus Aurea prior to 64, but his ambitious plans came to fruition only after the fire of that year. As noted in chapter 1, Nero was accused of having started the fire to further his own goals. Suetonius states that Nero directed servants to start the fire in various places. He tells us that Nero's men destroyed a vast number of tenements and mansions and that Nero "also coveted the sites of several granaries, solidly built in stone, near the Golden House; having knocked down their walls with siege-engines, he set the interiors ablaze" (*Nero* 38). Unlike his predecessor Tiberius, who had not taken advantage of fires in A.D. 27 and 36 to add to his own properties, Nero took possession of a huge tract of devastated land surrounding his palace.

The Domus Aurea complex included a grand palace and baths, and at its center was an artificial lake (on the site later occupied by the Colosseum) surrounded by extensive grounds. Built by Nero between 64 and 68, and finished by Otho, the Domus Aurea was intended to represent a sprawling Roman country villa placed in the center of Rome. A greater snub to the common people of Rome, living in densely packed and squalid conditions, can hardly be imagined. Tacitus says of this palace, "The marvels did not consist so much in gems and gold, materials long familiar and vulgarized by luxury, as in fields and lakes and the air of solitude given by wooded grounds alternating with clear tracts and open landscapes" (*Annals* 15.42). A pasquinade of the time suggests the impression its size made on the Roman mind: "All Rome is transformed to a villa!

1. Axel Boëthius, *The Golden House of Nero* (Ann Arbor: University of Michigan Press, 1960); C. C. Van Essen, "La Topographie de la Domus Aurea Neronis," *Meded. Koninkl. Nederlandse Akademie van Wetenschappen, afd. Letterkunde* n.s. 17 (1954): 372–88; Ward-Perkins, *Roman Imperial Architecture;* and Blake, *Roman Construction in Italy from Tiberius Through the Flavians.*

Romans, flee to Veii, if only the Villa does not also spread itself to Veii!"[2]

Scholars in general agree with Van Essen's assertion that Nero wanted to separate his villa from the rest of the city by extending it to and surrounding it with natural boundaries. He established a wide, shallow country valley of about two hundred acres between the Palatine, Caelian, and Esquiline hills. Though no maps of the estate exist, modern researchers usually consider the Servian Wall its eastern boundary. San Clemente is located inside this wall. After beginning the palace complex on the Palatine and Esquiline hills, Nero destroyed the temple built by his adoptive father Claudius on the Caelian and used its substructures for his own purposes. He converted the eastern face of the Caelian (just above the San Clemente complex) into a grand approach to the palace from the south. One would have to pass near the San Clemente site to use this entrance. From this, it appears highly probable that the land on which San Clemente sits was once a part of the Domus Aurea grounds. The significance of this is explored below.[3]

San Clemente is located in one of fourteen regions established by Caesar Augustus sometime between 10 and 4 B.C. (Fig. 1).[4] Our knowledge of the regions comes primarily from two fourth-century documents, the *Notitia* and the *Curiosum*. Augustus selected the Palatine hill as the center of the city; the Servian walls and the major roads into the city through the Servian gates were used as lines of demarcation. Eight regions were located inside the walls. Six regions comprised the area beyond the walls, one of which represented the area across the Tiber River (Transtiberinum or Trastevere). San Clemente is located in the third region, which includes the Oppian hill (part of the Esquiline ridge), the valley occupied by the Colosseum, and the narrow valley east of the Colosseum between the Oppian and Caelian hills. It is bordered by the Servian Wall on the east (Fig. 2). The region was called "Isis and Serapis" after the temple to that Egyptian religion built on the Oppian. This apparently

2. Suetonius, *Nero* 39.
3. Van Essen, "Topographie," 376. For the Servian Wall, see Ward-Perkins, *Roman Imperial Architecture*, 60; for the grand entrance, see Blake, *Roman Construction*, 53.
4. Lanciani, *Ruins and Excavations of Ancient Rome*, 87.

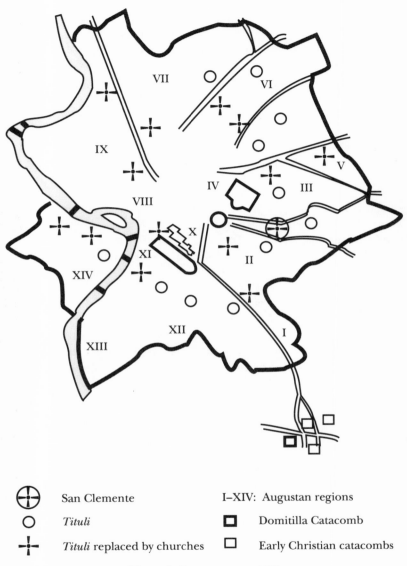

San Clemente

Tituli

Tituli replaced by churches

I–XIV: Augustan regions

Domitilla Catacomb

Early Christian catacombs

Figure 1: Rome, ca. A.D. 500.

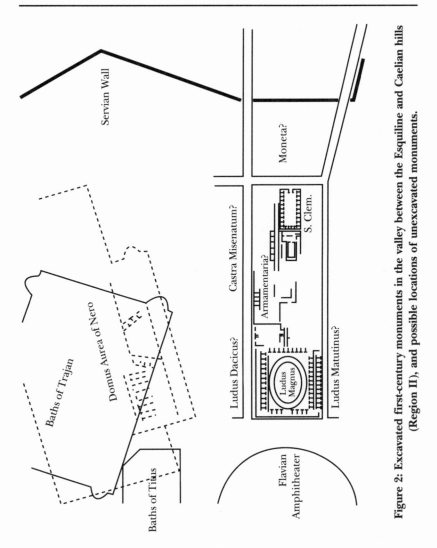

Figure 2: Excavated first-century monuments in the valley between the Esquiline and Caelian hills (Region II), and possible locations of unexcavated monuments.

was not its original name, since the temple was not built until the time of Caracalla or shortly thereafter.[5]

The only information we have on the private buildings of this region comes from the *Curiosum* and the *Notitia*. The *Curiosum* says that in the fourth century the third region included 18 grain storage buildings, 2,757 tenement buildings, and 60 private residences (built by and for the aristocracy).[6] The *Notitia* differs in recording the number of private residences as 160, but this is usually taken to be an error. Region XIII, on the perimeter of the city, appears to have been the most popular region with the upper class. It contained one private residence for every 19 tenement buildings. The least popular appears to have been Region III, the region of San Clemente, with one private residence for every 46 tenement buildings. However, these statistics should not be considered precise. The authors of the *Curiosum* and the *Notitia* or their sources seemed to have a penchant for symmetry. Regions III and IV both are said to have 2,757 *insulae*, and Regions XII and XIII both reportedly have 2,487 *insulae*. There are other examples of identical or similar counts in different regions. Though the regions were laid out so as to be as similar in extent as possible, it does not seem likely, taking into account the great variety in topographical features throughout the city, that two areas in Rome of the same size would have exactly the same number of *insulae* or *domus*. The Palatine region is said to be 11,510 Roman feet in circumference (3,418 meters) by the *Notitia* and *Curiosum*. But Lanciani, in a study of the marble map of Rome commissioned by Septimus Severus in the third century, discovered that it measured only 2,080 meters.[7] And while the Palatine was nine-tenths imperial palaces, the fourth-century reports tell us there were also 2,692 tenement houses and 89 private residences on this hill. Such a large number of buildings could not have been built on one-tenth of the Palatine's buildable land, so we must not rely uncritically on the information in these sources. Nevertheless, it appears safe to say that

5. Preller, *Die Regionen der Stadt Rom*, 124. The remains of the Temple of Isis and Serapis have never been located with certainty.

6. Ibid., 6; Lanciani, *Ruins and Excavations*, 88. The number of buildings in this region would not have changed much from the late first to the fourth century, since the third region was entirely built up by the earlier date.

7. Lanciani, *Ruins and Excavations*, 91.

the region in which San Clemente is found, although inhabited by some aristocrats, was less popular with them.

Archaeologists have not been able to locate the remains of all the public buildings that documentary evidence assigns to Region III in the late first century. Virtually all of this region was a part of Nero's Domus Aurea complex. Most if not all public buildings that had been in this area were either destroyed by the fire of 64 or by Nero afterwards. Not long after Nero's death, a new building program took place in this area under the Flavians. In an attempt to gain the goodwill of the people of Rome, the first Flavian emperor, Vespasian, used much of the land once encompassed by the Domus Aurea for public works.[8] He drained the artificial lake and in its place began construction of the most famous structure in the third region, the Flavian Amphitheater.

First dedicated just before Vespasian's death in 79, the Flavian Amphitheater was continually added to by Titus and Domitian. The Flavians hosted a wide variety of games and events in it. Men fought wild animals in jungles composed of imported tropical plants and gladiators fought one another. Occasionally, the arena was filled with water and mock naval battles were held. Various props and types of machinery were needed, and this necessitated a network of support buildings.

These support buildings include the Ludi, four training schools built by Domitian for the gladiators. The greatest of the four, the Ludus Magnus, is situated fifty meters east of the Colosseum (Fig. 2). Archaeologists first excavated the site in 1875. Its remains presently are visible at the intersection of the Via Labicana and the Via delle Sette Sale. The Ludus Magnus, the principal barracks of the gladiators who fought in the Flavian Amphitheater, was built during the reign of Domitian.[9] The gladiators were housed in rectangular rooms on upper levels surrounding a miniature amphitheater used for training. The lower level alone remains; all fourteen rooms on the north side are preserved, as are a few on the western and eastern sides. An underground tunnel led from the Ludus Magnus directly to the complex below the Flavian Amphitheater. The identity of the Ludus Magnus is based on documentary references, including the

8. Coarelli, *Guida Archeologia di Roma*, 123.
9. Blake, *Roman Construction*, 110, 125.

Curiosum and *Notitia*, and on a fragment of the Severan marble map of Rome. The three other gladiator training schools probably were nearby. They were the Ludus Dacicus, the Ludus Gallicus, and the Ludus Matutinos. The first two were named for the nationalities of the gladiators trained in them. Rodriguez-Almeida suggests that scant ruins from the first century just north of the Ludus Magnus may be those of the Ludus Dacicus.[10]

Region III contained two other Flavian Amphitheater support buildings: the Castra Misenatium and the Summum Choragium. Certainly they were built during the Flavian era, but possibly not before Domitian. The former was the barracks of sailors of the fleet of Misenum who were responsible for the awning suspended as a sunscreen over the amphitheater. Remains east and north of the Ludus Magnus, along the base of the Oppian hill, have been tentatively identified with the Castra Misenatium (Fig. 2). The functions of the Summum Choragium are unclear, beyond the fact that it serviced the amphitheater. Coarelli suggests that amphitheater machinery was repaired here. He believes the Choragium stood just east of the Ludus Magnus.[11] In the same valley, though technically in Region II, were the Spoliarum, where the armor of dead gladiators was removed, the Saniarium, a hospital for injured gladiators, and the Armamentarium, a warehouse of gladiator weapons.

In the late first century, Region III included three other major public structures. The baths of Titus and the baths of Trajan, built partly over the remains of the Domus Aurea palace, are located on the Oppian hill (Fig. 2). The mint of the imperial era, the Moneta, apparently was located in the same valley as the Colosseum support buildings discussed above. Its ruins, however, have not been identified.

We can draw several conclusions from this. First, since the Domus Aurea extended to the Servian Wall and included the Oppian and Caelian hills as well as the land between them, it must have included all of Region III. This means that when the Flavian dynasty came to

10. For the marble map, see Carettoni et al., eds., *Pianta Marmorea di Roma Antica*, 1:255; Lanciani, *Ruins and Excavations*, 386; Emilio Rodriguez-Almeida, "Forma Urbis Marmorea: nuove integrazioni," *Bullettino della Commissione Archeologica Comunale* 82 (1970–71): 105–35.

11. Samuel B. Platner, *A Topographical Dictionary of Ancient Rome*, rev. Thomas Ashby (Rome: Bretschneider, 1965), 105. Coarelli, *Guida Archeologia*, 131. There is no firm evidence for either suggestion.

power and inherited the lands confiscated by Nero, it controlled Region III. The great number of public buildings in this region, especially buildings connected with the Flavian Amphitheater, confirms this notion. The area provided an excellent stage for the Flavian program of public pacification. The land occupied the center of the city but there were relatively few preexisting structures. In addition, it was the site of the hated Domus Aurea villa. The great amphitheater replaced Nero's private lake. The public baths of the Flavian emperor Titus, and later those of Trajan, were erected over Nero's Oppian palace grounds. But during the first years of the Flavian dynasty, much of the land in Region III remained bare. The majority of the amphitheater support buildings in the valley between the Caelian and the Oppian were not built until the time of Domitian (81–96). This allows us to conclude that the land on which they were located remained in Flavian hands during this period. Thus, a Flavian must be responsible for any private construction in Region III during the Flavian era, especially construction in the vicinity of the public buildings. Two such private buildings lie below the San Clemente complex.

The Excavations at San Clemente

The present-day Basilica of San Clemente is located in Rome on the Via di S. Giovanni in Laterano, about midway between the Colosseum and the Basilica of St. John Lateran. For centuries scholars have considered it the fourth-century basilica that Jerome connected with the name of Clement. Jerome wrote in 392 that during a visit to Rome he had seen the church that preserved up to his day the memory of the name of Clement of Rome.[12] But in the mid-nineteenth century, Joseph Mullooly, then prior of the order of Irish Dominicans who have charge of San Clemente, began to doubt this assumption. He discovered discrepancies between traditional descriptions of the fourth-century church and the visible basilica. After years of study, he put his ideas to the test by excavating beneath the existing church.[13] In 1857, equipped with little more than pick and shovel, he began digging in the monastery's garden. The next

12. "Nominus ejus memoriam usque hodie Romae exstructa ecclesia custodit." Jerome, *De Viris Illustribus* 15. See p. 85 for a discussion of this reference.
13. For a detailed account of the excavations, see Boyle, *San Clemente Miscelleny* 1, 171–208.

year he uncovered the north aisle of a fourth-century basilica below the visible basilica. Debris had collected over the centuries in this dip between two of Rome's seven hills, causing the surrounding ground level to rise and eventually bury earlier structures. In the twelfth century, the walls of the earlier and much larger basilica had been strengthened and used (along with additional walls on this level) as a foundation for the present-day basilica.[14] The lower church, which centuries of debris had almost buried, was filled with rubble to provide a solid foundation for the new church. This made Mullooly's work slow and arduous. He made a brief excursion into a level below the fourth-century church, where he discovered a room that has come to be called the Mithras Anteroom (Fig. 3). In 1860 he discovered a tufa block wall belonging to a second building below the fourth-century basilica. He also excavated a city alley between the two buildings (Fig. 3). This level also was filled with rubble, presumably by fourth-century builders.

The Pontifical Commission for Sacred Archaeology, which had supported Mullooly's efforts after his initial discovery, temporarily withdrew official support of the excavation during 1860–61. But Mullooly continued to excavate. He was assisted unofficially by his friend G. B. De Rossi, the premier Christian archaeologist of his day. In late 1861 he explored the left aisle and part of the nave in the fourth-century basilica. Over the next several years, rubble was removed from the nave and narthex. In 1865 the remainder of the left aisle was cleared. Around the time of a visit by Pope Pius IX in 1866, a staircase was built from the sacristy above to the narthex of the lower church, and Mullooly excavated below the high altar. An ancient set of stairs down to the level below the fourth-century church was discovered and cleared in 1869. In 1870, on this lowest level, Mullooly made what some consider his most monumental discovery: an ancient sanctuary of the Mithras religion, complete with altar. In the same year, Mullooly fully excavated one room of the building next to the brick Mithras building, a multichambered tufa block structure. But water from an underground spring or a forgotten Roman aqueduct seeped into the excavations at this level, and in 1875 Mullooly had to abandon his work.[15]

14. Leonard Boyle, "The Date of the Consecration of the Basilica of San Clemente, Rome," *Archivium Fratrum Praedicatorum* 30 (1960): 417–27.

15. Guidobaldi, *Il Complesso Archeologico di San Clemente*, 13. See pp. 7–16 for a history of the excavations. Osborne, *Early Mediaeval Wall-Paintings*, 19.

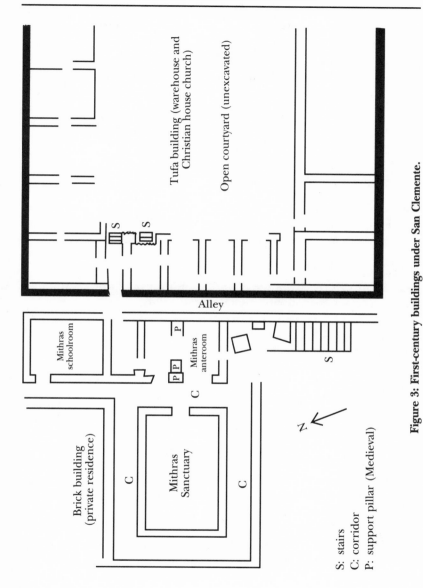

Figure 3: First-century buildings under San Clemente.

S: stairs
C: corridor
P: support pillar (Medieval)

Tufa building (warehouse and Christian house church)

Open courtyard (unexcavated)

Alley

Mithras schoolroom

Mithras anteroom

Mithras Sanctuary

Brick building (private residence)

Mullooly's task was monumental, and the results were well worth the effort. Flying in the face of conventional wisdom and at first with no financial backing, he pursued his theory. He published a compilation of his findings, including a compendium of traditions about Clement.[16] However, Mullooly was not a professional archaeologist, and even professionals in his day lacked today's knowledge and equipment for more accurate study and preservation of the evidence. We can only speculate about the amount of significant data that Mullooly may have discarded as rubble.

In 1882, the Dominicans installed scaffolding in part of the excavated area to raise the floor about four feet and allow visitors to see the remains above the water line. By the time Louis Nolan became prior of San Clemente in 1908, the water had risen about seven feet above the level of the brick building's floor. During 1912–14, a tunnel was constructed to connect San Clemente with the Cloaca Maxima drainage line, more than six hundred meters away. This effort succeeded in diverting the water and allowing excavation to proceed, although the sound of rushing water can still be heard. The corridor north of the Mithras sanctuary was excavated in 1924. Excavation of the west wing of the tufa building proceeded under Pius O'Daly during 1937–38. Under Raymond Dowdall, the rubble in the rooms of the north wing was cleared during 1940–45. The years 1963–71 witnessed a major project to restore the pavement of the subterranean basilica. Since that time, a number of minor excavation projects have been undertaken. The largest was the excavation of two more rooms in the tufa building.[17] At present, fifteen perimeter rooms in the tufa building have been excavated fully or partially. The courtyard has not been excavated, and no further major excavations are planned. Federico Guidobaldi of Italy's National Council of Restoration Research, assisted by resident Dominican archaeologist Paul Lawlor, continues excavation work at this site.

The San Clemente complex includes four buildings on five levels. The visible twelfth-century basilica sits atop the fourth-century basilica to which Jerome referred. Below this is a massive building built of large tufa blocks. Next to the tufa building, but on a higher

---

16. Mullooly, *Saint Clement, Pope and Martyr, and His Basilica in Rome.* Unfortunately, he does not talk about his excavations.

17. Nolan, *Basilica of San Clemente*, 210; Guidobaldi, *Complesso Archeologico*, 16.

level, is a brick building enclosing one of the best-preserved Mithraea in Rome. In addition, the tufa building underwent a major remodeling at some point that included raising the level of its floors.

The Tufa and Brick Buildings
at San Clemente

Since the basilica observed by Jerome was built in the fourth century, it could not have housed a first-century church. But it might have been built on the site of a first-century house church, so we must look at the origin and nature of the remains below the basilica. A building with a perimeter wall constructed of large Anio tufa blocks occupies the lowest level of excavations below San Clemente, some 11 meters below the current street level (Fig. 3). It measures 29.6 meters in width, and perhaps as much as 60 meters in length (its length has been traced 45 meters without termination). The tufa blocks are 60 centimeters thick, rusticated on the exterior side, and laid in a thin stratum of lime. Scholars have offered various theories concerning the date of its construction. Nolan thinks the walls date to republican times. Cecchelli believes that the tufa walls were built during the time of Augustus. Nash and Blake are confident that the walls predate the fire of Nero. Blake believes that if the walls were postfire, one would expect to find peperino or Gabine stones. Trinci places them in the postfire Neronian period. He points out that evidence of a great fire was discovered below the level of the walls, and that the only significant fire in this area during the first century was Nero's fire in 64. But while such tufa walls done in *opus quadratum* style (small tufa blocks set in a diamond pattern) date mainly to the Augustan era, as Cecchelli asserts, they were also common under Claudius, and continued to be used in construction in the second century. I agree with Guidobaldi's conclusion that since the walls rest on a stratum indicating a great fire, and since this area probably was burned in 64, this building must postdate the time of Nero. But it had to exist before the end of Domitian's reign (96) since the building next to it, built around 96 (see below), clearly was erected after it. Guidobaldi suggests that the tufa building may have been erected as part of Domitian's building project in this part of Region III. We do not know whether Domitian erected this building, but someone connected with the Flavian imperial household, which inherited this

Corridor between the tufa warehouse (right) and the later
brick residence (left). The brick wall was constructed using the
tufa wall for support.

area from its predecessors, must have been responsible for its construction. Thus, the tufa building was built under a Flavian sometime
between 69 and 96.[18]

Some have attempted to identify the tufa structure with one of
the buildings which have yet to be located among the remains. De
Rossi suggests that the tufa building was the Moneta, the Roman
mint in imperial times. Junyent and Jordan disagree, and Guidobaldi
finds no positive evidence of a connection to the Moneta. Since the
tufa building is located near the Ludus Magnus and other buildings
serving the Flavian Amphitheater, Guidobaldi thinks it may have
been part of this complex. For example, perhaps it was the Armamentarium mentioned in the *Curiosum* and the *Notitia*. However, no
one has discovered positive evidence for this identification. Junyent
expresses a view current in late nineteenth- and early twentieth-

18. Blake, *Roman Construction*, 28; Nolan, *Basilica of San Clemente*, 28; C. Cecchelli, *S. Clemente, Le chiese di Roma Illustrate* (Rome: Collegio San Clemente, 1930), 61; Trinci, "Osservazioni sulla basilica inferiore di S. Clemente in Roma," 96; Guidobaldi, *Complesso Archeologico*, 30–33.

century scholarship when he says that this could have been a private residence, perhaps the home of Clement of Rome.[19]

Modern archaeologists have usually identified the tufa building as a warehouse *(horreum)*.[20] Like a warehouse, its tufa walls have no external doors or windows. The walls are much thicker and the blocks larger than was normal for a private dwelling. The interior is composed of perimeter rooms of similar size on at least three sides of the building (the fourth side has not been excavated) which surround an inner courtyard (Fig. 3). The rooms have doorways 1.7 meters wide that lead to the inner courtyard. Windows above the doorways provided light for the rooms by way of the open-air courtyard. There was no intercommunication between rooms. Square holes in the partition walls indicate the existence of wooden rafters to support a second level over the perimeter rooms. The shape of the wall ends indicates that the original ceiling was of a barrel-vault design. The rooms are bare of decorations from this period. There might have been a residence on the destroyed second level, perhaps for the warehouse caretaker. Unfortunately, any evidence for this was lost when the upper level was demolished.

Comparisons with other ancient Roman warehouses support the notion that the tufa building was a warehouse. Its floor plan bears a striking resemblance to *horrea* on the Severan map of Rome and to first- and second-century *horrea* in the ancient port city of Ostia. The impenetrable outer walls and the inner cells independent of each other suggest a warehouse. The outer walls are thick enough to withstand the pressure of rooms full of grain. The rooms, which vary in size from 4.1 by 2.3 meters to 7.9 by 4.3 meters, are in the range of room sizes among the *horrea* of Ostia. Blake believes that the relatively small doorways to the individual rooms, with their travertine sills, suggest a warehouse for a commodity more costly than grain, but he offers no specific alternative. Guidobaldi considers it highly doubtful that this was a private or independent warehouse, since (1) all the independent *horrea* in this area were burned in the fire of 64,

19. Junyent, "La primitiva Basilica di S. Clemente e le Costruzioni Antichi Circostanti," 276; Guidobaldi, *Complesso Archeologico,* 30; Jordan, *Topographie der Stadt Rom im Altertum,* 1.3:302.

20. Giuseppe Lugli, *I Monumenti Antichi di Roma e Suburbio,* 3 vols. (Rome: Periodici Scientifica, 1931–40), 3:543; Blake, *Roman Construction,* 28–29; Nash, *Pictorial Dictionary of Ancient Rome,* 1:353; A. M. Colini and L. Cozza, *Ludus Magnus* (Rome: Monte dei paschi di Siena, 1962), 118 n. 7; and Guidobaldi, *Complesso Archeologico,* 29.

Two of the storage rooms that surround an open courtyard in the first-century tufa warehouse. A small congregation could have met in one of these rooms in inclement weather. The floor is third century.

Example of a travertine wall from the remains of a first-century Ostian warehouse.

and (2) the building is so close to the Ludi complex. He believes it was probably a depository for gladiators' weapons or other items connected with the amphitheater. But it is improbable that the Flavians would build a warehouse with such massive walls as a storage place for weapons or equipment. The site offers no positive evidence for this or indeed any other specific identification. It may be that if and when the inner courtyard is excavated, it will yield such evidence.[21] Guidobaldi probably is correct in concluding that the tufa and brick buildings functioned as a unit. Although they are near the Ludi complex, they lie on its edge and so need not have been a part of it. If built by a branch of the Flavian family, such as that of Clemens, they could have served a more private function. Their design and the materials used in their construction suggest such a function.

---

21. G. Rickman, *Roman Granaries and Store Buildings* (Cambridge: Cambridge University Press, 1971). I was able to confirm the similarities to *horrea* in Ostia, both in layout and in construction materials, during a trip to Italy. Hermansen, *Ostia: Aspects of Roman City Life,* 230; Blake, *Roman Construction,* 29; Guidobaldi, *Complesso Archeologico,* 30.

A Christian house church could have met within this warehouse. The inner courtyard, which served mainly to provide access to the perimeter storage rooms, could have accommodated several hundred worshipers. Of course, as indicated in chapter 2, it is unlikely that Christian assemblies reached this size in the first and second centuries. More likely, a warehouse like this would be used by a smaller group which could meet in one of the perimeter rooms in inclement weather. An incident related in the late-second-century *Acts of Paul* provides support for the use of warehouses as Christian meeting sites:

> There were awaiting Paul in Rome: Luke from Gaul and Titus from Dalmatia. When Paul saw them he was glad, so that he hired a barn outside Rome, where with the brethren he taught the word of truth. . . . A great number of believers came to him from the household of Caesar. . . .[22]

This story may not refer to a historical incident. But the readers of the *Acts of Paul*, less than one century removed from Clement's time, must have found acceptable the idea of Christians from the imperial household meeting in a barn or warehouse. In addition, at least two other *tituli* are built in part upon former warehouses. One is connected with St. Cecilia in Trastevere, and one lies west of the church of San Martino ai Monti.[23]

Converts to Christianity who had been exposed to the religious associations of Rome would have found this warehouse an obvious choice for clandestine worship, if it became available to them. The warehouse at San Clemente shows certain affinities to buildings designed for religious meetings in the first and second centuries. Such buildings served several basic functions: worship, banquets, and assemblies of members *(conventus)*. One of the more impressive examples of this is the "Seat of the Augustales," built in Ostia ca. 150–65. Its plan is similar to that of a warehouse: a central courtyard surrounded by a porticus and rooms. Its sanctuary as originally constructed measures 8.2 by 5.7 meters, about 30 percent larger than the larger rooms in the San Clemente warehouse. The sanctuary in the "Seat of the House Builders' Guild" is just slightly larger than the

---

22. *Acts of Paul* 11.1. See Wilhelm Schneemelcher, ed., *New Testament Apocrypha*, trans. and ed. R. McL. Wilson, 2 vols. (Philadelphia: Westminster, 1965), 2:383.
23. Peterson, "House-Churches in Rome," 270.

largest San Clemente rooms. In Ostia, the "Guild of the Shipowners" *(Schola del Traiano)*, built in the late third century, contains the largest and most impressive sanctuary room among the buildings of religious associations in that city. It measures 9.1 by 7.7 meters, a little more than twice the size of the largest rooms in the San Clemente warehouse. The point of all this is that this warehouse, or just one of its rooms, could have housed Christians in numbers similar to those of contemporary religious associations. It could have provided the kind of room otherwise available only in the residence of a sympathetic aristocrat.[24]

In order to assess the probability that the tufa warehouse was the site of a first-century house church, we must understand the nature of the first-century building next to it. A short time after the warehouse was erected, a new building was situated just west of it (Fig. 3). Although it was modified heavily in later years, we can tell how it was initially constructed. The walls are constructed of long and well-made red bricks 3.6 to 4 cm. thick, and the mortar joints are .9 to 2.1 cm. wide. The ceilings were once all barrel-vaulted, with a concrete having an aggregate of bits of yellow tufa. A large central room was surrounded by four corridors and more rooms on all sides. There was at least one upper level, which covered the entire building except for the central room. Some of the exterior walls of this second level remain, as does a wide stairway in the southeast corner. Large windows in the ribbed vault provided light for the central room and, through five doorways, for the surrounding rooms. The actual extent of the building is uncertain. Its eastern wall, which parallels the western wall of the tufa building, has been excavated to a length of 32.5 meters. Excavations to the west have proceeded 20 meters without finding a terminus.[25]

This brick building was built some time after the fire of 64. It is built upon the ruins of an earlier building with similar wall structures. A stratum of rubble 2.3 meters thick, composed of carbonized material, lies between this building and the earlier one. The depth of rubble accumulated within a short time suggests a violent destruction of the preceding building. As noted previously, the only major fire in this area was in 64, so it is logical to think that the earlier

24. Hermansen, *Ostia*, 62–63, 71, 111.
25. Blake, *Roman Construction*, 128.

building was destroyed at this time, and a new building raised later. The new building must postdate the tufa building, since its east wall is supported by the western tufa building wall via an arching bridge of bricks above an 80-cm.-wide alley (Fig. 3, Alley). Further evidence for a post-64 date is the fact that this alley conforms to the Neronian building codes passed as a result of the 64 fire.

A critical means of dating Roman brick buildings, the brick-stamp, helps us date this structure more precisely. Stamps indicating the names of current city officials were pressed into undried bricks. Brickstamps found below the brick building's eastern corridor (Fig. 3, C) refer to three officials who were active at the end of the first century and beginning of the second. These particular styles of brickstamps were most prominent in the latter years of Domitian's reign (ca. 90–96). Other brickstamps were found in the stairs (Fig. 3, S). Several date to the Neronian/Flavian times, and one dates clearly between 95 and 110. This evidence, which seems to point to a time of construction in the latter part of Domitian's reign, ca. 90–96, is not without problems. Romans often used bricks salvaged from earlier buildings in new projects. But the brickstamps suggest that all the bricks in this building were made within a very few years. Thus, it seems most likely that they were new bricks and the building was built during the 90s.[26]

The original function of this brick building is uncertain. Heavy successive remodeling has removed any remains of decorations on the walls and ceilings. Some of the floor tile is probably original. Peterson considers it an apartment house. Guidobaldi, while admitting it has the style of a private residence, suggests it may have served as a barracks for gladiators or others connected with the Flavian Amphitheater. A number of scholars consider it simply a *domus*, a private residence.[27] There is no firm evidence to prove or disprove any of these possibilities. However, the proximity of this building to the Ludi complex is suggestive. The Flavian household surely owned

26. Guidobaldi, *Complesso Archeologico*, 38, 48–49. For the 95–110 brickstamp inscription, see *CIL*, XV, 635b.

27. Peterson, "House-Churches in Rome," 268; Guidobaldi, *Complesso Archeologico*, 43. In favor of a *domus*, see Blake, *Roman Construction*, 128; "Flavius," in *Realenzyklopädie für protestantische Theologie und Kirche*, 62, cols. 2536–39; and Nolan, *Basilica of San Clemente*, 219.

this land, and one would not expect Domitian or another Flavian of his day to erect a private or public apartment building in this area. But the building clearly was designed as living quarters of some kind. So the building probably was either a public barracks connected with the Colosseum complex, as Guidobaldi suggests, or a private residence built by Domitian or a member of the Flavian family.

In later centuries, these two buildings underwent successive modifications. At some point, remodelers raised the pavement of the tufa building's perimeter rooms 60 cm. The original level of the inner courtyard was left untouched. At the same time, the interior walls were covered with a thick layer of plaster. Blake suggests that this plaster was in part a measure against water inundation caused by the rising ground level around the building. He believes that since the new floor level was equal to that of the brick building's ground floor, it probably was done when the latter was built. Guidobaldi places this modification at a later date, near the end of the second or beginning of the third century.[28]

The ground floor of the brick building was converted later into a Mithraeum: a sanctuary and connected rooms dedicated to the cult of the Persian deity Mithras. The central room described above became the sanctuary (Fig. 3). All but one of its five doorways were sealed up. Other doorways were closed, and new ones added. All the walls were covered in thick plaster, and some walls were decorated with designs in stucco or with paintings or mosaics. The other excavated rooms include an anteroom to the sanctuary (Fig. 3) where devotees prepared themselves for worship. Here excavators discovered a trough used to catch the blood from sacrificed animals. In the northeast corner of the building (Fig. 3), a well-preserved mosaic tile floor and wall paintings enhance what was probably a Mithras schoolroom. The only external access to this level discovered to date is the stairway mentioned above. This first level must have been underground by the time of the Mithras modifications. Devotees of this secretive cult, who typically used caves or rooms designed to look like caves, would find such a locale appealing. The date of these modifications is a matter of conjecture, but most place it at the end of the second or beginning of the third

28. Blake, *Roman Construction*, 128; Guidobaldi, *Complesso Archeologico*, 78.

**Third-century sanctuary of Mithras, one of the best preserved
in all Rome, in the brick building below San Clemente.**

century.[29] Probably the third-century owner converted to Mithraism
or sold the building to a Mithras devotee.

Around the mid-third century, the tufa building was used as the
foundation for a new structure. Two great foundation walls, 90 cm.
thick and parallel to the east-west tufa walls, were built between the
inner courtyard and the inner partition walls. This level was then
filled in with dirt and debris and a new structure was built. The new
walls have been dated to the mid-third century. In 1970, the neck of
a wine amphora dating to 216 was discovered in the debris in the
abandoned tufa building. In the same room another amphora dates
to the Severan age, no later than 230–40.[30] This level, then, could not
have been filled in much before the mid-third century. The new
building was very irregular in shape. It was probably a private dwelling of some sort. While it clearly was not an *insula*, the decorations
that remain do not identify its nature or function. We know only that

29. Junyent, "Primitiva Basilica di S. Clemente," 243; Guidobaldi, *Complesso Archeologico*, 49; and Nolan, *Basilica of San Clemente*, 219. Coarelli, *Guida Archeologia*, prefers
mid-third century.
30. Guidobaldi, *Complesso Archeologico*, 60.

it had a second level, but we know nothing about the nature of this upper floor.

At some point in the third or fourth century, the Mithraeum was invaded and the Mithras altar damaged. The cult was not stamped out, however, for the altar was repaired and the cult's practices reinstated. Probably as a result of the Theodosian edict of 395, which prohibited all forms of pagan worship, the cult was finally destroyed. The property later came into the hands of the Roman church.

During the fourth century, this building gradually took on the appearance of a Christian basilica minus its apse. The first level became a grand hall divided into three naves. Once the church took over the Mithras building, the Mithras altar was defaced, but the Mithras sanctuary, virtually untouched, was sealed up. The other rooms continued in use, however, as evidenced by a new pavement containing pieces of the Mithras altar. On this pavement was erected a pillar to provide support for a new structure above: an apse for the Christian basilica. This apse dates to the early fifth century, probably before the visit of Pope Zosimus to San Clemente in 417.[31]

Literary Evidence Pertaining to
the San Clemente Site

The San Clemente site clearly became a prominent part of the life of the early church in Rome. The critical issue is how early the site was used by and for Christians. Various documentary and inscriptional remains help determine how much we can assert with confidence.

The reference in Jerome mentioned earlier (*De Viris Illustribus* 15) makes it clear that by 385 the complex had been associated with Clement of Rome for some time. Since the apsed basilica was not built until a somewhat later date, Jerome had in mind the modified third-century structure into which it was incorporated. Guidobaldi is alone in calling this earlier structure an "unapsed basilica," but he has clear justification for such an identification. The building certainly was used for worship, and it was not the only example of a basilica that lacked an apse. Jerome calls it an *ecclesia* that preserves the *memoria* of Clement of Rome. The term *memoria* used in this context usually referred to a martyr's shrine, but tradition says that the remains of Clement were transferred to this site only in the

31. Ibid., 86.

ninth century. No one in Jerome's day believed that Clement's remains lay under San Clemente. Therefore, Jerome must have believed that the site preserved the memory of Clement in a different way.

Kirsch suggests that a church such as San Clemente could have become dedicated to the memory of a particular saint in various ways: (1) in celebration of a special occasion, such as the building of a basilica on the site; (2) in celebration of that martyr's festival in that church; or (3) as recognition of personal devotion to a saint by the owner of the site.[32] Since the third-century building was gradually transformed into a basilica, the first option seems unlikely. There is no other direct evidence with which to affirm or deny the other two options. But why would this site be chosen for a festival dedicated to Clement? Or why would the site's owner be especially devoted to this saint? Kirsch is right in suggesting, contrary to the views of earlier scholars such as De Rossi and Lightfoot, that Jerome's quote does not necessitate an organic connection between Clement and this site. Kirsch's ideas also make more sense than the theory that the name of Clement was associated with this site simply because a former owner of the building, perhaps its third-century donor, was named Clement, and this Clement later became confused with the saint. In this case scholars have greatly undervalued the strength of oral history among the illiterate and semiliterate who made up the bulk of the early Roman church.

The existence of a Mithraeum under the San Clemente complex has caused many to question a first-century Christian connection. Based on Guidobaldi's studies, it appears certain that the Mithraeum here was still functioning and the apse over this area not yet built when Jerome saw San Clemente. In other words, it was not the Mithras building that preserved the memory of Clement for Jerome, but the building next to it. A number of scholars, not knowing this, have dismissed the possibility of a first-century Christian church on this site due to the existence of this Mithraeum. The reasoning is that if this land belonged to Christians in the first century, it seems unlikely that it came into the possession of Mithraists in the second or third, then again fell into the hands of Christians in the third or fourth century. De Rossi tried to overcome this objection by positing that

32. Kirsch, *Die römischen Titelkirchen im Altertum*, 147.

the complex was confiscated from the Christians during the third-century persecutions of Decius or Diocletian. It was returned to the church when Emperor Maxentius decreed the restoration of (Christian) religious places *(loca ecclesiastica)*.[33] This theory lacks any direct evidence and has lost support in recent years. It is in conflict with evidence that dates the origin of the building's Mithraic use to the second century. It also conflicts with the fact that the Mithras altar was not destroyed completely until the late fourth or early fifth century. Therefore, if any building on this site correctly preserves the memory of use by Clement of Rome and other first-century Christians, it must be the tufa building.

The inscription on a bronze slave collar offers further documentary evidence for this site: "Hold me fast for I am a runaway; and return me to Victor the acolyte of the Dominicum of Clement." Below the inscription is the Constantinian monogram. Most scholars date this collar to early or mid-fourth century. Because of its use of the term *dominicum,* some assume that it refers to a private residence, but Cyprian tells us that the term *dominicum* was also used to denote a place of Christian worship.[34] This uncommon usage of the term may be due to the origins of Christian churches in private houses. Any fourth-century *dominicum* may have been simply a church, a private dwelling, or a private residence that was also used for worship. In addition, Christians in the fourth century did not normally name churches for a saint unless that saint had personal contact with that site. Buildings donated to the church typically retained the name of the owning family.[35] So we have evidence from early- to mid-fourth century that this site was the *dominicum,* a present or former private residence, named for a Clement.

CONCLUSION

We cannot be certain that the San Clemente complex was once the site of Clement's house church. We would need more positive evidence to assert this with a high degree of confidence. But I believe

---

33. Cited by Junyent, "Primitiva Basilica di S. Clemente," 236, who disagrees with this theory.

34. *CIL,* XV n. 7192. "Tene me quia fug et reboca me Victor i acolito a Dominicu Clementis." Cyprian, *De Opere et Eleemosyna* 19.

35. Nolan, *Basilica of San Clemente,* 209.

that the evidence in this chapter makes the connection more plausible than many have supposed.

As I suggested in chapter 2, the *titulus Clementis* was probably a charitable and administrative center of the Roman Christian community dating back to at least the third century. If so, then it likely was at least a house church in the second century. The site was in the hands of the Flavians in the late first century, having been part of Nero's Domus Aurea grounds they took over. During the Flavian era, when the land was probably still owned by the Flavians, a private warehouse and adjoining private residence were constructed on it. They may have been built by Flavius Clemens as a residence for part of his urban household and a warehouse for one of his business concerns. Domitilla, a sympathizer with Christianity, at the least, would have given Christians in her household burial plots and allowed them to conduct worship services. She might have allowed Christians to meet in this warehouse.

Later traditions, Jerome's comment being the most important, connect this site and probably the first-century warehouse with the author of *1 Clement*, a leader of the Christian congregations in Rome. No other explanations satisfactorily explain the strength with which early Christians connected this site with Clement. Although no Christian remains have been discovered on the first-century level of San Clemente, it is possible that the warehouse was used for Christian worship. The building is large enough to house a large congregation, and it would have provided a natural site for a clandestine Christian house church organized as a household or funeral association. When Domitian executed Clemens and exiled Domitilla in 96, this site would have been confiscated. Domitian was assassinated shortly thereafter by a group that included Stephanus, a freedman of Domitilla. Domitilla probably recovered her properties when the next emperor, Nerva, allowed her to return to Rome. Clement, who may have been a freedman of Clemens, could have in mind the various conflicts between Clemens and Domitian when he says that his letter was delayed by "sudden and repeated misfortunes and calamities" (*1 Clem.* 1.1).

Could a house church have survived so close to a complex full of gladiators? This question is less problematic than it at first seems. By the late 90s, Christians had not been persecuted in Rome for thirty years. In addition, gladiators were mostly slaves, former soldiers captured by the Romans in battle. They had no great love for Rome, and no particular motive to oppose the devotees of an illicit religion. In addition, the Christians meeting in this warehouse would have enjoyed the protection of its powerful owner.

In view of the evidence, therefore, it is probable that Clement's house church represented a small group of Christians who had benefited from the Roman system, unlike the majority of their poorer brothers. They were, in effect, a social elite among the congregations of Rome and had greater wealth, more education, and more hope for a comfortable life on earth.

5

THE SOCIAL CONTEXT
OF *1 CLEMENT*

Virtually no commentaries or monographs on *1 Clement* attempt seriously to analyze the letter's social context: what group or groups of Roman Christians it represents, how the larger Roman society would have looked at that group, and how the group identified itself in its social environment. This chapter attempts such a study and, at the same time, establishes a basis for investigations into *1 Clement* in later chapters. We will see that *1 Clement* represents the concerns and convictions of a Roman Christian congregation.

THE BACKGROUND OF *1 CLEMENT*

First Clement is about the same length as the Gospel of Mark but is composed of sixty-five chapters instead of sixteen. It purports to be written on behalf of the Roman church to address problems arising from strife and division within the Corinthian church. Numerous examples from the Old Testament as well as from history and pagan literature are presented to persuade the congregation to cast aside prideful schism and in humility renew its previous unity and harmony.

The Date of *1 Clement*

The date of composition of *1 Clement* is of vital importance here. I concur with most scholars, who believe that the letter was written about 93–97. The only specific internal evidence for this date comes from *1 Clem.* 1.1: "Owing to the sudden and repeated misfortunes and calamities (συμφορὰς καὶ περιπτώσεις) which have befallen us, we consider that our attention has been somewhat delayed in turning to the questions disputed among you. . . ." Most commentators take this as a reference to a recent persecution of Christians. Unlike Stuiber, who regards the verse as referring to no concrete event,

Mikat argues that it should be read in an "ordinary sense" that reflects an important occurrence in the Roman churches. Barnard argues that "sudden and repeated" sounds too serious to refer to simple internal domestic upsets. Rather, it must refer to external interference with the life of the church. This is usually linked with traditions about a persecution by the emperor Domitian in 95–96.[1] But as I suggested in chapter 1, it seems unlikely that a general persecution took place at this time. Domitian eliminated anyone he suspected of treason, and some Christians or sympathizers with Christianity fell into his net. His actions toward the end of his reign caused anxiety and probably some suffering within the church. As I indicated in chapter 4, if Clement had been a member of Flavius Clemens's household, he and his house church would have suffered some discomfort at this time.

The other internal evidence militates against a date much earlier or much later than 93–97. The church in Corinth is called "ancient" in *1 Clem.* 47.6. Although this could be a hyperbole rather than an attempt to describe the chronological age of the Corinthian church, it seems a term more likely to be used in the 90s or later, when the church at Corinth was over fifty years old, than at an earlier date when most of its original members would still be alive. In addition, Clement says that his emissaries to the Corinthians "have lived among us without blame from youth to old age" (*1 Clem.* 63.3). Since Christianity probably did not reach Rome until the late 40s or 50s, such a statement could hardly be made before the 80s, and seems more likely to refer to the 90s or later. Moreover, the author speaks of the apostles as though they belonged to a former era. He says that some of their successors had died by his time. A date later than the 80s or 90s is unlikely, since according to *1 Clement* some

---

1. Mikat, *Die Bedeutung der Begriffe Stasis und Aponoia für das Verstandnis des 1. Clemensbriefes*, 11–12. See also Stuiber, "Clemens Romanus I," 3:191; Barnard, *Studies in the Apostolic Fathers and Their Background*, 10. For persecution by Domitian, see Mikat, *Bedeutung der Begriffe Stasis und Aponoia*, 11; Barnard, *Studies in the Apostolic Fathers*, 12; Lightfoot, *Apostolic Fathers*, 1:346–58; Adolf von Harnack, "Der erste Klemensbrief," 61–62; Kleist, *Epistles of St. Clement of Rome and of Ignatius of Antioch*, 3; Cruttwell, *Literary History of Early Christianity*, 1:30; Richardson, ed., *Letter of the Church of Rome to the Church of Corinth*, 34; Hagner, *Use of the Old and New Testaments in Clement of Rome*, 1; Wilson, "First Epistle of Clement," 5; and Fuellenbach, *Ecclesiastical Office and the Primacy of Rome*, 1–3.

presbyters appointed with the apostles were still alive.[2] Since the author has no knowledge of a monoepiscopacy, which came to Rome around the mid-second century, the letter must have been penned before that time.

References to the Neronian persecution also support a date in the 90s. In chapter 5, the author refers to Peter and Paul as examples of suffering in "the days nearest to us" and in "our own generation." The passage gives the impression that these are events which occurred some years ago but still within living memory. *First Clement* 6 adds to these two martyrs "a great multitude of the chosen" who were victims of jealousy and who suffered "many indignities and tortures." As indicated in chapter 1, the author must have had in mind the persecution by Nero. In 7.1 he reminds himself and his readers that "we are in the same arena, and the same struggle is before us." The fact that the author felt it necessary to include this reminder suggests that these events, while within living memory, occurred a number of years previously.

External evidence for the date of *1 Clement* is scant. The first references to it are in Hegesippus, sometime around 150, and in Dionysius of Corinth, ca. 180. Jaubert and Mikat, following Van Cauwelaert, Harnack, and Lightfoot, find clear evidence that Polycarp used *1 Clement* in his letter to the Philippians, written about 135. Other external evidence focuses on the identity of the author, and will be dealt with in the next section. Less convincing is the suggestion of Mikat that Ignatius is referring to this letter when he says in his *Letter to the Romans* that "you taught others."[3]

Not all authorities accept a date in the 90s, however. Edmundson argues for sometime around 70, believing that the author's references to Peter and Paul imply only a short lapse of time since the event. He incorrectly believes that a terrible persecution of Christians took place under Domitian, and so he concludes that *1 Clem.*

2. *1 Clem.* 44.1–3. See Fuellenbach, *Ecclesiastical Office*, 1; Wilson, "First Epistle of Clement," 4; and Richardson, *Letter of the Church of Rome*, 34.

3. On Hegesippus and Dionysius, see Eusebius, *Historia Ecclesiastica* 4.22, 23. On Polycarp, see Jaubert, *Clément de Rome*, 18; Mikat, *Bedeutung der Begriffe Stasis und Aponoia*, 10; R. Van Cauwelaert, "L'Intervention de L'Eglise de Rome à Corinthe Vers L'an 96," *Revue D'Histoire Ecclesiastique* 31 (1935): 269; Harnack, *Klemensbrief*, 40; and Lightfoot, *Apostolic Fathers*, 1:149–52. Ignatius, *Letter to the Romans* 3.1. See Mikat, *Bedeutung der Begriffe Stasis und Aponoia*, 11.

1.1 refers to troubles too vague to apply here. He also errs in believing that a monoepiscopacy existed in Rome by the 90s. As a result of these errors, his arguments are not convincing.[4]

Robinson and Hooijbergh more recently have echoed Edmundson's arguments. They believe "misfortunes and calamities" (συμφορὰς καὶ περιπτώσεις; *1 Clem.* 1.1) refers to chaotic political events occurring in the wake of Nero's death. Hooijbergh says that the author's reference to Peter and Paul implies that the readers had personal memories of them. He adds that the emissaries to Corinth, Claudius Ephebus and Valerius Vito, could have reached old age as Christians by 69. He posits a very early origin for Roman Christianity, possibly as early as the middle 30s, but, as we saw in chapter 1, no evidence exists for such a position. He assumes that (1) monoepiscopacy existed in Rome by around 100 since Ignatius of Antioch, writing about this time, portrays monoepiscopacy as the norm in Asia Minor and (2) thus, *1 Clement* must have been written long before this time. As Dix points out, however, the existence of monoepiscopacy in one locale does not prove its existence in another; differing concepts of office existed side by side in Asia Minor in the second century. Some churches, including the church in Rome, were ruled by colleges of presbyters even as late as mid-second century. A reference to the Jewish Temple in *1 Clement* 41 suggests to Hooijbergh that the Temple still stood, so the letter must have been penned prior to its destruction in 70.[5] But Noll has pointed out that it was not unusual for early writers to speak of the Temple and its cult as though it still existed. Some scholars believe that Jews continued to worship and sacrifice in Jerusalem up to 135.[6] No solid case has been made for a composition date earlier than the 90s.

---

4. Edmundson, *Church in Rome in the First Century*, 180. See Barnard, *Studies in the Apostolic Fathers*, 5–18; Milburn, "Persecution of Domitian"; Merrill, *Essays in Early Christian History*, 148–73.

5. John A. T. Robinson, *Redating the New Testament* (Philadelphia: Westminster, 1970), 149, 327–35; A. E. Wilhelm Hooijbergh, "A Different View of Clemens Romanus," *Heythrop Journal* 16 (1975): 266–68, 275.

6. For colleges of presbyters, see G. Dix, "The Ministry in the Early Church," in *The Apostolic Ministry*, ed. K. E. Kirk (London: Hodder & Stoughton, 1947), 266–73; and R. R. Noll, "The Search for a Christian Ministerial Priesthood in 1 Clement," *Studia Patristica* 13 (1975): 230–64, esp. 251. For sacrifice in Jerusalem, see K. W. Clark, "Worship in the Jerusalem Temple after A.D. 70," *New Testament Studies* 6 (1960): 269–80.

E. T. Merrill believes that *1 Clement* was written sometime between 125 and 135.[7] He bases his argument primarily on a reference in the *Shepherd of Hermas*. Hermas, writing in the mid-second century, is told to send a copy of his visions to a Clement whose duty it is to send writings of the Roman church abroad (*Vis.* 2.4.3). The clearest reading of this text is that Hermas plans to give his work to someone named Clement who was alive at the time. Most scholars take this as a reference to the author of *1 Clement*, and this seems probable, although such an identification cannot be proven. Based on a reference to the *Shepherd* in the Muratorian Canon, which we consider in detail in chapter 6, Merrill believes that Hermas wrote around 125–35. Since Hermas indicates that Clement was still in office, the latter must have written around this time as well. Furthermore, the fact that Hermas does not make use of *1 Clement* suggests to Merrill that the latter work was written at the same time or shortly before the *Shepherd*. Merrill's date for the *Shepherd*, around 135, is based solely on the Muratorian Canon. As I will show in chapter 6, the validity of this source is questionable. Also, while Hermas may not have finished his work until 135 or later, he could have begun it during the late first or early second century. His reference to Clement occurs very early in the work, and, as Merrill concedes, Hermas could be referring to a different Clement. Merrill's position is not convincing, and it has failed to gain a following.

Christian Eggenberger dates *1 Clement* to a time between 118 and 125. He believes it reflects the ideology of Emperor Hadrian and of works as late as 118.[8] His hypothesis, while interesting, is too speculative to overcome the evidence presented above for a date in the 90s.

The Occasion of *1 Clement*

The author of *1 Clement* refers to the occasion of his letter in 1.1, 3.3, 44.6, and 47.6. He indicates that a small group of young men incited the Corinthian congregation to remove the existing church leadership which had performed "blamelessly." Word of this reached Rome, and Clement issued the letter to admonish the Corinthians to reinstate their former leaders and expel the usurpers. Very little

---

7. Merrill, *Essays in Early Christian History*, 225.
8. Eggenberger, *Die Quellen der politischen Ethik des 1. Klemensbriefes*, 182.

information is given about the precise situation in Corinth. I am interested here not so much in what the letter can tell us about the Corinthian situation, but what it tells us about the issues facing the Roman churches.

First Clement was written not as an affirmation of Roman primacy, but as the action of one sister church helping another restore peace and unity. The author states in 63.4 that the letter is directed "to your speedy attainment of peace." He never asserts the authority of the Roman church, nor does he appeal to it as an example. Rather, he writes as an interested friend who appeals to commonly held beliefs. Harnack supports this position. He considers the dispute in Corinth as "without any basis in principle." Van Cauwelaert asserts that the envoy was sent to Corinth based on the principle of the church's unity: one part has the responsibility to assist another in times of trouble. In addition, Van Cauwelaert shows the close relationship between Rome and Corinth. As a Roman colony, Corinth and Rome shared social relations, civic spirit, and national sentiment. Van Cauwelaert maintains that members of both churches belonged to the working classes. In light of this, Goodspeed's comment that the Roman church was "looking about for some church that needed instruction" appears gratuitous.[9]

As Wilson points out, the author of *1 Clement* assumes from the start that the deposed presbyters were not at fault in any respect. Rather, he blames those who have removed them from office and the congregation that allowed this action. One might argue that he does not mention the errors of the deposed leaders since his audience was well acquainted with them. However, since the usurpers were challenging the blamelessness of the leaders, one might expect Clement to use more specific evidence in defending their innocence. He labels the motive of the usurpers "jealousy and envy" but does not consider their case beyond this. He may have lacked more specific information, or, if he possessed a full account, for some reason he did not deem it worth debate. Brunner represents the thinking of a number of authors when he asserts that Clement had more interest in expounding his views on church office than in the situation at

---

9. Harnack, *Einführung in die Alte Kirchengeschichte*, 91–92; Van Cauwelaert, "L'Intervention de L'Eglise de Rome à Corinthe," 282–83; Goodspeed, *History of Early Christianity*, 12.

Corinth. Meinhold argues that Clement's view of the conflict reflects not the actual incident, but his own interests and those of the Roman church, especially regarding the topic of officeholder authority. But, in making his case, Meinhold reads later Roman assertions of primacy into a document from an earlier period.[10]

The author of *1 Clement* does not question the innocence or authority of the expelled presbyters. He makes several brief but strong statements identifying them as the successors to the apostles and their authority. But he devotes far more space to affirming the importance of unity and peace within the church and to decrying disorder and rebellion in any form. Although the author addresses the Corinthian situation, he sees in it larger issues with which the Roman church also must deal. In particular, he wants peace and harmony restored in Corinth, since internal congregational strife (ἄπονοια and στάσις) may cause the authorities to suspect the religion of not supporting the Pax Romana. The letters between Emperor Trajan and Pliny the Younger, written during the early second century while the latter was governor of Bithynia, provide valuable insight into this issue.[11] Trajan's attitude toward the discovery of Christians in Bithynia suggests that the state avoided persecuting Christians unless someone brought a charge against them. Trajan preferred to ignore their existence whenever possible. But Christianity was not a legal religion, so someone accused of being a Christian by a legitimate witness had to be tried. In the absence of evidence to the contrary, we can assume that this situation obtained in Rome and Corinth only a few years earlier, in the late 90s.

The churches in both Rome and Corinth arose in the shadow of the ideology and military might of the Roman Empire. Both cities were controlled by rulers who did not recognize the legitimacy of Christianity but were willing to look the other way as long as Christianity's presence was not brought to their attention. The author of *1 Clement* saw in the Corinthian uproar a threat to this tenuous peace with the state. Any insurrection within the church, especially in

---

10. Wilson, "First Epistle of Clement," 18; Brunner, *Die theologische Mitte des ersten Klemensbriefs*, 100–107; Meinhold, "Geschehen und Deutung im Ersten Clemensbrief," 97.

11. Mikat, *Bedeutung der Begriffe Stasis und Aponoia*, 39; Pliny the Younger, *Letters* 10.96, 97.

Rome, could cause a repeat of the Neronian persecution. The author did not need more details to know that this kind of disturbance was likely to attract the attention of the state.

The Authorship of *1 Clement*

The earliest extant manuscripts of *1 Clement* do not name the author. The letter simply identifies itself in 1.1 as the work of "the church of God which dwells in Rome." In a subscription added to the Coptic version (probably known to Clement of Alexandria), the work is called "The Epistle of the Romans to the Corinthians."[12] The *Shepherd of Hermas* is the earliest source to mention a Roman Christian author named Clement (*Vis.* 2.4.3), however, the work does not connect *1 Clement* with this person. By the late second century, Christian writers began to identify the author of *1 Clement* as a person named Clement. Dionysius of Corinth, writing around 180, speaks to the Romans of the "earlier epistle which Clement wrote on your behalf" to the Corinthians, which was customarily read in the church at Corinth. But he says nothing more about Clement's life and work. At about the same time, Irenaeus says that *1 Clement* was written by a Clement who was bishop of Rome. Clement of Alexandria, sometime around the year 200, likewise ascribes the letter to Clement, whom he identifies as an "apostle." Later testimony appears to be dependent on these witnesses.[13] As a result of these references, scholars of early Christianity conclude with virtual unanimity that a prominent member of the Roman church named Clement wrote the letter now called *1 Clement.*

THE ROMAN SOCIAL CONTEXT
OF *1 CLEMENT*

First Clement provides a great deal of evidence, both overt and subtle, about the social composition of the Christian group with whom its author associated. We can examine specific references to occupations and to individuals whose social status can be determined, as well as evidence of a more general knowledge of the ideologies of

---

12. Lake, *Apostolic Fathers,* 1:121.
13. Dionysius: quoted in Eusebius, *Historia Ecclesiastica* 4.23. Irenaeus, *Adversus haereses* 3.3.3. Merrill, *Essays in Early Christian History,* 228.

the classes. This approach assumes that persons with more intimate knowledge of the upper classes had greater contact with them and may have been part of them, while those who had a greater understanding of the lower classes had more association with them and may have belonged to them. Before demonstrating how *1 Clement* looks at each social class, we must understand the nature of those classes.

The Ruling Elite

Rome had a clearly defined class structure.[14] The senatorial class was at the pinnacle of the social pyramid. By the early empire, this class included some nine hundred senators and their families. This tiny percentage of the empire's population was known only by reputation outside the capital, but its presence dominated life in the city. The senators' grand urban villas filled Rome's central sections, and their clients among the urban plebs constituted an important group. Members of this class usually held the highest governmental offices in Rome.[15] Their wealth far surpassed that of individuals in other classes with but few exceptions. One of the requirements for membership in this class was property worth 250,000 times a laborer's daily wage. Whether in farms, ranches, urban homes, or country villas, most of a senator's wealth was invested in land. For example, Pliny the Younger thus invested some seventeen million of his twenty million sesterces.

The equestrian class, although below the senatorial class in power and prestige, still was part of the ruling elite in imperial Rome. Romans became *equites* if (1) they could claim two generations of free birth and (2) they possessed about one-half of a senator's wealth. Roman law allowed *equites* unlimited participation in commerce, trading, and government contracts, all of which it denied to senators. Nonetheless, *equites* tended to emulate their social betters; even those who engaged in business generally invested their profits in land. While most *equites* in the early empire were wealthy men whose ancestors were free Romans or provincials, the descendants of freed slaves, from the early first century A.D., began to enter this class.

14. This section follows Tacitus's taxonomy (*Histories* 1.4). The Latin word used for class by Tacitus and other Latin authors is *ordo*. "Class" seems a more useful translation than "order."

15. MacMullen, *Roman Social Relations*, 89; Christ, *Romans*, 69.

The wealth of the ruling elite was not an end in itself, but a means to an end. It was needed to gain the honor conferred by a high social status. With it, these people built large public buildings that bore their names and proclaimed their greatness and beneficence. With it, they bought slaves and retained clients who followed them through the city giving visual testimony to their power. They principally sought the respect of fellow members of the ruling elite and reveled in opportunities to contrast their high estate with the low estate of their social inferiors. This theme underlies almost all Roman literature.

The Roman elite highly esteemed formal education. Boys and girls in the aristocracy were sent to elementary schools at age seven, where they were taught the fundamentals of reading, writing, and arithmetic. The boys' education continued in the grammar schools, which taught mainly Greek but also some Latin literature and grammar. In their teens, they attended the schools of rhetoric. These schools sought to prepare them for their future as leaders of Rome. The education again was bilingual; its goal was to train students to imitate the great Latin and Greek orators of the past. These young aristocrats then usually went on a "grand tour" of the empire, especially of intellectual centers in the East such as Athens, Rhodes, or Alexandria. Roman nobles never questioned the need for many years of formal education.

As we have observed, Clement was not a member of the senatorial or equestrian classes. He and his group did, however, have firsthand knowledge of the ruling elite and so must have had contact with it. While Clement ultimately has in mind *spiritual* pride as he writes to the church in Corinth, his visual images of prideful people demonstrate his familiarity with the proud upper classes of Rome. When Clement speaks of the rich and the great, he makes desire for honor rather than wealth and luxury the motivating factor in their lives. Clement seems to have in mind the aristocracy when he tells the Corinthians that the "rich boast in their wealth, and the strong in their strength" (13.1; cf. Jer. 9:23, 24). They "praise themselves" (αὐτεπαινέτους, a term found in Greek literature only in Clement) and "boast in the pride of words," whereas Moses, though great, did not use "great words" (30.6; 21.5; 17.5). Clement borrows from the language of Rome's lower classes when he calls them "haughty" (59.3). To Clement they are "preeminent in repute," possess "glory and honor," are "lofty," and filled with the "pomp of pride" (16.2; 57.2; 59.3; 61.1). He may have in mind the importance the elite placed on eloquent rhetoric when he says that the wise should manifest their wisdom not in words but in deeds (38.2).

Clement mirrors the ruling elite's high estimation of education in his letter. He commends the elders at Corinth, who have "studied the oracles of the teaching of God" (62.3). The Corinthian Christians have demonstrated a "perfect and secure knowledge," "studied the holy Scriptures" and "the oracles of God," and have a "good understanding of the sacred Scriptures" (62.3). Although the object of their study was quite different from that of the upper classes, in repeatedly drawing attention to their knowledge Clement shows more affinity with this group than with the lower classes for whom education was an unimportant luxury.[16]

The *Populus Urbanus*

Just below the senatorial and equestrian classes in legal status was the freeborn Roman citizenry. This group included those Romans who were not quite wealthy enough to belong to the equestrian class down to the poor who were dependent on the daily grain dole. Tacitus makes a sharp distinction, however, between Romans who supported themselves adequately and the destitute. Thus, I will include only the former group in this category. Tacitus calls it the *populus integer*, or the "respectable populace"; he may have in mind passages in Livy in which the *integer populus* is contrasted with the poor.

Although of lower legal status than freeborn Romans, some freed slaves who had gained citizenship, particularly those from the imperial household, earned considerable wealth and gained a status virtually equal to that of "respectable" Romans. However, it is misleading to make freed citizens and freeborn Romans part of a single economic "middle class." They did not have a unified class consciousness, and they performed only some of the functions of the modern middle class. Also included in the *populus urbanus* were freeborn Greeks, perhaps with Roman citizenship, who had voluntarily

---

16. The educated Greeks and others who had been enslaved and brought to Rome constituted a very small group, and so are a relatively insignificant factor.

migrated to the capital and taken up business there. These groups shared a desire to rise in wealth and status.[17]

Unlike the aristocracy, members of the *populus urbanus* generally could not and did not avoid manual labor, at least not until they became wealthy enough to do so. This group included rich and experienced freedmen who invested in risky shipping enterprises or who operated a number of businesses. It included Roman citizens who owned their own shops or crafts businesses and worked alongside their one slave or free laborer. These citizens put a high value on honesty in business dealings. They preferred a person's promise to collateral.[18] In imitation of the aristocracy, they feasted as lavishly as they could afford. The less wealthy among them joined street or craft associations, where they could find comradeship and share the cost of great banquets and funeral expenses. In this group, as among the *equites*, we find people who had some degree of upward social mobility. A far greater percentage of people among the *populus urbanus* and the *equites* saw an increase in their wealth and status over their lifetimes than any other group.

Clement and his house church probably belonged to this class. As I indicated in chapters 1 and 2, an imperial freedman and another freedman of high standing belonged to Clement's house church. As we have seen, Clement himself probably was an imperial freedman. *First Clement* thus implies the existence of at least one Christian house church which was led by imperial freedmen and drew its members at least in part from dependents of the imperial household and from dependents of other aristocratic families. *First Clement* says nothing directly of the most numerous members of this class, the freeborn Romans or foreigners who supported themselves financially. He may have in mind such a one, however, when he speaks of an "employer" (ἐργοπαρέκτης; 34.1).

The Slaves

A sizable percentage of Rome's residents were slaves. In first-century Italy, slaves made up between 25 and 40 percent of the population.

17. Herbert Hill, *The Roman Middle Class* (Oxford: Oxford University Press, 1952). On respectable populace, see Tacitus, *Histories* 1.4. The Penguin Classics edition of Tacitus unfortunately paraphrases *populus integer* as "respectable middle-class Romans" (*Tacitus: The Histories*, trans. K. Wellesley [New York: Penguin, 1964], 23 [1.4]). See also Livy 9.46.11, 13, 14.

18. MacMullen, *Roman Social Relations*, 65.

A significant percentage of the rest of Italy probably was freedmen or descended from freedmen. Slaves belonging to the households of the wealthy or moderately wealthy in some ways lived a better life than did the free poor of the city. Unlike the free poor, they were normally assured three meals a day, lodging, clothing, and health care. Urban slaves who were being prepared for posts in the government bureaucracy received a superior education. Even many slaves who were not in the imperial bureaucracy were better educated than the freeborn poor. Most slaves, while working for their masters, could earn and save money toward buying their freedom. The most fortunate slaves, as indicated earlier, were those belonging to the emperor. Some imperial slaves, even before manumission, had their own slaves. When acting on behalf of the emperor, they had authority over freeborn Romans. Former imperial slaves more than once rose to wealth and prominence, and joined the *populus urbanus.*

Clement was probably at one time a slave. His work alludes frequently to slavery. Like the apostle Paul, he calls Christians the slaves (δοῦλος) of God, and identifies God as their Master (δεσπότης). Clement makes more use of the word δεσπότης than any New Testament or early church author. While it appears in the New Testament once in every forty thousand words of text, it appears in *1 Clement* once in every four hundred words. Brunner thinks this is part of Clement's focus on ecclesiastical authority and the powerful God behind it. Clement's focus, however, is not on ecclesiastical authority as such, but on peace and order. Servile obedience to God as Master is Clement's solution to disorder and division in the Christian community.[19] Such a positive or at least neutral attitude toward the experience of slavery suggests that slavery had worked for Clement and his friends. That is, it had provided a maximum of benefits and security with a minimum of injustice and inhumanity. Clement's allusions to slavery make more likely the truth of the suggestion that Clement and many of those in his house church were trusted slaves of the emperor or the great houses, who usually were better treated (see chap. 4). They could appreciate the sense of security and stability that the slave system at its best provided. Although Clement does not condemn the institution of slavery, he

---

19. Brunner, *Die theologische Mitte des ersten Klemensbriefs,* 121–23; Wilson, "The First Epistle of Clement," 65.

did not consider that a slave held an ideal position in life. For example, he laments the fact that the patriarch Joseph fell into slavery (4.9). He praises as a great sacrifice the recent actions of Roman Christians who had sold themselves into slavery for the sake of others (55.2).

The Poor

At the bottom of the social pyramid were the free poor. Tacitus calls them the "shabby people" (*plebs sordida*), those who frequented the circus and theaters (*Histories* 1.4). He seems to place them alongside the slaves who were not dependents of the great houses and "spend-thrifts and bankrupts." The poor spent most of the day working to meet immediate needs—if they could find work. Many were tenant farmers or descendants of farmers who had lost their property through indebtedness. A few were able to move out of this class, but others who had fallen into overwhelming debt were continually moving in. This group may have constituted as much as one-third of the population of Rome. The arenas of Rome attracted destitute Roman citizens, where, during the fifty-seven days of public games each year, they could forget their problems. In the first and second centuries A.D., every citizen age eleven and above in the city of Rome was entitled to the dole. This grain allotment probably supplied only two-fifths of the food needs of the average family,[20] so the poor had to supplement their income. The state did not provide for the needs of the aged, widows, orphans, the disabled, or the sick. As a result, once poor Romans used up their paltry savings, they joined the destitute "rabble" of the city, which caused Cicero and Tacitus so much consternation. The slave with a master of inadequate resources would find it much harder to earn his freedom. Once such a slave earned his freedom, he often found himself competing unsuccessfully with cheap slave labor without the economic support of his former master. The poor descendants of non-Roman freedmen were beyond Tacitus's notice, but comprised a sizable portion of Rome's population. They attempted to support themselves with the simple

20. On one-third, see MacMullen, *Roman Social Relations*, 93. The minimum age of grain-dole recipients may have been 14. Hopkins, *Conquerors and Slaves*, 38; Geoffrey Rickman, *The Corn Supply of Ancient Rome* (Oxford: Oxford University Press, 1980), 187–95.

trades and skills they possessed, often working at jobs that poor citizens considered too menial.

A prayer in *1 Clement* demonstrates concern for the plight of the poor and those in serious need in Rome:

> Save those of us who are in affliction, have mercy on the lowly, raise the fallen, show yourself to those who ask, heal the sick, turn again the wanderers of your people, feed the hungry, ransom our prisoners, raise up the weak, comfort the fainthearted . . . (59.4)

While it is difficult to distinguish between social and theological categories in this passage, Clement clearly refers, in part, to Christians who were poor in an economic sense. The "hungry" (present participle of πεινάω) certainly refers to them. Clement probably uses the term "lowly" (ταπεινός) here to refer to the poor in an economic sense, even though he uses this term elsewhere as a positive theological category (30.2; 55.6).[21] Most of Clement's terms in this passage refer not to the chronically poor, but to those in temporary need: those "in affliction" (ἐν θλίψει), the physically "sick" (ἀσθενεῖς), "prisoners" (δέσμιος), the "weak" (ἀσθενήω), and the "fainthearted" (ὀλιγοψυχήω). Clement identifies himself and his group only with this category of temporary need: "those of us in affliction" and "our prisoners." This suggests that Clement and his group were in closer contact with Christians who suffered temporary need than they were with those in continuous poverty.

Clement accepts the low status of the poor in Roman society. In the traditions of the New Testament and Septuagint, he says that the rich have been made rich by God. He adds, however, that the poor have been made poor (πτωχίζοω) by God as well (59.3). Included in this stratum of urban poor is the "good laborer" who can honestly receive payment from his employer, and the "lazy and careless" worker who has neglected his work and so feels shame at not having earned his pay (34.1). This apposition may indicate that Clement blamed the poor who could not provide for their families. For Clement, the poor in Rome are the "small" as opposed to the "great" of the Roman ruling elite (37.4). While these terms come not from Latin but from Greek, the small/great dichotomy depicted here reflects the basic distinction made by the aristocracy between them-

---

21. Walter Bauer, *Greek-English Lexicon of the New Testament*, 811–12.

selves and everyone else. While Clement knew of poor Christians, he identified most closely with those whose basic material needs were cared for and who suffered, at worst, intermittent physical need.

CONCLUSION

The *Letter of the Romans to the Corinthians*, commonly known as *1 Clement*, expresses the beliefs and concerns of a segment of the Roman congregations. Although written to address problems in a distant church, it reflects the life experiences of its author, Clement, and those Christians close to him. These Christians probably were imperial freedmen and slaves or the freedmen and slaves of the great houses of Rome. Clement's attitudes toward the various social classes confirm this notion. He demonstrates an intimate knowledge of the ruling elite's values. He understood that they valued honor over wealth. He agreed with their high estimation of education. Although he shows a personal dislike of slavery and poverty, he also reflects the elite's attitudes toward slaves and the poor. The slave's submission to his master was for Clement a symbol of the peace and concord that comes when Christians submit to God. Clement showed a genuine concern for those in momentary need, but, like the upper classes, he had little to say about the perpetually poor.

6

THE SOCIAL CONTEXT OF
THE *SHEPHERD OF HERMAS*

Unlike studies of *1 Clement*, several works on the *Shepherd of Hermas* have analyzed its social context. Most notable among these is Carolyn Osiek's *Rich and Poor in the Shepherd of Hermas*, which focuses on "rich" and "poor" as theological categories. Osiek does not, however, consider in detail the social identity of the Christians behind the *Shepherd*.

In this chapter, I will introduce and analyze the *Shepherd* using the same categories I used in chapter 5, and I will compare the attitudes toward the various classes of Roman society in the *Shepherd* and *1 Clement*. We will then see how and why those attitudes differ.

THE BACKGROUND OF
THE *SHEPHERD OF HERMAS*

The *Shepherd of Hermas* records a series of visions from God to a Christian in Rome. It is composed of five *Visions*, twelve *Mandates* or commandments, and ten *Similitudes* or parables. *Visions* 1–4 are written in the form of Jewish apocalypse. *Vision* 5 probably was once an introduction to the *Mandates*. The *Mandates* are composed in the style of Jewish-Hellenistic homily. The *Similitudes* are not true parables in form but are closer to the "parables" of Enoch.[1]

The Date of the *Shepherd*

The *Shepherd* was widely disseminated and very popular during the early centuries of Christianity; a Latin version of the Greek text probably dates to the second century. The *Shepherd* quickly achieved an

---

1. Snyder, *Shepherd of Hermas*, 11. Citations to the *Shepherd* in this chapter are by *Vision* (*Vis.*), *Mandate* (*Mand.*), or *Similitude* (*Sim.*), followed by book, chapter, and verse. Roman numerals, normally used with this format, are converted into Arabic numerals. A conversion table for this and the other standard system of citation appears in the preface.

honored status among Christians. Irenaeus introduces a quote from it with the words, "Well said the Scripture. . . ." Since Irenaeus does not name the work, it probably was well known by his audience among the Gallican churches. Clement of Alexandria likewise quotes it and accepted the divine character of its revelations. Origen with reservations proclaims it "divinely inspired" and "authoritative scripture." Tertullian bears witness to the significant effect the *Shepherd* had on liturgical practices by the year 200. The *Shepherd* is treated as a canonical document by nearly all third-century Greek theologians who mention it. Writing in the fourth century, Eusebius is the first major Greek author to deny it a place among the "accepted books," but he still considered it useful for instruction.[2]

Evidence from the Muratorian Canon

The most important external testimony to the date of the *Shepherd*'s composition is the Muratorian Fragment. L. A. Muratori found preserved in a manuscript from the seventh or eighth century a fragment of an early Roman canon. The Canon probably was written in the last decades of the second century. It denies apostolic authority to the author of the *Shepherd* and says that the *Shepherd* had been written recently by the brother of Pope Pius I (140–55):

> In the city of Rome, Hermas composed the *Shepherd* most recently, in our times, while his brother Pius was sitting in the chair of the church of the city of Rome. And for that reason it is appropriate that it be read, but not publicly among either the prophets, since their number is complete, nor among the writings of the apostles, until the end of times.[3]

The authenticity and accuracy of this reference to Hermas have been widely debated. A number of scholars, including Dibelius, Robinson, Giet, Reiling, Turner, and Osiek, conclude from it that the *Shepherd* was written at least in part by a man alive at mid-second century and

---

2. For the Latin version, see Cruttwell, *Literary History of Early Christianity*, 111. Irenaeus, *Adversus haereses* 4.20; Eusebius, *Historia Ecclesiastica* 5.8. Clement of Alexandria, *Stromata* 1.17, 29; 2.1, 9, 12. Origen, *Commentary on Romans* 16.4; idem, *De principis* 1.3.3; 2.1.5; 3.2.4.

3. "Pastorem vero nuperrime, temporibus nostris, in urbe Roma Herma conscripsit, sedente cathetra urbis Romae aeclesiae Pio episcopo fratre eius. Et ideo legi eum quidem oportet, se pupulicare vero in eclesia populo neque inter profetas conpletum numero, neque inter aposstolos in fine temporum potest." L. Duchesne, *Le Liber Pontificalis*, 3 vols. (Paris: Cyrille Vogel, 1886–92), 1:132. My translation.

thus, while parts of it may have been composed at an earlier date, its final redaction dates to this time.[4] Others have found reasons for questioning the Canon's accuracy. Virtually all scholars agree that the monoepiscopate did not exist in Rome at the time referred to in this fragment. Indeed, the *Shepherd* gives no indication that a single bishop ruled in Rome. Osiek dismisses the significance of this inaccuracy by pointing out that anachronisms regarding the monoepiscopate were common in Roman Christian authors from the late second century.[5] However, even this kind of error serves to cast doubt on the accuracy of other details.

Several scholars have questioned the Canon's assertion that Hermas was the brother of Pius. Joly incorrectly assumes that the author of the *Shepherd*, who describes his slave origins in *Vis.* 1.1, could not possibly have known who his brother was.[6] Slaves in Rome did at times know and maintain contact with relatives who belonged to a different master, but such knowledge was not common. In addition, A. S. Barnes suggests another way to account for the Canon's identification of Hermas with Pius. In the *Roman Breviary* account of the feast of Pope Pius, the building in which Pius lived was called "Pastor" (or "Shepherd"). Barnes says that this became confused in the *Acts of Pastor and Timotheus*, which makes "Pastor" the brother of Pius. He concludes that the author of the Canon was misled by this tradition and added his own misinformation.[7] Barnes's argument is interesting if purely conjectural. While far from conclusive, it shows that one need not accept the connection between Hermas and Pius if it is untenable on other grounds.

A more serious basis for questioning the Canon's accuracy is its author's bias against the *Shepherd*. The Canon's flat rejection of the *Shepherd*'s spiritual authority runs counter to the sentiment expressed in every other Christian author up to Eusebius. This has caused A. C. Sundberg to question the early date generally assigned to the Canon.

---

4. Martin Dibelius, *Der Hirt des Hermas* (Tübingen: J.C.B. Mohr, 1923), 421–22; J. Armitage Robinson, *Barnabas, Hermas and the Didache* (New York, 1920), 42; Stanislaus Giet, *Hermas et les pasteurs* (Paris: Presses Universitaires de France, 1963); Reiling, *Hermas and Christian Prophecy*, 24; Turner, "Shepherd of Hermas and the Problem of Its Text," 193; David Hellholm, *Das Visionenbuch des Hermas als Apokalypse* (Lund: C. W. Gleerup, 1980); Osiek, *Rich and Poor*, 11.

5. Osiek, *Rich and Poor*, 12.

6. Joly, *Hermas: Le Pasteur*, 17.

7. Barnes, *Christianity at Rome in the Apostolic Age*, 212.

This is significant, because the Canon's evidential value is based in large part on its assumed early date. This date is based in turn on the statement that the *Shepherd* was written "most recently." But Sundberg demonstrates that the term "most recently" (*nuperrime*) need not refer to the Canon author's time. Rather, it most likely is used to distinguish the present age from the apostolic age. The *Shepherd* must not be read with the Old Testament Scripture (the "prophets"), which are complete, nor with the writings of the apostolic era, since it was not written in either period.[8]

If written in the second century, the Canon must have opposed the *Shepherd*'s popularity for more localized reasons. Snyder suggests that the Canon operates under the bias of Hippolytus, who fought against a doctrine of second repentance similar to that expressed in the *Shepherd*. Hippolytus opposed Callistus in this matter of a second repentance, and Callistus used the *Shepherd* as support for his position. Hippolytus would have welcomed the assertion that the *Shepherd* did not represent binding authority.[9] Although there is no clear evidence of a connection between Hippolytus and the Canon, it is significant that the sentiment expressed in the latter may represent one side of a heated theological debate. That is, if its author had a point to prove, he may have been willing to use an obscure reference such as the one in the *Acts of Pastor and Timotheus* in order to assign the *Shepherd* a clear post-apostolic date of origin.

Finally, J. B. Lightfoot questions the fidelity of the single seventh- or eighth-century Latin manuscript that preserves this fragment of the Canon. Passages from this manuscript, which can be compared with citations in other manuscripts, contain a number of errors.[10]

Firm conclusions about the origin and accuracy of the Canon are not possible based on the present evidence. Sundberg points out that even the supposed Roman origin of this work is not above question. Even if it originated in Rome, it may be much later than second century, based on a liberal understanding of *nuperrime*. If the Canon is Roman and only several generations removed from the time of Pius, its accuracy is still called into question by its mistake regarding monoepiscopacy at Rome and the possibility of a confusion of identities as suggested by Barnes. Finally, the author of the Canon may

---

8. A. C. Sundberg, Jr., "Canon Muratori: A Fourth-Century List," 35.
9. Snyder, *Shepherd of Hermas*, 22.
10. Lightfoot, *Apostolic Fathers*, 360.

have had a theological axe to grind, and so his objectivity cannot be above question. Thus, the Muratorian Fragment provides only tentative data for the date of the *Shepherd*. It presents secure evidence only that the author of the Canon believed that the *Shepherd* was not written *after* the time of Pius.

Internal Evidence

Vision 2 presents the clearest internal evidence for a date. Here the church personified tells Hermas to send a copy of this vision to Clement: "Thus Clement will send it to the cities abroad, since that is entrusted to him (ἐπιτέτραπται)" (*Vis.* 2.4.3). If this refers to the author of *1 Clement*, written around 96 as established above, then at least the initial *Visions* must date to the late first century. Some scholars consider this reference to Clement too obvious. Osiek points out that, while Grapte is called on to share the new revelation with the widows and orphans of the Roman Christian community, Hermas does not feel the need to say that this is her duty as he does of Clement. As a result, the reference to Grapte seems more natural, while that to Clement seems contrived. This implies that Hermas wishes to identify his work falsely with an earlier era, and so must be sure his audience knows he is referring to the author of *1 Clement*. Osiek, who does not completely reject the authenticity of this statement, does not go so far as to assert duplicity on Hermas's part. But if *Vision* 2 is not an authentic contemporary reference to Clement, then Hermas or a later redactor sought to mislead readers in order to place the work at the end of the apostolic era.

If Hermas did this, he would be acting in direct contradiction to his character and teachings as represented in the work. In addition, the author of the *Shepherd* intended to read the work to his contemporaries. He could not have deceived them about whether or not Clement was still alive. Beyond this, Hermas could have had a more straightforward and innocent motive for this wording: he may have felt the need to defend giving an order (on behalf of "Ecclesia") to one of his leaders by reminding Clement that he was responsible for disseminating such new revelations to the other churches. Most scholars accept the reference to Clement as genuine. Cases against it seem to be built more on a preference for the testimony of the Muratorian Canon than on any independent evidence or reasoning.

The presence or absence in the *Shepherd* of allusions to theological issues in early Roman Christianity also provides evidence for its date. Hermas describes the leaders in the church as a collegial presbyteral government rather than a monoepiscopacy. Thus, the *Shepherd* probably was completed by mid-second century at the latest. Passages such as *Sim.* 5.7 seem to reflect a knowledge and rejection of some form of Gnosticism. For example, the *Shepherd* appears to reject the dualism of body and spirit common to Gnostic sects:

> See to it, lest the idea enter your heart that this flesh of yours is mortal, and you abuse it in some defilement . . . defile neither the flesh nor the spirit; for both are in fellowship, and neither can be defiled without the other. (*Sim.* 5.7.1, 4)

It is unlikely that this passage could have been composed earlier than the late first or early second century. On the other hand, the *Shepherd* lacks even one reference to Montanism, which came to Rome around the year 135. Thus, the work probably was completed before that date. Osiek suggests that the adoptionist Christology in the *Similitudes* "corresponds more smoothly" to later second-century Rome.[11]

A more tentative piece of evidence comes from Hippolytus. A reference in Hippolytus may date most of the *Shepherd* as early as 100. Hippolytus writes that in Rome Alcibiades the Elkesaite taught a doctrine of second repentance: Christians who had fallen into sinful ways had not forever lost their salvation, but could regain it through repentance. Alcibiades claimed his view derived from a teaching that originated in the third year of Trajan's reign (100). W. J. Wilson observes that this concept is very similar to that expressed in *Mandates* 4 and 12 and *Similitude* 8 of the *Shepherd*. Since Hermas presents this doctrine as a new revelation, Alcibiades could refer to the *Shepherd*. Alcibiades may have been wrong about the date this doctrine originated, but Wilson correctly asserts that Alcibiades had no obvious reason to falsify his information.[12]

---

11. On Montanism, see Barnard, *Studies in the Apostolic Fathers*, 155–56; Osiek, *Rich and Poor*, 7.

12. W. J. Wilson, "Career of the Prophet Hermas," 55–57. This idea was first advanced by Adolph von Harnack in *Geschichte der altchristlichen Literatur*, 4 vols. (Leipzig, 1897), 2.1: 266 n. 2.

More problematic are suggestions by Wilson and Snyder that references to persecution in the *Shepherd* can be related to historical events.[13] Wilson relates the persecution mentioned in the *Visions* to the reign of Domitian, and the reference to persecution in the *Similitudes* with the reign of Trajan. Snyder believes that the persecution mentioned in the *Visions* refers to the time of Trajan. But these views have several weaknesses. First, these references do not necessitate a literal and general persecution in Hermas's past. Second, we possess no clear evidence for a general persecution of Christians in Rome under either Domitian or Trajan (though probably some Roman Christians were prosecuted under both). As a result, these suggestions cannot help us establish the date of the *Shepherd*.

Based on the foregoing discussion, the testimony of the Muratorian Canon probably is in error and part or all of the *Shepherd* dates to the late first century. The work was probably written in stages, by either the same author or a succession of authors. The *Visions* almost certainly date to the time of Clement,[14] and the final portions of the work were done no later than 135. Arguments for a later second-century adoptionism are not conclusive enough to challenge the other evidence presented.

The Authorship of the *Shepherd*

The *Shepherd* claims to be the work of one Hermas, a former slave residing in Rome. The social identity of this person was discussed at length in chapter 1. Hermas wrote at least the first four *Visions*, and may have written the entire work over a period of years.

The piecemeal nature of the *Shepherd* has caused many to assert multiple authorship. For example, the revelations in *Visions* 1–4 are made by the church personified as a woman. But in the *Mandates* and *Similitudes*, an angel in the guise of a shepherd presents the revelations. *Similitude* 9 seems like an interpolation into an earlier work: it repeats and reinterprets the vision of the tower as a parable of the universal church in *Vision* 3, and it is three times as long as the

13. Wilson, "Career of the Prophet Hermas," 27–30; Snyder, *Shepherd of Hermas*, 22–24.

14. Reiling, *Hermas and Christian Prophecy*, 24; Dibelius, *Hirt des Hermas*, 453; Robert Joly, "Judaïsme, Christianisme et Hellènisme dans le Pasteur d'Hermas," *La Nouvelle Clio* 5 (1953): 394–406, esp. 397; Daniélou, *Theology of Jewish Christianity*, 39.

next longest *Similitude.* Bonner and Reiling show that the *Shepherd* probably circulated in some places from the second century without *Visions* 1–4, which were most likely written first. This indicates as a minimum that the two parts were written at different times, and perhaps that they were written by two or more authors. A number of passages show signs that the original author or another person reworked the writings at a later time. *Vision* 5 probably originated as an introduction to the *Mandates,* since many manuscripts call it an "apocalypse" rather than a "vision" like the first four. Giet asserts that the *Shepherd* was composed by three authors writing between 100 and 150. Peterson also holds to multiple authorship. He believes the *Shepherd* was produced by a Roman Christian "Schulbetrieb." Recent scholars, however, have asserted single authorship.[15]

The issue of multiple authorship cannot be settled easily. There is no overwhelming reason to assume more than one author if one does not posit a writing period longer than the adult life of one man. Hermas could have written the *Visions* as a middle-aged man during Clement's life and still have been alive to finish them around 135. If more than one author is responsible for this work, their similar attitudes indicate that they shared social status and place within the Roman Christian community. If the differences in social location and ideology between the supposed multiple authors were significant, there would be much less debate over multiple authorship. For the sake of convenience, I treat the *Shepherd* as the work of✓ one person. But my conclusions would not change if a different person or persons wrote the later parts of the *Shepherd,* since they probably would have belonged to the same part of Roman Christianity as did Hermas.

We asserted in the last chapter that *1 Clement* represents not simply the values and attitudes of one man, but those of the house church or house churches he led. Does the *Shepherd* likewise represent the thinking of a segment of Roman Christianity? The answer is

15. On circulation without *Visions* 1–4, see Bonner, ed., *Papyrus Codex of the Shepherd of Hermas,* 13–14; and Reiling, *Hermas and Christian Prophecy,* 22–23. On reworked passages, see Daniélou, *Theology of Jewish Christianity,* 39. On three authors, see S. Giet, "L'Apocalypse d'Hermas et la Pénitence," *Studia Patristica* 111:1 (1961): 288–302; and Erik Peterson, *Frühkirche, Judentum und Gnosis* (Freiburg: Herder, 1959), 271–83. On single authorship, see, e.g., Reiling, *Hermas and Christian Prophecy,* 22–24; √ and Pernveden, *Concept of the Church in the* Shepherd of Hermas, 13.

not as certain as it was for *1 Clement*. Hermas does not represent himself as having a following, and he had no official standing among the Roman churches. Hermas almost certainly was part of a congregation. *Mandate* 11 makes clear his commitment to congregational life. The "true prophet" in this passage only functions within the context of a local "assembly" of Christians. Hermas would have shared his message with fellow worshipers, and as a result of his message, he might have gathered around himself a congregation of like-minded believers. His absolute claim to special divine revelation would leave fellow Christians with only two alternatives: reject him as insane or accept his spiritual guidance. While some may have chosen the former response, it is probable that some chose the latter. Hermas did not wish to pursue philosophical contemplation or even a life of teaching. Rather, he wished to see a practical and immediate reform of Christian behavior. This practicality and urgency would tend to attract followers or at least admirers. The wide popularity enjoyed by the *Shepherd* in later years both in Rome and abroad suggests that many early Christians found his message attractive. Not all of Hermas's values would be reflected in such a group, but it is probable that, as his ministry progressed and his views became known throughout the congregations of Rome, he would attract Christians who agreed with his definition of the church and his attitude toward society. As we shall see, the Roman Christian leaders Hermas seeks to reform seem resistant to his message. If so, he might well have established a group in protest against the dominant leaders.

Hermas may or may not have led a group of like-minded Christians. But as the most "average" Roman Christian to leave behind a body of writing, he undoubtedly represents the beliefs and concerns of a segment of Roman Christianity. As noted in chapter 1, Hermas was a former slave with little education, wealth, or status. Very few such people in antiquity have left behind a record of their lives and thoughts. Hermas's very ordinariness makes quite probable the representative nature of his work. Roman Christians who agreed with Hermas may not have been united formally under him or another leader. But their views still count, and to the degree that they represent a unique interpretation of Christianity over against that of Christians like Clement, they may be said in broad terms to represent the ideology of part of the Roman churches.

The Occasion of the *Shepherd*

Hermas believed that he was the recipient of divine revelation. The *Shepherd* is presented as the result of visions and revelations made to Hermas first by a woman who represents the church (*Visions* 1–4). The remainder of the text consists of revelations made by an angel in shepherd's garb. Dibelius interprets all the autobiographical elements allegorically. Reiling questions the certainty of this view. But even Dibelius believes that Hermas was convinced he had received a core of genuine revelation (i.e., that fallen Christians have one chance to repent). However, K. D. MacMillan believes the entire work is a clever allegory meant to discredit those in the Roman church who had an interest in revelation. Davison shows the flaws in MacMillan's view. Van Deemter asserts that the *Shepherd* was intended not as a literary fiction but as an apocalypse.[16]

The purpose of Hermas's work is to communicate a divinely authorized message to the church. He repeats his central message four times: in *Vis.* 2.2.4, *Mandates* 4 and 12, and *Similitude* 8. Early Roman Christianity had taught that a Christian who fell into sin could not be forgiven. Hermas announced that postbaptismal sin can be forgiven, but only one time. Hermas also indicates concern that Christians should live out their faith in constant obedience to God. He is aware of Christians whose new-found wealth has caused them to reject former associations with poorer Christians. They have become preoccupied with the concerns of the material world, and value it above the next life. Hermas's message includes a rebuke of the Roman church. The woman Ecclesia says, "You shall say, then, to the leaders of the church, that they reform their ways in righteousness, to receive in full the promises with great glory" (*Vis.* 2.2.6).

THE ROMAN SOCIAL CONTEXT OF THE *SHEPHERD*

Clearly, Hermas, the author of the *Shepherd*, was a contemporary of Clement, the author of *1 Clement*. While Hermas's purposes in writ-

16. For a summary of scholarly views, see Davison, "Spiritual Gifts in the Roman Church," 74–75; Dibelius, *Hirt des Hermas*, 419; Reiling, *Hermas and Christian Prophecy*, 25; R. van Deemter, *Der Hirt des Hermas: Apokalypse oder Allegorie?* (Vitgever: W. D. Meinema, 1929), 157.

ing his work differ from Clement's, the *Shepherd* reveals just as much about the social identity and outlook of its author and Christians like him as *1 Clement* reveals about Clement and his congregation.

The Ruling Elite

While Clement shows a close familiarity with the values of the ruling elite, Hermas has little direct knowledge of them, and so probably had little or no contact with them. *Mandate* 7 may reflect some knowledge of their ability to inspire fear in the lower classes when it reads that where there is "glorious might" there is also fear, since everyone who has might gains the fear of others (*Mand.* 7.2). This appears to be the view of someone far down the social scale. At first glance, Hermas seems to address the upper classes when he warns Christians against having "lands and costly establishments and buildings and vain dwellings" (*Sim.* 1.1, 4). But here and in other similar passages he addresses people who acquired their wealth during their lifetimes. They buy land in imitation of the aristocracy, but they do not belong to the upper classes. The *Shepherd* represents the views of Christians with less social status and less direct contact with the Roman elite than those behind *1 Clement.*

The *Populus Urbanus*

Hermas condemns the conspicuous consumption by wealthy Roman Christians who are members of the *populus urbanus.* Hermas's descriptions of the rich are much more appropriate to freeborns and freedmen who have gained surplus wealth during their lifetimes. The rich for Hermas are concerned to accumulate an abundance of luxuries and to be involved in many affairs of "business" (πραγματεία). Aristocrats, whose wealth was secure and who generally avoided business entanglements, were more interested in pursuing education, power, and honor.

Hermas probably has in mind successful Roman freeborns and imperial freedmen when he condemns the luxury of many feasts and "various and unnecessary foods" (*Mand.* 6.2.5). A little later he again warns against evil luxury, much eating, the extravagance of wealth, boastfulness, haughtiness, and pride (*Mand.* 8.3, 4; cf. *Mand.* 12.2.1). The aristocracy favored lavish banquets, and their social inferiors who could afford it imitated them. Conspicuous consumption was one of the few ways a wealthy member of the lower classes could imitate the elite—it was far more difficult to buy honor and social status.[17]

The targets of Hermas's invective were those who had an over-abundance of possessions and rejoiced in their wealth (*Vis.* 3.9.5, 6). Hermas recounts a parable about a master whose many slaves worked his vineyard and fields. The master put a slave in charge of the vineyard while he went abroad. This master must have been a successful member of the *populus urbanus*, since a senator or *equite* would have had a permanent manager to care for each of his estates.

Hermas clearly has in mind successful members of the urban populace when he criticizes Christians who are involved in many affairs of "business" (πραγματεία; *Sim.* 9.20.1–4). They are "mixed up with business and riches, and heathen friendships, and many other occupations of this world . . ." (*Mand.* 10.1.4). Aristocrats in general did not occupy their minds with commerce any more than was necessary.

Hermas appears to be attacking Christians of the sort that made up Clement's house church: well-connected imperial freedmen and freedmen of the great houses who had far more opportunity to increase their wealth and status by involvement in commerce than almost any other group.[18] Hermas warns Christians not to go after the wealth of the heathen (*Sim.* 1.10). He laments the fact that some Christians had become "rich and in honor among the heathen." They "put on great haughtiness and became high-minded, and . . . lived together with the heathen" (*Sim.* 8.9.1). These Christians had gained material wealth and a position of respect in the Roman social hierarchy, and their Christian piety suffered for it.

These examples suggest that Hermas knew of "rich" persons only in terms of successful freeborns and freedmen below the aristocracy. This is confirmed by the fact that his former owner, Rhoda, belonged to the *populus urbanus* (see chap. 1). Hermas was also a member of this class. Thus, when Hermas criticizes "wealthy" Christians, he probably has in mind people like Clement and his congregation who, although technically members of his own class, enjoyed opportunities and material success beyond his reach.

---

17. Samuel Dill gives a number of examples of this in "The Society of Freedmen," in *Roman Society From Nero to Marcus Aurelius* (Cleveland: Norwood, 1956), 100–137.
18. Osiek, *Rich and Poor*, 127–32, also takes this view.

The Slaves

A number of Hermas's parables allude to slavery. He writes of a slave who disappoints his master and of one who was faithful to his master and honored by him (*Mand.* 12.2.1; 5.2.2–9). He gives us a number of insights into his relationship with his former owner, Rhoda, both as slave and as freedman. Hermas identifies himself and other Christians as the slaves of God (e.g., *Vis.* 1.2.4; 4.1.3; *Mand.* 3.4; *Sim.* 8.6.5). But, unlike Clement, he never uses the human slave-master relationship as a metaphor of order and harmony. Rather, the implication of these passages is that Christians owe God the same obedience that masters require of their slaves.

Neither Clement nor Hermas ever condemns slavery outright or instructs Christian slaveowners to free their slaves. Although both prefer freedom to slavery, their acceptance of the institution of slavery demonstrates that they do not challenge the basic categories of Roman society. Their frequent allusions to slavery indicate that both their congregations included a significant number of slaves or ex-slaves. The slaves and ex-slaves in Clement's group, however, have a more intimate awareness of the ideology of the upper classes, so they may have begun life as slaves of the aristocracy (see chap. 5). Those in Hermas's group, on the other hand, probably belonged to members of the *populus urbanus*.

The Poor

Hermas, while not poor himself, shows a greater knowledge of the Roman Christian poor and greater concern for their plight than does Clement. Since Hermas is exhorted by the *Shepherd* to give to "those who lack" (*Mand.* 2.4; *Sim.* 5.3.7), he does not count himself among the poor. He refers seven times to "those who lack" (ὑστερούμενος, substantive of ὑστερέω). Unlike *1 Clement*, which never refers to the chronically poor, in these passages the *Shepherd* refers to those in a continuous state of poverty. They are contrasted with the rich among the churches, who should help them deal with their hunger (*Vis.* 3.9.2–6). The need of the poor is so great that they may "groan" (στενάζω) to God and bring condemnation down on the rich if they are not helped (*Vis.* 3.9.6). "Those who lack," along with orphans and widows, are for Hermas those persons especially in need of material help (*Mand.* 8.10; *Sim.* 5.3.7; 9.27.2). They include homeless people sheltered by good Christian leaders (*Sim.* 9.27.2).

Osiek observes that Hermas never directly addresses the poor. They are mentioned only as objects of oppression by church officers, as objects of charity, or as the godly counterparts to Hermas's addressees.[19] This is probably because he takes the side of the oppressed when he condemns wealthy Christian oppressors who, while making up part of the "church" in Rome, are not part of the group of Christians with whom Hermas identifies.

Hermas's congregation probably included some poor people. He demonstrates an ability to look at society from their perspective when he says that the one without might is despised by all men (*Mand.* 7.2). He turns this into a spiritual lesson when he implies that Christians should not be concerned about how society perceives them, but about how God perceives them.

Although Hermas never advocates renunciation of material possessions, he seems to identify with the poor when he affirms that the poor man is spiritually superior to the rich. Since the rich Christian is caught up in his possessions and worldly responsibilities he, unlike the poor Christian, ignores the things of God (e.g., *Mand.* 8.10). Clement, on the other hand, assumes that the leaders of the congregation are its most spiritual members, regardless of personal wealth or lack thereof. Economic categories are never equated with spiritual maturity or immaturity in *1 Clement*. This difference suggests that Hermas was more sensitive to the very real dilemma of economic deprivation facing a part of Roman Christianity. Clement and his congregation, more isolated from the realities of chronic poverty, show little awareness of this dilemma.

CONCLUSION

Clement was a leader in the Christian community at Rome who in the 90s wrote a letter to a sister church in Corinth. He wrote *1 Clement* out of concern that the beliefs and practices of the Corinthian Christians were not in line with the principles of Christianity as understood by himself and those he represented. He wrote on behalf of a house church or house churches composed of Christians who associated closely with one another and shared common beliefs and values. They probably included a large proportion of slaves and

19. Ibid., 46, 55.

freedmen, some with imperial connections. Clement was literate and educated to some degree in the literary traditions though not in the philosophical traditions of his day.

At about the same time in Rome, a very different kind of author was beginning to express his beliefs. Hermas probably began writing during Clement's time and may have added to his work until his death sometime prior to the middle of the second century. He wrote to Roman Christians, probably the only ones he knew much about, but he also believed that his message needed to be shared with all the churches. He may have attracted a group of like-minded Christians as he shared his message. Thus, like Clement, Hermas represents a group of like-minded individuals within the larger body of Roman Christians. Unlike Clement, Hermas almost certainly had no connection with the imperial household, nor does he appear to have received much if any formal education. The purpose of his work is straightforward: to convince Christians that an authentic divine revelation had been made through him.

While both *1 Clement* and the *Shepherd* probably were composed by Christians in the *populus urbanus*, the status of those Christians was quite different. Clement's group possessed a relatively high status among ex-slaves: they were Roman citizens, and had some hope to see their economic and social lot continue to improve over their lifetimes and those of their children. Hermas and those who identified with his message, on the other hand, came from the lower levels of the *populus urbanus*, where freedom from slavery often meant not knowing where one's next meal would come from. Hermas seems less satisfied with the institution of slavery. He shows more concern for the plight of those who cannot feed themselves and their families, and greater anger at Christians who could help them but choose not to. We now turn to the question of how these differing social identities led to different conceptions of how Christians should relate to one another and to the larger Roman society.

7

SOCIAL RELATIONS AMONG THE
FIRST ROMAN CHRISTIANS

We have seen that *1 Clement* and the *Shepherd of Hermas* represent unique social identities within Roman Christianity. Clement and his congregation enjoyed a higher social status than did Hermas. The dominant Roman system of society had worked for Clement, while Hermas had suffered economic deprivation. Clement and those who associated with him understood and respected the Roman elite, while Hermas and his followers sympathized with the poor and held the rich responsible for their predicament. We now examine how the different social attitudes of Clement and Hermas caused them to define Christianity and, specifically, relations between Roman Christians, very differently. Clement showed greater affinity for Roman ideology in his description of six areas of Christian social relations: rules of household behavior, hospitality, responsibilities between Christians, membership in the congregation, congregational order, and congregational discipline.

THE ROMAN *FAMILIA* AND CHRISTIAN
HOUSEHOLD RULES

For the Roman aristocracy, the household was the basic structure of the state. Its health was considered essential to the stability of the state. In ancient Roman law, the only person with full political rights was the *paterfamilias*, the male head of the Roman household. He held nearly unlimited power *(patria potestas)* over his wife and children, as well as over his clients, slaves, and other legal dependents. He could have an unwanted new-born infant abandoned, sell his son into slavery, and even have his wife or children executed. Other laws also served to protect and maintain the position of the *pater.*[1]

1. Cantarella, *Pandora's Daughters*, 113–14. See also Crook, *Law and Life of Rome*, chap. 4, "Family and Succession"; and Pierre Grimal, *The Civilization of Rome*, trans. W. S. Maguinness (New York, 1963), 119.

These laws were changed dramatically as time went by, so that by the period of the early empire, the *patria potestas* had lost most of its legal power. Nevertheless, the *pater* still had considerable influence over his adult sons. A son, even though a Roman citizen and in spite of his age and rank, could own nothing while his *paterfamilias* lived. Only heads of households among the aristocracy benefited from the laws enforcing the *patria potestas*. The households of the *populus urbanus* apparently were not always organized in this way. This was particularly true of slaves and noncitizen foreign residents of Rome, since their marriages were not recognized by Roman law. Codes of behavior written by Romans were usually addressed to the *paterfamilias* only. Women, children, and slaves normally were addressed in the third person. Adherence to the *patria potestas* became for the aristocracy a symbol of traditionalism, that is, an ideology, under the empire.[2]

Although both Clement and Hermas define the Christian family in terms of the Roman household (*familia*), Clement does so to a greater extent. Clement and Hermas present codes of household ethics (*1 Clem.* 1.3; 21.6–8; *Shepherd, Mand.* 8.10). Such codes in the New Testament typically focus on three levels of submission and obligation: wives to husbands, slaves to masters, and children to parents.[3]

Christian household codes may have their origins in Stoicism or in the ethical teachings of Plato and Aristotle. Stambaugh and Balch claim that household codes in the New Testament may have been an attempt to impose on Christian family life a more patriarchal order, patterned on the Greco-Roman household.[4] These codes usually define relationships between members of individual households, not relationships between members of a house church.

The two codes in *1 Clement* are similar in content and parallel in structure. In 1.3, Clement tells the Corinthian Christians:

2. Daube, *Roman Law*, 75–76; and Stambaugh and Balch, *New Testament in Its Social Environment*, 123–24.

3. Aune, *New Testament in Its Literary Environment*, 196. See also David L. Balch, *Let Wives Be Submissive: The Domestic Code in 1 Peter* (Chico, Calif.: Scholars Press, 1981); and D. Lührmann, "Neutestamentliche Haustafeln und antike Oekonomie," *New Testament Studies* 27 (1980): 83–97. Codes of household ethics in the New Testament are found in Col. 3:18—4:1; Eph. 5:21—6:9; 1 Pet. 2:13-21; 3:1-7; 1 Tim. 2:1—6:2; and Titus 2:1-10.

4. Stambaugh and Balch, *New Testament in Its Social Environment*, 55.

> For you did all things without respect of persons, and walked in the laws of God, obedient to your rulers, and paying all proper honor to the older among you. On the young, too, you enjoined temperate and seemly thoughts, and to the women you gave instruction that they should do all things with a blameless and seemly and pure conscience, yielding a dutiful affection to their husbands. And you taught them to remain in the rule of obedience and to manage their households with seemliness, in all circumspection.

In 21.6–8, he returns to this theme:

> Let us respect those who rule us, let us honor the aged, let us instruct youths in the fear of God, let us lead our wives to that which is good. Let them exhibit the lovely habit of purity, let them show forth the innocent will of meekness, let them make the gentleness of their tongue manifest by their silence, let them not give their affection by factious preference, but in holiness to all equally who fear God. Let our small children share in the instruction which is in Christ, let them learn . . .

These passages represent the earliest codes of household ethics, intended for the general membership of a congregation, in which only the *paterfamilias* is addressed directly. The codes in Col. 3:18—4:1, Eph. 5:21—6:9, and 1 Pet. 2:13-21 and 3:1-7, also written to a general audience, address wives, husbands, children, fathers, slaves, and masters in the first person.[5] The codes in 1 Tim. 2:1—6:2 and Titus 2:1-10 are each addressed to a specific individual charged with supervising the behavior of Christians. The two passages from *1 Clement* quoted here address all categories of family members in the third person. Unlike the New Testament codes, *1 Clement* does not present the proper behavior of husbands and fathers toward the family beyond their responsibility to govern its conduct. This indicates a subtle shift in Clement's thinking. He sees the *paterfamilias* as ultimately responsible for the spiritual welfare of his entire household.

The influence of the *paterfamilias* on Clement also appears in how he thinks of church officeholders. Clement and his group appear to see the church officeholder as the *paterfamilias* of a congregation household *(familia)*. Concern for the officeholder's personal behavior, like that of the Roman *paterfamilias*, is overshadowed in *1 Clement* by a concern to spell out his authority over and respon-

---

5. Fathers and children are not mentioned in the 1 Peter passages.

sibility for the members of his congregation. In chapter 44, Clement labels unjust the removal from office of men who were appointed by the apostles and their successors, and who have served blamelessly for many years (44.2–3; cf. 42.1–5). Although he characterizes them as "blameless" (ἀμέμπτως) three times in this chapter, he tells us almost nothing about the current situation in Corinth. This suggests that Clement supported the ousted leaders more on principle than from a thorough knowledge of the situation. For Clement, once a presbyter is appointed, he is untouchable (like a *paterfamilias*). All others must respect his position, be content in their own places, and not aspire to positions to which they have not been appointed (41.1).

In contrast to the New Testament codes of household conduct mentioned above, *1 Clement's* codes devote a disproportionate amount of space to the duties of wives. Also in contrast to the New Testament codes, they are concerned solely with regulating the behavior of women rather than delineating their privileges and responsibilities. They are to act from a pure conscience, show the proper affection and obedience to their husbands, show equal affection to all Christians, manage their household with the proper attitude, exhibit purity and meekness, and speak little. This greater emphasis on wives may be a reflection of the fact that the decline of the *paterfamilias'* power had been accompanied by a rise in the power and independence of women in the aristocracy, much to the chagrin of their husbands.[6] Clement, because of his respect for aristocratic ideology, may have shared the *paterfamilias'* frustration over their loss of power. In addition, the women in Clement's congregation may have imitated the more independent behavior of their mistresses.

Clement's instructions for children in 21.6–8 also differ from the New Testament codes of household ethics. Whereas in the New Testament codes the focus is on obedience and respect to parents and elders, in *1 Clement* the focus is on instruction in the basics of the Christian faith. While the education of children was generally thought to be basic to obedience, the shift in emphasis from the received Christian tradition is significant. This focus on education

6. Cantarella, *Pandora's Daughters*, 135–59. She records a number of complaints along this line by classical authors.

could reflect an increased concern among second-generation Christians that the received faith be transmitted to the new generation. But it also may reflect the high value placed on education among the Roman aristocracy.

The great omissions in Clement's codes of household ethics, when compared to those in the New Testament, are instructions to slaves and masters. Clement's audience, like his congregation, undoubtedly included slaves. It is unlikely that his congregation included Christian slaveowners, however, since they would have had to be fairly wealthy. Clement's house church probably was composed of slaves and freedman clients of the Roman aristocracy. Whether or not the Corinthian congregation included slaveowners, it appears that Clement's concerns in this area were shaped more by his own experiences than by his knowledge of the situation in Corinth.

Clement appears to have combined New Testament principles with the Roman upper-class ideal of the *paterfamilias* who exerts ultimate power and authority over his household. Such a model lends itself to the main point of Clement's letter, that order and harmony must reign in the community if dire consequences are to be avoided. Hermas accepts the Roman concept of *patria potestas*, but in a more general and less complete sense than does Clement. The closest that Hermas comes to a code of household ethics is in *Mand.* 8.10:

> Next hear the things which follow: To minister to widows, to look after orphans and the destitute, to redeem from distress the servants of God, to be hospitable, for in hospitality may be found the practice of good, to resist none, to be gentle, to be poorer than all men, to reverence the aged, to practice justice, to preserve brotherhood, to submit to insult, to be brave, to bear no malice, to comfort those who are oppressed in spirit, not to cast aside those who are offended in the faith, but to convert them and give them courage, to reprove sinners, not to oppress poor debtors, and whatever is like to these things.

Osiek says that the material in this verse comes from traditional lists of virtues, church order material, codes of household ethics, and the traditional theology of the "pious poor." The only obvious link to the codes in the New Testament and *1 Clement* is the command to "reverence the aged." Osiek takes this verse to imply that the Christian community is "by extension one household," since the form of a code of household ethics is extended to include various duties among members of the congregation.[7]

Hermas speaks at length about his own family. Hermas is the "head" (κεφαλή) of his household (*Sim.* 7.2). This is different from Paul, who in Eph. 5:23 makes the husband the head only of the wife. The change is subtle, but significant. The *paterfamilias* was the head of the entire household.

Unlike the New Testament and *1 Clement*, the *Shepherd* depicts the head of a household, Hermas, as having direct responsibility for the sinfulness of his family:

> But it is not for this that God is angry with you, but in order that you should convert your family, which has sinned against the Lord, and against you, their parents. But you are indulgent, and do not correct your family, but have allowed them to become corrupt. For this reason the Lord is angry with you, but he will heal all the past evils in your family, for because of their sins and wickedness you have been corrupted by the things of daily life. . . . Do not cease, then, correcting your children, for I know that if they repent with all their heart, they will be inscribed in the books of life with the saints. (*Vis.* 1.3.1, 2)

If the head of the household obeys God's commands and corrects his family in piety, they will be saved (cf. *Sim.* 5.3.9). If he neglects God's commands, the entire household will not be saved (*Mand.* 12.3.6). This includes his wife as well, whose sins apparently stem from her inability to control her tongue (*Vis.* 2.2.3; 2.3.1).

These passages seem to give Hermas the absolute power of a spiritual *paterfamilias*, but the power is limited in that Hermas is, in a sense, held hostage by the behavior of his family. Their sins affect his life on earth as well as his eternal destiny. The threat he issues, that their sins would bring down condemnation on the entire family, is a powerful weapon. But this does not seem like the kind of weapon a *paterfamilias* of the aristocracy would have used.

Similitude 7 relates that the "shepherd (angel) of punishment" has been sent to afflict Hermas and his household. Hermas is told that he is being punished so harshly because of the great sins of his family. He protests that he should not be punished, "even if they have done such things." The shepherd explains that his family

---

7. Osiek, *Rich and Poor*, 61.

"cannot be punished in any other way, than if you, the head (κεφαλή) of the household (οἶκος), be afflicted. For when you are afflicted, they also will necessarily be afflicted, but while you prosper, they cannot suffer any affliction" (*Sim.* 7.3). Hermas must be referring to affliction caused by economic deprivation. The health or happiness of his family members could be removed on an individual basis. But if they are to suffer material loss, the one who feeds and shelters them must also suffer material setbacks.

Hermas, like those in the lower classes of Roman society, was affected by the aristocracy's concept of the *patria potestas*. The power of the Christian *paterfamilias* over his family in spiritual matters is made quite strong by Hermas, and to this degree he follows the Roman aristocratic model. But this power is mitigated by the power of his family to disobey him and thus cause his own ruin, both materially and spiritually. In addition, references to Hermas's past leniency with his household suggest that he has not based his prior relationship with it on the *paterfamilias* model. Hermas adopted about as much of this model as one would expect of a member of the lower classes who had no real contact with the aristocracy.

Unlike Clement, Hermas never attempts to apply this model in a systematic way, nor does he expand the model to include the place of leaders over the congregation. If Hermas does see his congregation as a household, as Osiek believes, his concepts do not come from Roman ideology.[8] The idea of the family in *1 Clement* clearly has been influenced by Roman ideology to a greater degree than has the idea of the family in the *Shepherd*.

FRIENDSHIP AMONG THE ROMAN ELITE AND CHRISTIAN HOSPITALITY

Clement and Hermas place a higher emphasis on the importance of hospitality within the Christian community than do the authors of the New Testament, probably as a result of the influence of Roman aristocratic notions of friendship. Again, *1 Clement* is more influenced by these Roman ideas than is the *Shepherd*.

Friendship among the elite was very important, since their social life was based primarily on personal relationships. Political princi-

8. Ibid., 61–62.

ples sometimes mattered less than personal links. MacMullen observes that, in Rome, "clearly the sense of hierarchy ruled behavior."[9] Senators and *equites* competed for the respect of peers. Senators formed long-term alliances based on their knowledge of one another's family backgrounds, friends, and connections by marriage. A wealthy Roman walking through the city, to avoid the public embarrassment of encountering a fellow aristocrat he did not know or could not remember, would be accompanied by his *nomenclator,* a slave who could give him the name and a short biography of any fellow member of the elite.

Gift giving among the rich sometimes reached excessive proportions. Obligations between "friends" *(amici)* were not formally defined, but, as is often true of unwritten law, they were more important than many formal regulations. The letters of Pliny the Younger provide us with contemporary examples. They depict a network of mutually obligatory friendships among the elite. For example, Pliny tells Romalius Firmus:

> Your father was a close friend of my mother's and uncle's, and a friend to me too, as far as our difference in age allowed; so there are sound and serious reasons why I ought to try to improve your position.[10]

Pliny then gives him 300,000 sesterces in order to raise him to the rank of an *equites.* He demonstrates the reciprocal nature of Roman friendship when he adds that "the length of our friendship is sufficient guarantee that you will not forget this gift." Pliny agrees to help a friend of Suetonius the biographer attain a military tribunate, as he once helped Suetonius (*Letters* 3.8). Pliny could ask for favors as well. He once persuaded the emperor to raise a young equestrian friend to senatorial rank (*Letters* 2.9). He asks Socius Senecio to grant a tribunate to the relative of a mutual friend (*Letters* 4.4).

Hospitality in various forms existed in Hellenistic society prior to the first century A.D. and had by that time become a significant part of the ideology of the Roman aristocracy. Country villas of

---

9. On personal links, see Grimal, *Civilization of Rome,* 308; and MacMullen, *Roman Social Relations,* 112.

10. Pliny the Younger, *The Letters of the Younger Pliny,* trans. B. Radice (Middlesex: Penguin, 1963), 1.19. See also A. N. Sherwin-White, *The Letters of Pliny* (Oxford: Oxford University Press, 1966), 44–45, 129–31.

the elite could be counted upon to provide shelter for the traveling aristocrat.[11]

While Clement has nothing to say about the Roman elite's notion of friendship, Hermas demonstrates an acquaintance with it. In the parable of the wealthy landowner and the faithful slave, Hermas has the master hold a meeting with his heir and "his friends whom he had as counselors" (*Sim.* 5.2.6). These friends clearly are not members of his household, but peers within his class who give each other advice.

More significantly, Hermas condemns the imitation of upper-class friendships among the wealthy Christians to whom he writes. He probably has in mind Christian imitators of this ideology among the imperial freedmen and freedmen of the great houses when he says that spiritually weak Christians can be made bitter "because of daily business or of food or some trifle, or about some friend, or about giving or receiving, or about some such foolish matters" (*Mand.* 5.2.2). The proximity of the phrases "some friend" and "giving or receiving" indicates familiarity with the Roman practice of gift giving between *amici*, and the onerous burden it could be.[12] Hermas repeats this theme later, when he says that weak Christians become corrupted through being "mixed up with business and riches, and heathen friendships, and many other occupations of this world" (*Mand.* 10.1.4). The coupling of business, wealth, and "heathen friendships" is not incidental in a society where strategic relationships were key to the accumulation of honor. Since Hermas addresses Christians in a social situation very similar to that of Clement's congregation, it is possible that Clement and his friends had fallen without realizing it into the kinds of practices condemned by Hermas. This could explain *1 Clement's* silence on this subject.

Hospitality (φιλοξενία) was important to both Clement and Hermas. They show a greater concern for this practice than do the New Testament authors, a concern they may have learned from Roman society. The Greek word for hospitality is absent from the Septuagint and used only six times in the New Testament. But it is

11. Ladislaus Bolchazy discusses Livy's extensive use of this concept in *Hospitality in Early Rome* (Chicago: Ares Press, 1977), 43–78.

12. Hermas could have in mind the *sportulae*, gifts given by patrons to clients who attended them for a day (see p. 131).

used six times in *1 Clement* and three times in the *Shepherd*.[13] Since several of the New Testament letters in which it occurs had some connection with Rome, they may also have been influenced by the example of hospitality among the Roman aristocracy. Romans was written to a congregation or congregations in Rome, and 1 Peter probably was written from Rome. Many scholars think Hebrews was written to or from Rome.

Hospitality is for Clement an important factor in relations within the Christian community. Clement calls the Corinthians' character "magnificent in its hospitality" (1.2) in reference to how they had received Christian visitors from Rome in the past. Clement offers the example of Abraham's "faith and hospitality" toward the angels, Lot's "hospitality and piety" toward the same angels, and Rahab's "faith and hospitality" toward the spies of Israel (10.7; 11.1; 12.1). In 35.5 he lists "inhospitality" among the serious sins of those who rebel against God.

Hermas places a high priority on hospitality in his list of things that flow from a virtuous soul: "to be hospitable, for in hospitality may be found the practice of good . . ." (*Mand.* 8.10). Since this passage is addressed to behavior within the congregation, it implies that the congregation is the proper locus of hospitality. He praises the bishops and "hospitable men who at all times received the servants of God into their houses gladly and without hypocrisy" (*Sim.* 9.27.2).

Thus, like Roman aristocrats, Clement and Hermas place high priority on hospitality within their groups of Christians. The idea of showing hospitality toward strangers and unbelievers in Heb. 13:2 is absent from *1 Clement* and the *Shepherd*. Hospitality became a vital form of service among the early Roman Christian congregations, although it had become an irritating burden for the Roman upper classes. Since the Christians associated with Clement and Hermas were not aristocrats, none of them participated directly in the Roman ideology of friendship. But as slaves and ex-slaves, they probably participated in the Roman system of patronage.

13. Bauer, *Greek-English Lexicon of the New Testament*, 868. The NT references are: Rom. 12:13; 1 Tim. 3:2; 5:10; Titus 1:8; Heb. 13:2; and 1 Pet. 4:9. The references in *1 Clement* are: 1.2; 10.7; 11.1; 12.1; 12.3; and 35.5; and in the *Shepherd of Hermas: Mand.* 8.10 (2x); and *Sim.* 9.27.2. See Koenig, *New Testament Hospitality*; Donald W. Riddle, "Early Christian Hospitality, a Factor in the Gospel Transmission," *Journal of Biblical Literature* 57 (1938): 141–54.

ROMAN PATRONAGE AND OBLIGATIONS
AMONG CHRISTIANS

Clement and his congregation came to accept social distinctions among themselves as a basis for ordering their relationships. That is, through the influence of Roman ideology, they came to accept hierarchy as natural to Christianity. In contrast, Hermas accepts the need for interdependency, but he does not base the value of a Christian on his social identity.

During the Republic, and particularly after the plebs won the right to elect their own magistrates, patricians developed the ties of responsibility and duty with their social inferiors commonly referred to today as the patron-client relationship. The plebs became *clientela* of the *patroni*. They owed them deference and specific responsibilities such as joining their retinue during public appearances. Seneca observed that this reciprocal exchange, which he called *beneficia*, was a custom "which more than any other binds together human society."[14]

Patronage remained an important social basis of the aristocracy in the early empire period, even though it had lost its earlier political significance. Public attendance on one's patron was required, and often consumed the better part of a patron's morning hours if not the entire day. Clients provided an aristocrat with a retinue that accompanied him around the city or ornamented his receiving room, thereby announcing the aristocrat's social importance. For his day's attendance, the patron rewarded the client with a small basket (the *sportula*), which generally contained food and small presents. Trajan restricted its value to six and one-quarter sesterces per day, a small remuneration if the client had to attend to the errands of his patron for the better part of the day.[15]

Sometimes a client was invited to a patron's banquet table simply to witness the latter's wealth and power, not out of genuine friendship. In such cases the client could expect to be the butt of jokes and

14. Seneca, *De beneficiis* 1.4.2: "De beneficius dicendum est et ordinanda res, quae maxime humanam societatem adligat." Cf. Saller, *Personal Patronage Under the Early Empire*, 119 n. 1. See also Juvenal, *Satires* 1.46; 7.142; Ludwig Friedländer, *Roman Life and Manners Under the Early Empire*, 4 vols., trans. L. A. Magnus (New York: Ayer Co. Pubs., 1913), 2:195–202.

15. Christ, *Romans*, 97; H. G. Pflaum, *Abrégé des Procurateurs Equestres* (Paris, 1972), 19; Friedländer, *Roman Life and Manners*, 197.

to receive food and wine far inferior to that of honored guests, as Juvenal laments (*Satires* 5). Freedmen, who as slaves had been part of the *familia* of the *paterfamilias*, normally in freedom became his clients. In the first century, the free citizen owed only moral obligations to his patron, but the freedman owed him legal obligations as well. Augustus used this relationship in establishing the imperial bureaucracy. As a result, members of the *familia Caesaris*, imperial slaves and freedmen, were recognized as special representatives of imperial authority, and they came to exert at times greater influence than many aristocratic members of the ruling elite.[16]

Clement and Hermas show a familiarity with the patron-client relationship, and build their concept of relations within the Christian community in part on this model. Clement says, "The great (μεγάλος) cannot exist without the small (μικρός), nor the small without the great; there is a certain mixture among all, and herein lies the advantage" (37.4). Clement emphasizes the importance of order and stability to the proper functioning of society and the mutually beneficial nature of the patron-client relationship at its best.

Clement also says:

> Let the strong care for the weak and let the weak reverence the strong. Let the rich man give help to the poor and let the poor give thanks to God, that he gave him one to supply his needs. (38.2)

Like a Roman patron, the strong (ἰσχυρὸς) and rich (πλούσιος) Christian has a responsibility to lend aid to the weak (ἀσθενῆς) and poor (πτωχὸς) Christian. The way in which Clement juxtaposes strong/weak and rich/poor implies that, for him, both appositions had an economic aspect. In other words, he identifies the "strong" Christian with the materially "rich" Christian. Clement says that the weak Christian should show "reverence" (ἐντρεπέσθω) for the strong Christian. Grant and Graham assert that Clement's commands to the strong are the same as the commands to the strong in Rom. 15:1-2. But they add that enjoining the weak to respect the strong was Clement's "own idea of order."[17] More likely, however, is that Clement's idea arose not in a vacuum but from the Roman patron-client relationship. Since ἐντρεπέσθω is the same word Clement uses for

---

16. P. A. Brunt, *Social Conflicts in the Roman Republic* (New York: W. W. Norton, 1971), 48; and Weaver, *"Familia Caesaris,"* 5–6, chap. 22.

17. Grant and Graham, *First and Second Clement*, 23.

reverence for God, it conveys for him more than a superficial respect. This passage accurately describes Roman social relations: if the poor were dependent on the patronage of the elite, the elite were just as dependent on the clientage of slaves and clients who staffed their palaces, managed their businesses, and guarded their persons.

Clement appears to accept social distinctions among Christians as a basis for ordering relationships within the community on the model of Roman patronage. He makes only one significant change: unlike Roman aristocrats, rich Christians are not to use their retinue of needy clients for ostentatious display. Rather, they are to care for those with legitimate needs.

Hermas also asserts that rich and poor Christians benefit one another. But he alters the Roman model further, so that the poor man shows gratitude not to his patron but to God. In *Similitude* 2, the common Roman use of elms to support growing grape vines is presented as applying "to the servants of God, to the poor and the rich":

> The rich man has much wealth, but he is poor with regard to the Lord, being busied about his riches. . . . But when the rich man rests upon the poor, and gives him what he needs, he believes that what he does to the poor man can find a reward with God, because the poor is rich in intercession and confession. . . . The rich man, therefore, helps the poor in all things without doubting. But the poor man, being helped by the rich, makes intercession to God, giving him thanks, for him who gave to him, and the rich man is still zealous for the poor man, that he should lack nothing in his life, for he knows that the intercession of the poor is acceptable and rich toward the Lord. Therefore the two work together to complete the work, for the poor works in the intercession in which he is rich . . . this he pays to the Lord who helps him. And the rich man likewise provides the poor, without hesitating, with the wealth which he received from the Lord . . . and has fulfilled his ministry rightly. (*Sim.* 2.4–7)

In this passage, the rich man is responsible to help provide the material needs of the poor. Hermas adds that a Christian cannot have both wealth and a strong relationship with God. This notion departs from Clement, who equated "strong" with "rich," and from Roman ideology, which equated wealth with strength, honor, and effectiveness. According to Hermas, the rich man's low spirituality can be mitigated only by providing for the material needs of the poor, as the elm provides support for the vine. Like the elm, the rich man by nature cannot produce fruit (*Sim.* 2.3, 5). But when he supports the poor man, who like the vine naturally produces fruit, he increases the fruitfulness of the poor man. In helping the poor man, the rich man is able to produce fruit as well.

The poor Christian in this passage has no responsibility toward his rich benefactor except to pray to God on his behalf. He is not charged to show either deference or gratitude, in opposition to *1 Clement.* He is to show gratitude to God for providing assistance through the rich man. An additional responsibility of the poor toward God is mentioned in *Mand.* 2.5. The one who receives material support must be in true "distress" (θλίβω). Apparently the rich Christian is responsible only to help poor Christians who cannot provide their own basic sustenance. This passage further supports the idea that Hermas possessed an intimate knowledge of Rome's poorer classes, and knew the difference between subsistence poor and those below the subsistence level.

Thus, Hermas stood the patron-client relationship on its head. Unlike Roman patronage, which had as its ultimate purpose building the prestige of the patron, the purpose of mutual support for Hermas was to sustain the true spiritual warriors of Christianity: the "pious poor." He probably was affected more in this concept by Jewish and Christian traditions than by Roman society.[18] Clement also rejects the ultimate purpose of Roman patronage. But he accepts the basic Roman assumption that great and small can assist one another, and that they can contribute equally to the community. The key influence of Roman ideology on *1 Clement* in this section is its hierarchical nature. Unlike the *Shepherd*, in which rich and poor support one another and in which the poor are more spiritual, *1 Clement* reflects Roman ideology when it implies that those with power and wealth in the churches have far more to offer the congregation than do their powerless and poor brothers.

ROMAN CITIZENSHIP AND MEMBERSHIP
IN THE CHRISTIAN COMMUNITY

Roman citizenship was highly esteemed in the first century. Those who possessed it were entitled to special protection by the Roman

18. Regarding the theology of the pious poor, see Osiek, *Rich and Poor,* 16–38.

government from the accusations of noncitizens and from the more extreme forms of punishment. Citizens were held in honor above noncitizens, even if they were of slave origin. Some, like the centurion in Acts 22:28, had paid large sums of money to obtain their Roman citizenship. The word πολιτεύομαι in antiquity originally had the meanings "to be or live as a citizen," "to act as a citizen (by taking part in political life)," or "to share in state government, to rule the state." The more diluted sense of "conduct" is first found in Maccabees, where it is used only in this sense.[19] Paul uses πολιτεύομαι to mean "conduct" in Phil. 1:27.

Clement thought of membership in his congregation like citizenship in the secular state. *First Clement* incorporates the larger society's respect for Roman citizenship into its view of Christianity. Clement says that the Corinthians were adorned by their "virtuous and honorable" citizenship (πολιτεία; 2.8). Like Maccabees and Paul, Clement uses πολιτεύομαι in the broader sense of "to conduct," but the fact that he uses the word seven times suggests that his familiarity with Roman citizenship made him consider the term a fitting expression of conduct within the community. Clement says that the peace of the Christian community was upset by dissension and schism because Christians pursued their own selfish desires and did not live out their citizenship in a civil manner (3.4). Those who "live without regret as citizens of God" (ταῦτα οἱ πολιτευόμενοι τὴν ἀμεταμέλητον πολιτείαν τοῦ θεοῦ) would rather leave the community than cause strife (54.4). The Christian martyrs conducted themselves in an exemplary fashion (6.1). Similarly, those who live in the "fear and love" of God are willing to suffer torture (51.2). Christians who perform good and virtuous deeds in harmony (ὁμόνοια) are acting as citizens worthy of God (21.1). Clement asserts that the Corinthian presbyters were removed despite their behavior as good citizens in the Christian community (44.6).

The *Shepherd* is silent on the subject of citizenship. While Hermas's writings do not specifically devalue Roman citizenship, they do not treat it as a fitting metaphor of the Christian life.

---

19. Hermann Strathmann, *"Polis,"* in *Theological Dictionary of the New Testament,* ed. G. Friedrich, trans. G. W. Bromiley, 10 vols. (Grand Rapids: Wm. B. Eerdmans, 1968), 6:517–18.

CIVIL HARMONY AND
CONGREGATIONAL ORDER

Clement admired the order and stability of Roman society. The basic imperative of the Christian congregation's authority structure for Clement was not personal ability or moral character in its leaders, but the need to preserve harmony.

Civil war (στάσις) was endemic in the city-states of the ancient Greeks. They strove for the often-elusive ideal of concord (ὁμόνοια). Plato defined στάσις as internal and domestic hostility and as fighting among those united by nature. In this way a city is divided against itself.[20] The Greek city-state, prior to Roman intervention, had suffered as much from στάσις as from external war.[21] Rome itself had endured long periods of civil war prior to the establishment of the principate under Augustus.

But imperial power significantly reduced στάσις in the first century, and contemporaries readily attributed the Pax Romana, or Roman peace, to the power of the emperor. Strabo writes that while in the past Italy had been torn by factions,

> never have the Romans and their allies thrived in such peace and plenty as that which was afforded them by Augustus Caesar from the time he assumed the absolute authority. . . . (*Geography* 6.4.2)

This peace and the accompanying general prosperity were the great advantages of Roman rule, as recognized by pro-Romans such as Nicolaus of Damascus, advisor to King Herod of Judaea.[22]

It is no exaggeration to say that the Pax Romana was one of Rome's most effective noncoercive policy tools. Most people in the interior provinces, and especially the residents of Rome, had no fear of foreign attack. By the time of Clement and Hermas, the elimination of pirates in the Mediterranean Sea allowed a more continuous and predictable flow of trade. The far-flung Roman highway system, made possible by the absence of rebellion within the empire and maintained at great expense, allowed for uninterrupted travel and commerce as never before in history.

---

20. Plato, *Republic* 5.470.

21. Chester Starr, *Civilization and the Caesars* (New York: Oxford University Press, 1965), 105.

22. See Emilio Gabbe, "The Historians and Augustus," in *Caesar Augustus: Seven Aspects*, ed. Fergus Millar and Erich Segal (Oxford: Clarendon, 1984), 61–63.

According to Clement, the proper role of Christians is to support this peace, not to contest it or upset it. Clement demonstrates a knowledge of and a respect for the Pax Romana in the contrast he draws between the terms for peace and its absence. His term for peace (εἰρήνη), used twenty-four times, is linked to the word for concord or harmony (ὁμόνοια), used fourteen times. His main term for the absence of peace is dissension (στάσις), used sixteen times. To στάσις are linked strife (ἔρις), used eight times, schism (σχίσμα), used five times, and danger (κίνδυνος), used three times in this context.

The interaction of these terms with one another is a key to *1 Clement*'s basic theme. Clement believes that, just as Rome remains in peace because all obey the emperor, the Christian community will remain in peace when all obey God, the Master, by remaining in submission to the congregation's leaders.

The announced purpose of *1 Clement* is to restore peace to the Corinthian church. Its former leaders had been ousted by the congregation, and a new group installed (1.1). Clement ignores the possibility that the existing leadership of a congregation might need correction or replacement. Rather, he follows the lead of the Roman ruling elite, which held that the most grievous error in society was to challenge the existing social order—especially those on top. In the same way, in *1 Clement* the most grievous error is for the average Christian to rebel against the authority of the appointed leaders. According to Clement, this expulsion of the Corinthian leaders is a case of dissension (στάσις) and has disrupted the stability of the congregation.

Clement believes that the Corinthians's present internal dissension is in direct opposition to the Roman ideal of peace and concord. Love, which may be the Christian equivalent of Roman consensus, "allows no schism, love makes no dissension, love does all things in concord" (49.5). Prior to the ouster of the old presbyters, "a profound and rich peace was given to all . . ." (2.2); they enjoyed "righteousness and peace" (3.4); and all "dissension and all schism was abominable" to them (2.6). But the change in leadership meant the end of peace. Thus, Clement writes to address

> the abominable and unholy dissension, alien and foreign to the elect of God, which a few rash and self-willed persons have made blaze up to such a frenzy (απονοια) that your name, venerable and

famous, and worthy as it is of all men's love, has been much slandered. (1.1)

This *stasis* is held responsible for causing the Christians in Corinth to lose faith in God and to stop obeying God's commands (3.4).

The new leaders at Corinth apparently ruled with the active support of the congregation. In addition, Clement seems to have no direct knowledge of these leaders. Nevertheless, he calls them "men who rush into strife and dissension" (14.2). He considers them the "leaders of dissension and disagreement" rather than "those who live in love and fear." Thus, they put their own goals above the "common hope . . . our tradition of noble and righteous harmony (ὁμόνοια)" (51.1–2). This "common hope" appears to be Clement's version of the Pax Romana. Clement exhorts the new leaders at Corinth to leave the community so that it will have peace (54.2). In chapter 55, he refers to examples "from the heathen" of "many kings and rulers" who have sacrificed themselves or gone into voluntary exile in order to end dissension. Thus, the ancient Greek concern for concord, which had become a political reality in the cities of the Roman Empire, provides the standard for conduct in the church.

Clement clearly considers any instance of conflict within the Christian community very dangerous. This sentiment cannot be accounted for simply by the teachings of Christianity which he had received, although they certainly played a part. Clement is aware of the New Testament's teachings about the unity of the body of believers and the impropriety of dissension. He believes that God, as Master of the Christian, is due as much obedience as the emperor receives from his subjects.

In contrast to Clement, Hermas draws an unmistakable distinction between the goals of Christianity and the goals of the state. He never uses the term στάσις, and uses ὁμόνοια only twice. Far from providing the church with a model of organization, the state is by nature diametrically opposed to the church:

> He said to me, "You know that you, as the servants of God, are living in a strange country, for your city is far from this city. If then you know your city, in which you are going to dwell, why do you here prepare lands and costly establishments and buildings and vain dwellings. . . . For the Lord of this city will say: 'I do not wish you to dwell in my city, but go out from this city, because you do not use my law.' " (*Sim.* 1.1–3)

This is the only passage in which Hermas refers to secular authority. Unlike Clement, who calls the leaders of the state "our rulers and governors upon the earth" (60.4), Hermas contrasts God as Lord of the heavenly city with the Roman emperor as the "Lord of this city." He openly advocates hostility toward the world's systems, not imitation of them.

The *Shepherd* attempts to promote peace within the congregations, since division implies sin. But unlike *1 Clement*, it does not borrow from Roman ideology to support its conception of peace. It represents those who have found only grief from relationships with the state, whereas *1 Clement* represents those who value their relationship with the state and see no essential conflict between its forms and their Christian faith. These Christians, who enjoyed greater social status and economic stability, found it easier to see the secular society as worth imitating.

THE ROMAN ARMY AND DISCIPLINE WITHIN THE CHRISTIAN CONGREGATION

Clement does not borrow only from the general Roman notions of citizenship and civil harmony. He also considers the Roman army, the emperor's principal instrument for maintaining the Pax Romana, a fitting model for discipline and obedience in the church. In his well-known tribute to the army, he says:

> Let us consider those who serve our generals, with what good order, habitual readiness, and submissiveness they perform their commands. Not all are prefects, nor tribunes, nor centurions, nor in charge of fifty men, or the like, but each carries out in his own unit the commands of the emperor and of the generals. (37.2–3)

Jaubert thinks he refers here to the Jewish military, since he mentions a rank that existed in Jewish civil and military organization but not in the Roman army: one "in charge of fifty" (πεντηκόνταρχος). A number of references to Israel's leadership or army use this rank. Grant and Graham conclude on this basis that Clement does not have in mind the Roman army but Jewish precedents.[23]

23. Lightfoot, *Apostolic Fathers*, 2:114–15; Osiek, *Rich and Poor*, 80. For "in charge of fifty," see Exod. 18:21, 25; Deut. 1:15; 1 Macc. 3:55; and Josephus, *Antiquities* 3.71. See also Jaubert, *Clément de Rome*, 80; idem, "Sources de la Conception Militaire de L'Eglise en *1 Clement* 37," 74–84; and Grant and Graham, *First and Second Clement*, 64–65.

This view, however, raises a number of problems. Jewish sources that use this term also use another term not mentioned by Clement: one "in charge of ten soldiers" (δεκαδάρχος). Furthermore, this view does not explain why Clement calls them "our generals" in the same way he calls Roman officials "our rulers" in 60.2. As Grant and Graham admit, he does not refer in 37.2 to Christian leaders. They translate *basileus* as "emperor."[24] Clement probably does not have Old Testament leaders in mind, since he never calls them "our leaders" elsewhere. He does not refer to the contemporary Jewish army, since it no longer existed by his time, and he could hardly refer to the leaders, military or civilian, of a nonexistent nation as "our generals." Presumably Clement never served in the Roman army, but he had an extensive knowledge of the Old Testament. It appears most likely that he had in mind the Roman army, but he erred in his reference to those "in charge of fifty" because of his knowledge of the Old Testament.

It is very significant that a first-century Christian would refer to Roman military leaders as "our generals." Clement could have condemned the army for dealing in bloodshed, as would later church fathers such as Tertullian. He certainly was aware that soldiers following Nero's orders had rounded up Christians and executed a "vast multitude" (*1 Clem.* 6.1). But Clement felt no conflict of loyalty. The government, with the army as its instrument, performed God's will as it maintained the Pax Romana. The Neronian persecution was the result of "jealousy and envy" by unnamed persons rather than the conscious opposition of the state (5.2—6.2).

In contrast to the divisions among the Corinthians, and in contrast to divisions Clement probably witnessed among the Roman congregations, the army was for him a model of discipline. The discipline of the Roman soldier, celebrated throughout Roman literature, meant that each soldier, whatever his unit (τάγμα), was always ready for action and always obedient to the commands of the emperor. As a result, peace was maintained. Clement uses the term τάγμα, a technical military term for bodies of troops of differing

---

24. The term "our fathers," used by Clement of OT patriarchs (60.4; 62.2), refers to the spiritual heritage of Roman Christians and has a very different meaning. On "emperor," see Grant and Graham, *First and Second Clement*, 65.

numbers, to refer to the church.[25] He applies this principle directly to the Christian community in 41.1: "Let each one of us, brethren, be well pleasing to God in his own unit (τάγμα)." Christians should obediently fulfill the responsibilities of the place assigned them in the body of Christ, whether high or low, and should not desire a different place. Only in this way will harmony be maintained. Since for Clement the army served to enforce God's will, it is understandable that he used a military metaphor to urge Christians not to be "deserters" (λειποτακτεῖν) from God's will (21.4).

Thus, Clement sees the church as analogous to the army, and the church's leaders are like the army's officers. If the church is to function harmoniously, its members—like soldiers—must accept without question the directions of their leaders. This use of the Roman army as a model is a further sign of the influence Roman society exerted on Clement's congregation.

Hermas, on the other hand, does not use the Roman army as a model for church relations or authority. He makes no direct reference to the army. He does use the same military term (τάγμα) to describe the church, but he uses it in a nonmilitary sense.[26] In a parable of the church as a tower, he depicts believers standing "rank by rank" or "in their proper ranks" (τάγματι τάγματι; *Sim.* 8.2.8; 8.4.2). Hermas uses this expression to describe the place of Christians in God's eyes, based on the degree of obedience to God's commands evidenced in their lives.

CONCLUSION

The way in which *1 Clement* is affected by Roman ideology suggests that the Christians behind it were not representative of even a majority of Christians in Rome. Rather, it represents the beliefs of a small group of Christians who enjoyed far more material wealth and worldly hope than most Christians, and so found their religion in harmony with their society. They could overlook past persecutions of Christians and the present nonacceptance of Christianity by

---

25. Bauer, *Greek-English Lexicon*, 810. He sees this military sense in *1 Clem.* 37.3 and 41.1.
26. Ibid.

Rome only because they believed the government was essentially benevolent.

As well-treated slaves of the aristocracy, they understood and appreciated the Roman *patria potestas* ideology of the family. They saw the father in their families as the *paterfamilias* from whom all other family members were to learn their duties. Clement treated his congregation as a single household based on this model: church leaders, like the *paterfamilias*, deserved unquestioning honor and obedience, and followers must know and remain in their proper places in the hierarchy.

Clement's group also was affected by the Roman elite's notion of hospitality. It was more concerned with hospitality than were other earlier Christian authors. The members focused more on hospitality among Christians, that is, among members of the household, than on hospitality toward non-Christians. The *Shepherd* criticizes well-off Christians, the kind of Christians behind *1 Clement*, for imitating the idea of reciprocal "friendship" among the upper classes.

The members of Clement's congregation, as slaves and freedmen of the aristocracy, also apparently found the Roman system of patronage more acceptable than did the slaves and freedmen behind the *Shepherd*. Thus, Clement saw it as a natural model for relationships within the church. Wealthy Christians should behave like good patrons of poorer Christians, showing concern for them and providing for their needs. In return, poorer Christians should act like good clients, showing honor and deference to their patrons.

Unlike the majority of Christians of slave or freeborn Greek origin, the Christians behind *1 Clement* probably included many freedmen who were successful citizens, having received citizenship upon manumission. Thus, Roman citizenship provided them an important model for relations within the church: patrons and clients alike must be good citizens, and do their part for the good of the group. Clement also uses the example of the state to define the good of the group. He identifies the church with the Roman state and its Greek antecedents when he uses the terms στάσις and ὁμόνοια. For the church as well as for society, concord (ὁμόνοια) is the ideal, and dissension (στάσις) is the great enemy. The members of Clement's group saw themselves as good citizens of a state that had brought concord to the Mediterranean world and that provided a model for the church. The Roman army, likewise, presented the church with a model of discipline, order, and unquestioning obedience which resulted in the establishment and maintenance of the Pax Romana.

All this is not intended to show that Clement's notions of the church's identity and relations in the church were based solely or even primarily on the Roman model. He quotes extensively from the Old Testament and frequently from the New Testament, as well as from other Jewish literature. Rather, it shows that Clement and his group began a process of recasting the traditions they had received in the mold of Roman ideology. This process would continue and ultimately dominate the church in Rome, despite the fact that it originated within a small segment of Roman Christians.

Hermas's group probably represented the larger number of Christians in Rome in that it did not have much contact with the Roman elite and its ideology was not much affected by the Roman example.

Hermas shows an awareness of the Roman system of patronage, but he alters it so that the poor man shows gratitude to God, not to his patron. This shows a greater sensitivity for the awkward position in which a Christian was placed who was the recipient of benevolence from a fellow Christian. In a sense, Hermas turns the patron-client relationship on its head by making the pious poor the true warriors of Christianity. Hermas and his group also see the state as diametrically opposed to Christianity and its practices. The kind of acceptance of society that *1 Clement* represents is viewed by Hermas as improper and as a dangerous compromise of God's truth.

It appears probable that the higher a Christian's social status in Rome, the more likely the Christian was to adopt the values of the surrounding society. Since the Roman congregations probably represented socially homogeneous groups of Christians at various places in the social order, this tendency would have contributed to disunity among the congregations. This would have led a group such as Clement's to search for ways to bring about the organizational unity it believed was essential to harmony in the church. Its solution was to impose on the churches an identity in imitation of the Roman elite's notions of discipline, order, and hierarchy. If true, this conclusion challenges the notion of scholars such as George La Piana, who believed that these changes took place when Latin converts to

Christianity took over in Rome and brought about a "Latinization" of the church.[27] In fact, the beginning of this "Latinization" preceded the introduction of Latins into the Roman churches.

In this chapter I have used a static model of class distinctions and social status. In the next two chapters the sociological theories of Max Weber and Bryan Wilson are used as dynamic models of analysis. Their application demonstrates the changes in the very nature of Clement's congregation that their identification with Roman society helped promote. It suggests that Hermas's thinking arose in protest against Clement's group, and thus presented the kind of threat to disunity that Clement condemned.

27. La Piana, "The Roman Church at the End of the Second Century," 204.

8

BISHOP AND PROPHET IN
ROMAN CHRISTIANITY

The source of authority to which a leader appeals in order to legitimate the position of leadership reveals a great deal about the nature
of the group. Nearly all Christian leaders in the apostolic era
appealed to charismatic authority. They claimed to receive their
authority to speak or lead directly from Jesus Christ. The apostle
Paul's claims of authority are the most obvious example of this.
Hermas, considered by tradition a prophet, appealed to charismatic
authority. Clement, called a bishop of the church, appealed to traditional authority. In this chapter I suggest that Clement and his congregation had moved away from the more typical Christian form of
authority legitimation.

MAX WEBER'S IDEAL
AUTHORITY TYPES

"All ruling powers, profane and religious, political and apolitical,
may be considered as variations of, or approximations to, certain
pure types. These types are constructed by searching for the basis of
legitimacy, which the ruling power claims."[1] So proclaimed Max Weber
in setting forth his concept of authority structure ideal types. An
ideal type is not a description of reality nor need it exist anywhere in
its pure form. It is not an average of similar structures. Rather, it is a
one-sided accentuation of certain properties, a synthesis of the many
phenomena of the thing typified. Thus, an ideal type is not an end
in itself, but a means of "revealing concrete cultural phenomena in
their interdependence, their causal conditions and their significance."[2] It helps historians focus on the data that concern them and

1. Weber, "Social Psychology of the World Religions," 294.
2. Weber, " 'Objectivity' in Social Science and Social Policy," 90.

to work out their theories. Such an approach is unpopular with some because it seems to impose modern theories on ancient society. But historians cannot avoid looking at antiquity through the lens of their own culture, and this is not necessarily a problem. The more serious problem is being unaware of one's subtle and unstated biases. Weber sought to make clear the characteristic features of the relationship between a theoretical model and empirical data. Modern historians do not ask the same questions of early Christianity that second-century Christians would ask, and they must be cognizant of this fact.

Weber believed that authority systems and relations of authority were the building blocks of society. He developed criteria for three main types of authority, based on how leaders seek to establish the legitimacy of their authority without direct coercion, and on how authority is accepted by the ruled: charismatic, traditional, and rational-legal (bureaucratic).[3]

Charismatic authority arises in times of crisis to challenge the prevailing system on the basis of a leader's unique personal qualities. The charismatic leader attracts a following by appeals to personal revelation or ability. The governed submit because of their belief in the extraordinary quality of the specific person and the revelation. An irrational form of authority, charismatic authority is unstable. Transfer of such authority is problematic at best. If the transfer is successful, it generally leads to a routinization and evolution of the movement into one of the two other types of authority.[4]

Charismatic domination typically is exercised by the prophet. "The genuine prophet, like the genuine military leader and every true leader in this sense, preaches, creates, or demands *new* obligations—most typically, by virtue of revelation, oracle, inspiration, or of his own will. . . . The legitimacy of charismatic rule thus rests upon the belief in magical powers, revelations and hero worship."[5] It repudiates the economic exploitation of the "gifts of grace" as a source of income. It does not always demand a renunciation of property. But it despises "traditional or rational everyday economiz-

---

3. Weber, *Economy and Society,* 1:226.
4. Ibid., 1:242, 245.
5. On prophet, see Weber, *Economy and Society,* 1:243; on legitimacy, see idem, "Social Psychology of the World Religions," 296. See also idem, "Politics as a Vocation," 79.

ing" and the pursuit of a regular income devoted to this end. Charismatic leaders are usually supported by voluntary donations or by forced expropriation. "In traditionalist periods, charisma is *the* great revolutionary force." Rather than working from without by altering the social system, it "may effect a subjective or internal reorientation born out of suffering, conflicts, or enthusiasm."[6]

Traditional authority rests upon respect for what actually, allegedly, or presumably has always existed. Weber called it the "authority of the 'eternal yesterday,' the mores sanctified through the unimaginably ancient recognition and habitual orientation to conform."[7] It generally adopts a cyclical view of history supported by an underlying idea of renewal. It scorns innovation, and resists any attempts to change the existing order. The person in the traditionally sanctioned position of authority, who is thus bound by tradition, is owed strict obedience.

Weber identified a number of kinds of traditional authority. The most elementary kind is "gerontocracy," in which the group is ruled by elders who are most familiar with the sacred traditions. "Patriarchalism" refers to a group, such as a household, usually organized on both economic and kinship bases. A particular individual, designated by a definite rule of inheritance, governs the group. In both cases, consent of the governed is based on a belief that the rule is performed in the interest of all members. The members are thus not subjects. "Patrimonialism" arises when administrative and military forces develop as "purely personal instruments of the master." Here the group members are treated as subjects.[8] Authority becomes the leader's personal right.

Rational-legal, or bureaucratic, authority is based on impersonal laws rather than on personal loyalty. Its hallmark is a professional routinization and rationalization of all political and social processes. Weber asserts that it has replaced traditionalism as the basis of Western society in the modern era. Obedience to the one discharging statutory obligations is expected. Domination is exercised by a "servant of the state." Submission is based not upon belief in a charismatically

6. Weber, *Economy and Society*, 1:245.
7. Weber, "Politics as a Vocation," 78–79.
8. Weber, *Economy and Society*, 1:231.

gifted person, nor upon sacred tradition, but upon an impersonal bond to the broadly defined "duty of office."[9]

Many scholars have suggested that charismatic authority dominated early Christianity, giving way to traditional forms of authority under the Roman Catholic church. John Gager suggests that the authority of Jesus and some of his early followers was charismatic. Gager also describes Paul's authority as charismatic, resting on personal revelations from the religion's founder. At the same time, however, Gager asserts that the immediate context of Paul's authority was a sense of tradition, "both the old tradition that he reinterprets and the new one that his reinterpretation creates." As a result, "the tension in the early communities is between charisma and office, not between charisma and tradition."[10]

Weber's ideal authority types provide a suggestive approach to the comparison of *1 Clement* and the *Shepherd*, since their authors are held by tradition to be, respectively, a bishop and a prophet at Rome.

TRADITIONAL AUTHORITY
IN *1 CLEMENT*

Many of Clement's assertions were beliefs unique to him or significant modifications of earlier beliefs. But he sought legitimacy for them in the sanctions of tradition, not in his abilities as a leader or in personal claims of divine authority. He attempted to show that nature, humankind in general, and righteous people in particular have always upheld the behavior he advocated. In doing so, he appealed to what Weber called the "authority of the 'eternal yesterday.' "[11]

Nature, from creation to the present, exemplifies for Clement the order and harmony he wished to restore at Corinth. At God's command, the heavenly bodies, night and day, the seasons, and the winds all cooperate together in harmony:

> The heavens moving at his appointment are subject to him in peace; day and night follow the course allotted by him without hindering each other. Sun and moon and the companies of the

9. Weber, "Politics as a Vocation," 79; idem, "Objectivity in Social Science," 299.
10. Gager, *Kingdom and Community,* 69–70.
11. Weber, "Politics as a Vocation," 78–79.

stars roll on, according to his direction, in harmony, in their appointed courses, and do not swerve from them at all. The earth teems according to his will at its proper seasons and puts forth food. . . . The seasons of spring, summer, autumn, and winter give place to one another in peace. . . . The stations of the winds fulfill their service without hindrance at the proper time. (20.1–4, 9–10)

Even if the content of this passage was influenced by Stoic thought, as scholars have suggested, this would not affect the conclusion that Clement appeals to tradition to legitimize his views.[12]

First Clement also fulfills the Weberian ideal type of a group based on traditional authority in that it held a cyclical view of history with an underlying idea of renewal. The passage from *1 Clement* 20 quoted above presents a cyclical view in the way it depicts night perpetually succeeding day and the seasons continually giving way to one another. Renewal, implicit within a cyclical view of history, is evident in Clement's references to the cycles of day and night, the sowing and harvesting of crops, and the Phoenix myth (chaps. 24–25).

Clement also sought legitimacy in tradition when he appealed to pagan traditions of harmony. He used examples of pagan kings who were willing to sacrifice themselves for the sake of harmony to encourage the new leaders at Corinth to step down (55.1). The Roman government was part of this tradition of pagan governments that, according to Clement, rightly placed a high value on harmony. It peacefully coexisted with Christianity as long as a jealous person or group either within or outside the Christian community did not provoke it. Persecution was blamed on "jealousy and envy," and despite the Neronian persecution Clement could refer to the state as "our rulers and governors on the earth" (5.2; 60.4—61.1–2).

Like the leader who appeals to traditional authority, Clement demands unquestioning obedience to leaders and claims that ultimately it is in the best interests of all members of the group. Using the Old Testament, Clement shows that jealousy (like that of the usurping leaders at Corinth) has always caused problems for the righteous (chap. 4). The patriarchs' behavior, without exception, displayed obedience, repentance, faith in God, and humility—all qualities the Corinthians needed. Abraham was rewarded for obedi-

---

12. See Van Unnik, "Is *1 Clement* 20 Purely Stoic?" 181–90. Van Unnik answers his question in the negative.

ence in all his actions (chap. 10). Lot was rescued from Sodom because of his piety (11.1). Rahab was saved because of her faith and hospitality (12.1). The kind of humility needed by the Corinthians was exemplified by Elijah, Elisha, and Ezekiel (17.1), Abraham (17.2), Job (17.4), and Moses (17.5–6). Clement concludes this section by saying:

> The humility and obedient submission of many men of such great fame have rendered better not only us, but also the generations before us, who received his oracles in fear and truth. Seeing then that we have received a share in many great and glorious deeds, let us move on to the goal of peace, which was given us from the beginning. (19.1–2)

This tradition was continued by Judith in intertestamental times, and by early Christians such as Paul, Peter, and the Roman Christians in Nero's time (chaps. 5–6). According to Clement, righteous men had never been cast out by godly men, thus the men who cast out the "blameless" Corinthian presbyters were ungodly (44.3–6; 45.3). Clement even argued that the Corinthians had behaved correctly in the past, so that he was not advocating a new behavior but a return to the old virtues. The people Clement cites in his examples were obedient to God, not to human leaders. Nevertheless, Clement uses their examples to persuade the Corinthians to submit to human leaders.

However, they must submit not to any leaders, but rather to the deposed presbyters whose positions are sanctioned by tradition. This fits with Weber's assertion that traditional authority scorns innovation.[13] This notion is clear in Clement's attitude toward the change in leadership in Corinth. He was absolutely opposed to the innovators, even though he does not seem to have possessed a thorough knowledge of the situation. In chapter 44 he states that the presbyters are blameless and so should not be removed. But most of his efforts are devoted to arguing a priori against any change in existing authority. He gives no clear information about the identities of the new leaders in Corinth. He does not accuse them of heretical teaching. They may have been charismatics, or they may have been opposed to the old leadership for other reasons. What is certain is that they were able to persuade the church body to depose the old

13. Weber, *Economy and Society,* 1:242.

presbyters. Clement calls them the "enemies of God" (36.6), "rash and self-willed" (1.1), who rush into strife (14.2), yet he seems to know nothing about them except that they had ousted the rightful Corinthian presbyters. A list of their doctrinal or behavioral errors would have bolstered his argument, but he does not present one. This suggests that Clement resisted change in principle, and so sought to return the Corinthian community to its former, and to his mind proper, leadership. There was no room for compromise or negotiation in Clement's position: "You, therefore, who laid the foundation of the sedition, submit to the presbyters, and receive the correction of repentance, bending the knees of your hearts" (57.1).

First Clement exemplifies the traditional authority ideal type in that obedience is owed not to the most capable, nor to the one empowered by the Spirit, but to the leader who holds the tradition-sanctioned position of authority. Obedience is owed to the Roman state, which is empowered by God as are all governments (60.4; 61.1). In addition, Clement links obedience to the deposed elders with obedience to the apostles and Christ, and ultimately to God himself:

> The Apostles received the gospel for us from the Lord Jesus Christ, Jesus the Christ sent from God. The Christ therefore is from God and the Apostles from the Christ. . . . [The apostles] appointed their first converts, testing them by the Spirit, to be bishops and deacons of the future believers. (42.1–2, 4)

Though not arguing for Clement's use of traditional authority, Grant and Graham support it when they point out that in this passage the "orderliness of apostolic order thus serves to prove its divine origin."[14] Clement adds that if any of these leaders should die, "other approved men should succeed to their ministry" (44.2). The congregation was expected to consent to such successors (44.3). Although Clement appealed for authority to apostolic tradition, not to new revelation, his work is the first to advocate a self-perpetuating church leadership. Perhaps he repeats here an oral teaching of Paul. But, more likely, this is a later theological development, since none of Paul's extant writings suggest apostolic succession. The Corinthian church, which Paul founded and fostered, apparently was not aware of this teaching. Clement presents it as new information and indi-

---

14. Grant and Graham, *First and Second Clement*, 71.

cates that the Corinthians acted in a contrary manner. Clement was seeking to legitimize a new ideology of leadership by attributing it to earlier Christian tradition.

Thus, *1 Clement* offers a clear example of traditional authority. Absent are the rational arguments of Paul. Absent also is Paul's appeal to divine inspiration as the ultimate source of his authority. Rather than appeal to reason or to charisma, Clement appealed to traditions that appeared to support his views, even though they came from widely disparate sources: Jewish, Christian, and pagan.

CHARISMATIC AUTHORITY IN
THE *SHEPHERD OF HERMAS*

Hermas legitimated his authority by an appeal to personal knowledge and ability. Unlike Clement, he did not appeal to past tradition. His only mention of a past authority is a passing reference to the lost *Book of Eldad and Modad* (*Vis.* 2.3.4). Hermas claimed the right to be heard because he was the recipient of visions and revelations from God. He says, "A revelation was made to me, brethren" (*Vis.* 2.4.1). The "angel of repentance" told him to "write my commandments and the parables" (*Vis.* 5.5). He copied Ecclesia's book letter for letter, with the intention of reading it to the church (*Vis.* 2.1.4). Hermas identified as a new revelation of God the central teaching of the *Shepherd*: that a Christian who had fallen into sin could be forgiven once, but only once (*Vis.* 2.2.5). Rather than try to demonstrate its universal validity by examples from the past, as Clement might have done, he simply indicates that it was revealed to him in a vision. Hermas quotes the revealers directly, so that the reader is made to feel a part of the visions. He wanted to convince his audience that none of the teachings presented were his own ideas, but that they came straight from the mouth of God.

Weber looks for a key to identifying charismatic authority in the leadership that arises to challenge the prevailing system in a time of crisis.[15] Hermas exemplifies this ideal type when he challenges the existing leadership in Rome. Hermas is told to rebuke the church leadership: "You shall say, then, to the leaders of the church, that they reform their ways in righteousness, to receive in full the prom-

15. Weber, *Economy and Society,* 1:242.

ises with great glory" (*Vis.* 2.2.6). In *Vision* 3, the current church leadership in Rome is compared unfavorably with first-generation Christian leaders. In the past, the church was led by

> the Apostles and bishops and teachers and deacons who walked according to the majesty of God, and served the elect of God in holiness and reverence. . . . And they always agreed among themselves, and had peace among themselves, and listened to one another. . . . (*Vis.* 3.5.1)

The apostles and teachers "preached to all the world, and taught reverently and purely the word of the Lord" (*Sim.* 9.25.2). By contrast, the contemporary leaders were compared to poisoners:

> Therefore I speak now to the officials of the church and to those who take the chief seats. Do not become like the poisoners. For while the poisoners carry their drugs in bottles, you carry your drugs and poisons in your hearts. You are hardened, and will not cleanse your hearts. . . . How will you correct the chosen of the Lord if you yourselves suffer no correction? Correct one another, therefore, and be at peace among yourselves. (*Vis.* 3.9.7–10).

The assertion that the leaders refuse to be corrected probably refers to previous contacts between them and Hermas. While the leaders in Hermas's golden age "always agreed among themselves" (*Vis.* 3.5.1), the contemporary leaders had disagreements that threatened to rob them of life (*Vis.* 3.9.9). The past leaders always "had peace among themselves, and listened to one another" (*Vis.* 3.5.1). The present leaders lacked this peace. They are commanded to correct one another and to "be at peace among yourselves" (*Vis.* 3.9.10).

Hermas's experiences as presented in the *Shepherd* are consistent with James Davies's list of the determinants of a charismatic upsurge: feelings of insecurity or anxiety about basic needs, the frustration of expected demands due to rising expectations, and the persistence of unresolved conflicts between internal or external forces.[16] Hermas had suffered and continued to suffer economic deprivation, as we saw in chapters 1 and 6 above. He is told in his visions that the loss of wealth had made him able to receive the revelations. When he continued to suffer economically and complained, the angel of repentance told him that this was punishment for his family's sins. Since

---

16. James C. Davies, "Charisma in the 1952 Campaign," *American Political Science Review* 48 (1954): 1083–1102. Quoted in Hill, *Sociology of Religion*, 162.

Hermas was a freedman who had at one time succeeded in business, one would expect his failure in business to present itself as a frustration of rising expectations. With regard to the persistence of unresolved conflicts, Hermas was troubled by the conflict between wealthy Christians who were living like pagans and the demands of the Christian tradition. Specifically, he predicted a great persecution within their generation which would catch them unprepared (*Vis.* 2.2.7).

Scholars agree that Hermas intended to rebuke the leaders of the church in Rome, not just in foreign cities. However, no one has systematically explored the implications of this notion.[17] Hermas surely had little or no contact with Christians outside of Rome. As we saw in chapter 1, he was probably rather poor and uneducated. Also, he was told to have Clement send his book "to the cities abroad," while Hermas himself was told to read the book in Rome. This implies that, unlike Clement, Hermas had no contacts outside Rome. Unlike the New Testament revelation, which depicts Christ addressing "the seven churches of the province of Asia" (Rev. 1:4), the only congregation Hermas specifically mentioned was the one in Rome ("this city").

The focus of Hermas's rebuke probably is the Christian leadership in Rome. Hermas believed that some contemporary leaders no longer maintained the moral standards he considered appropriate. Ecclesia tells Hermas, "In this city you shall read it yourself with (μετὰ) the elders who are in charge of the church" (*Vis.* 2.4.3). This suggests the willing cooperation of the elders, but Hermas expected cooperation to result from their acceptance of him as a source of divine revelation. This had not yet been tested at the time of *Vision* 2. The note of cooperation sounded here does not contradict or diminish the charismatic nature of Hermas's authority. He does not ask the leaders to evaluate the book and decide if it should be read to the people and distributed abroad, as we might expect of Clement. Rather, he expects them to submit to God's commands as related through himself. Hermas comes across in the *Shepherd* not as a philosopher or theologian, but as an earnest if common man who

17. E.g., Grant and Graham, *First and Second Clement*, 20–21; and Osiek, *Rich and Poor*, 14.

wished to remedy the problems he had witnessed in the congregations of Rome.

Like the typical religious charismatic leader in Weber's model, Hermas is presented in the *Shepherd* as a prophet with a unique and authentic message from God. Scholars debate whether Hermas considered himself a prophet. Barnard says he claimed to be a prophet, but Reiling believes he saw himself merely as a reporter of the prophets (the church personified and an angel) rather than as a prophet.[18] However, the *Shepherd* depicts Hermas as a prophet in the sense that Weber used the term. This can be seen by comparing Hermas's assertions about true and false prophets with how he looked at himself. In such a comparison, we must distinguish between a prophet's functions and his personal qualifications. Hermas, while functioning differently from the "true prophet" in *Mandate* 11, fulfills the personal qualifications of the true prophet. He is told that the true prophet can be determined by his life:

> Test the man who has the Divine Spirit by his life. In the first place, he who has the spirit which is from above is meek and gentle, and lowly-minded, and refrains from all wickedness and evil desire of this world, and makes himself poorer than all men, and gives no answers to anyone when he is consulted, nor does he speak by himself (for the Holy Spirit does not speak when a man wishes to speak), but he speaks at that time when God wishes him to speak. (*Mand.* 11.7–8)

By contrast, the false prophet

> exalts himself and wishes to have the first place (προτοκαθήδρα) [in the congregation], and he is constantly impudent and shameless and talkative, and lives in great luxury and in many other deceits, and accepts rewards for his prophecy, and if he does not receive them he does not prophesy. (*Mand.* 11.12)

Hermas, though he never called himself a prophet, possessed the virtues of the true prophet and went to great lengths to distance himself from false prophets. He "abstains from every evil desire and is full of simplicity and innocence" (*Vis.* 1.2.4). Unlike the false prophet who lived in luxury, but like the true prophet who made

---

18. Barnard, *Studies in the Apostolic Fathers*, 153; and Reiling, *Hermas and Christian Prophecy*, 169.

himself poorer than all, Hermas was useful to God. Ecclesia tells him, "When you were rich, you were useless, but now you are useful and helpful for the Life" (*Vis.* 3.6.7).

Deprecating references to Hermas in the *Shepherd* are intended to convey his meekness and humility, not to suggest his inadequacy. Since meekness and humility are qualities of the true prophet, these references actually support the assertion that Hermas thought of himself as a prophet. Hermas confesses, "I have never yet in my life spoken a true word, but have always spoken deceitfully with all men . . ." (*Mand.* 3.3). Obviously, this is hyperbolic. It may have referred only to his business dealings before his repentance. Hermas was rebuked repeatedly for his impertinence in wanting the visions and parables explained to him. But this passage actually serves to demonstrate his eagerness to receive the revelation.

Hermas was constantly astounded and humbled by what he heard. This has led some scholars to suggest, incorrectly, that he never thought of himself as a prophet. For example, when the Lady tells him to sit on the bench beside her, he says, "Lady, let the elders (πρεσβύτεροι) sit first" (*Vis.* 3.1.8). Pernveden believes Hermas is subordinating himself to the church leaders in this passage.[19] But it is not certain that he was referring to church officeholders. And even if he had had the Roman presbyters in mind, he probably intended to contrast his humble rejection of any honor with the pride of the false prophet who wished to have the "first place." Thus, Hermas's self-deprecating comments are not in conflict with passages that commend his godly character. Like the true prophet, he was meek and did not exalt himself.

At the same time that the *Shepherd* portrays Hermas as humble and self-deprecating, it skillfully establishes his unique claim to personal qualifications and authority. Hermas resists evil temptations, maintains a spiritual innocence, and is called "the temperate" (*Vis.* 1.2.4). His place belongs with the righteous, not the apostates and heathen (*Vis.* 1.4.2), and he is a worker of "righteousness" (*Vis.* 2.2.7). While Hermas subordinated himself to the righteous men of a past golden age, the *Shepherd* represents him as the most worthy person then alive. The Lady tells him:

It is not because you are more worthy than all others that a revela-

19. Pernveden, *Concept of the Church in the* Shepherd of Hermas, 144.

tion should be made to you, for there were others before you and
better than you to whom these visions ought to have been revealed.
(*Vis.* 3.4.3)

Others more worthy than Hermas have existed, but they all belonged
to the past. Thus, the *Shepherd* considers the contemporary leaders
no more worthy than Hermas to receive the revelation. Though
subtle, this statement represents a direct challenge to the authority
of officeholders in Roman Christianity.

The *Shepherd* depicts Hermas as an authentic prophet, even
though Hermas did not function like the "true prophet" of *Mandate*
11, about whom he writes:

Therefore, when the man who has the Divine Spirit comes into an
assembly of righteous men who have the faith of the Divine Spirit,
and intercession is made to God from the assembly of those men,
then the angel of the prophetic spirit rests on him and fills the
man, and the man, being filled with the Holy Spirit, speaks to the
congregation as the Lord wills. (*Mand.* 11.9)

All of Hermas's visions occur while he is alone. He brings his messages to the congregation but does not receive them in its presence.
One similarity between Hermas and the true prophet is that both
provided a message from God instead of simply answering the questions of his audience (*Mand.* 11.5). Rather than implying that
Hermas was not a prophet, the differences between him and the
true prophet in *Mandate* 11 can be seen to place Hermas above the
true prophet: he possessed all the qualities of the prophet and had
received divine revelation, but he was not dependent on the congregation's intercession for his message. This distinction would not have
been lost on the readers in Hermas's congregation and elsewhere.
The prophet in *Mandate* 11, whom we might call a "congregational
prophet," had a more limited function: he provided God's message
to an individual house church. Thus, Hermas was presented in the
Shepherd as a unique but authentic prophet.

For Weber, the ultimate proof of a leader's charismatic authority
is the personal following the leader attracts. Unfortunately, we have
no information about how Roman Christians responded to Hermas
during his lifetime. But in the second century, Clement of Alexandria and Irenaeus give tacit recognition of his charismatic authority
when they testify to the divine authority of the *Shepherd* (see chap. 6).
The *Shepherd* was popular and considered as Scripture by large seg-

ments of the early church. Even the Muratorian Canon of Rome, which rejects its divine authority, commends the *Shepherd* to personal study. This indicates that the *Shepherd* was popular in second-century Rome. As suggested in chapter 6, some of Hermas's contemporaries probably would have found his message attractive. Hermas, who valued congregational involvement (see *Mandate* 11), would have been a member if not a leader of a house church when he began to write and spread his message. It appears probable that a man with the message and compulsion of Hermas would attract a following, at least in his own congregation. For example, he would have appealed to Christians who had experienced economic deprivation, and who were concerned about dissension among Roman congregations.

Like the charismatic leader in Weber's theory, Hermas repudiated economic exploitation. The true prophet makes himself "poorer than all men" and does not accept money for his prophecies (*Mand.* 11.8, 12). The *Shepherd* also criticizes Christians who pursue wealth to the exclusion of their religious duties. Rich Christians were considered spiritually weaker than poor Christians (*Vis.* 3.6.5). But unlike some charismatic leaders, Hermas did not deny the need for a steady income, nor did he demand the renunciation of property. Christians can have one business (*Sim.* 4.5) and can provide an appropriate level of support to their families (*Sim.* 1.6).

Hermas thus exercised charismatic authority. His sole sources of legitimacy were divine inspiration and personal ability. He challenged the prevailing system at Rome and demanded a new obligation of followers: in order to be saved, they must repent of former sins and never sin again. His book gained respect around the empire relatively quickly and was popular in Rome in the second century, suggesting that he also gathered a personal following in Rome.

CONCLUSION

Both Clement and Hermas represent modifications of Jewish and Christian traditions prior to their time. *First Clement* disguises the modifications by claiming that its views enjoy the authenticity of ancient tradition. Since most house churches in the first generation of Christianity probably were under charismatic authority, authority in Clement's congregation may have been charismatic at one time. But that charisma had routinized into traditional authority by

Clement's time. The rest of the Roman congregations ultimately would follow this development. Hermas's group represents a resurgence of charismatic authority, arising in protest against the ideology of groups like Clement's and attempting to recapture what it considered the golden age of the church: the apostolic era, when charismatic authority predominated.

Prior to Paul's arrival in Rome, the Roman Christian community enjoyed a period of anonymity and peace. A few years later, however, it had become visible enough to be Nero's scapegoat. This suggests that Paul's ministry had a significant impact. Since he probably exercised charismatic authority, he may have been able to establish charismatic authority as normative in Rome. But the Neronian persecution, the delay of the Parousia, and the unique challenges of organization within a pagan metropolis combined to alter the outlook of the next generation. This is not surprising, since charismatic authority is often not transferred to the successor of the charismatic leader, but becomes routinized, or transformed into traditional or legal authority. However, as Michael Hill suggests, charisma can remain latent within the institution.[20] It normally would routinize into traditional authority in the ancient world, and this appears to be the case at Rome. Hermas, by contrast, represents a resurgence of latent charismatic authority.

20. Hill, *Sociology of Religion*, 172.

9

EVOLVING CONGREGATIONS IN ROMAN CHRISTIANITY

We have observed that Clement, far more than Hermas, had accepted certain aspects of Roman society and incorporated those into his definition of Christianity (chap. 7) and that Clement's congregation developed from a congregation based on charismatic authority into one based on traditional authority (chap. 8). We now consider the way these changes affected the nature of Clement's congregation and the effect they had on the future of Christianity in Rome.

SECT ANALYSIS
IN SOCIOLOGICAL THEORY

The earliest Christian congregations arose for the most part as sects of Judaism. Even those congregations not associated with Judaism generally identified themselves as groups in protest against the larger society or another religious group. While Hermas and those Christians who identified with him and his message continued to see themselves in protest against society, Clement's congregation had ceased to do so. Instead, it had adopted a world-accepting attitude that described proper Christian attitudes and behavior not only by examples taken from the Old and New Testaments, but also by examples from secular history and non-Judeo-Christian mythology. The differences and ultimate conflict in worldviews between *1 Clement* and the *Shepherd* can best be seen by asking each text questions derived from sociologist of religion Bryan Wilson's model of sect analysis.

A Short History of Sect Analysis

Max Weber and his pupil, Ernst Troeltsch, developed the ideal types of the church and the sect to aid the study of Christianity's origin and development. Based on his study of European Christianity, Weber saw a dichotomous relationship between two parts of Christianity, which he called the "church" and the "sect."[1] The church is an institution including the just and unjust, while the sect is composed only of believers. Discipline in the church is authoritarian. In the sect, while harsher, discipline rests on voluntary submission. Asceticism is valued by both: for the church it is an additional, unrequired work; for the sect, however, it is essential, for it is the rational planning of one's whole life in accord with God's will. The church accepts the world as it is; the sect rejects it. The church is dominated by a professional ministerial group, while the sect is generally led by the laity. Churches are characterized by office charisma, sects by personal charisma. Weber believed that sectarian groups develop toward a more church-based organization as their charismatic authority is routinized.

Troeltsch based his study on medieval Roman Catholicism and took a different view of the relationship between sect and church—one of dialectical opposition. He felt that sect and church each expressed something unique and valid in the Christian gospel, and that sects could be found within the "church," mainly in the form of religious orders.[2] In general, he accepted Weber's description of the characteristics of sect and church, adding that the sect is connected with the lower classes and the disaffected, while the church utilizes the state and the ruling classes and becomes part of the existing social order. Troeltsch hesitated to apply his theory to Christianity prior to the eleventh century, since he believed that a permanent division between sect and church occurred only in the Middle Ages and before then the major Christian tradition fluctuated between sect and church.

H. Richard Niebuhr, who studied twentieth-century churches in the United States, created a new debate with his addition of a third category to those of church and sect: the denomination. "By its very

1. The following is based primarily on Weber, *Protestant Ethic and the Spirit of Capitalism*, 144–54; Weber, *Economy and Society*, vol. 2; Hill, *Sociology of Religion*; and Stephen Kalberg, "The Role of Ideal Interests in Max Weber's Comparative Historical Sociology," in *A Weber-Marx Dialogue*, ed. Robert Antonio and Ronald Glassman (Lawrence, Kan.: University Press of Kansas, 1985), 46–67.
2. Troeltsch, *Social Teaching of the Christian Churches*, 2:723.

nature the sectarian type of organization is valid only for one generation."[3] As the first generation bears children, it begins to realize the need for education and discipline within the institution. The new generation, however, rarely adopts the zeal of its parents. In addition, the sect finds it increasingly difficult to maintain isolation from the world. Asceticism encourages hard work and thriftiness, which in turn often lead to improved economic conditions. As a result, the sect evolves into a denomination. Unlike the church, the denomination is not universalistic and restricts its appeal to the respectable middle class. Unlike the sect, it possesses a more world-compromising ethic and has developed a specialized role for the minister. Although Niebuhr is thinking more of the modern United States than of ancient Rome, he could just as well have the first century in mind when he writes:

> Theological opinions have their roots in the relationship of the religious life to the cultural and political conditions prevailing in any group of Christians. This does not mean that an economic or purely political interpretation of theology is justified, but it does mean that the religious life is so interwoven with social circumstances that the formulation of theology is necessarily conditioned by these.[4]

Liston Pope found that the mere increase in size reorients the sect toward a more world-compromising ethic. As it grows in size, it attracts more wealthy members. In the case of a "rising sect," the older members who do not rise economically tend to drop out. Pope uses these criteria to quantify the evolution from sect to church.[5]

The preceding theories all have value but are limited somewhat to modern times. J. M. Yinger attempts a more comprehensive typology of Christian groups. He developed six categories of analysis: (1) the universal church, exemplified by thirteenth-century Roman Catholicism; (2) the ecclesia, a church bound by geography and class, such as German Lutheranism; (3) the denomination, an organization in harmony with the state, for example, Methodism; (4) the established sect, a transition group between sect and church; (5) the

3. H. Richard Niebuhr, *The Social Sources of Denominationalism* (New Haven: Yale University Press, 1929), 19–20.
4. Ibid., 16.
5. Liston Pope, *Millhands and Preachers* (New Haven: Yale University Press, 1942), 119.

cult, which is noninstitutional and unified solely by common beliefs; and (6) the sect. The sect, possessing a higher level of organization and self-consciousness than the cult, is divided into three subtypes: acceptance sects, which are middle class and concerned with personal failure; aggressive sects, which are lower class and concerned to reform evil society; and avoidance sects, which are pessimistic and emphasize the next life.[6]

Bryan Wilson's Analysis
of Sect

Many of the questions asked in the sect-church debate would prove helpful if applied to early Christianity. R. A. Markus asserts that, despite Troeltsch's reservations about applying sect-church typology to early Christianity, there are similarities between first- and second-century Christian communities and the sect. The theory considered most relevant to a study of first-century Christianity is Bryan Wilson's, whose work has influenced a number of recent studies of early Christianity. John Elliott, for example, applies Wilson's theory to the group that composed and the groups that read 1 Peter. Derek Tidball uses it in a more general way to suggest an analysis of New Testament Christianity. In a significant article, Robin Scroggs uses Wilson's theory along with those of other sociologists to analyze the data for Jesus and the early church in Palestine.[7]

In an influential early article, Wilson challenges the notion that a sect-type organization never survives the first generation. He accepts the terminology of sect and denomination, and proceeds to enumerate subtypes of sect. In later works, he broadens his ideas to encompass contemporary religious groups outside Christianity. Rather than calling these groups "sects," he defines them as groups in protest against other religious groups or against society. This

---

6. John Milton Yinger, *Religion, Society and the Individual* (New York: Macmillan, 1957), 148–54.

7. R. A. Markus, "The Problem of Self-Definition: From Sect to Church," in *Jewish and Christian Self-Definition*, ed. E. P. Sanders, 2 vols. (Philadelphia: Fortress, 1980), 2:1–15; Elliott, *Home for the Homeless*, chaps. 2, 3; Derek Tidball, *The Social Context of the New Testament* (Grand Rapids: Zondervan, 1984), 107–9; Robin Scroggs, "The Earliest Christian Communities as Sectarian Movement," in *Christianity, Judaism and Other Greco-Roman Cults*, 5 vols., ed. Jacob Neusner (Leiden: E. J. Brill, 1975), 2:1. The most recent commendation of his theories is in Wayne A. Meeks, *The Moral World of the First Christians* (Philadelphia: Westminster Press, 1986), 99 n. 1.

distinction provides a more appropriate approach to early Christianity as well. Wilson writes that "Christianity itself was only a Jewish sect at the beginning."[8] In defining the sect, Wilson avoids Troeltsch's limiting categories of organization, doctrine, and practice.

According to Wilson, the sect is a voluntary association. Members have to prove to sect authorities a claim to personal merit, such as knowledge of doctrine, a conversion experience, or recommendation by other members. The children of members may be required to submit to the same proofs. A key tension for sects is how to incorporate the second generation. The factors involved include the sect's standards of admission, how rigorously the children have been kept separate from the world, and whether the sect is individual- or family-oriented.[9]

The sect emphasizes exclusiveness. "Typically, the sectarian is identified by his sect allegiance in a way which is not true for other men: it becomes the most important thing about him."[10] Those considered unworthy, who have contravened doctrinal, moral, or organizational precepts, are often excluded from the group.

The sect's self-identity is of an elect, a gathered remnant, possessing special enlightenment. It has a strong conception of "us" in contradistinction to "them." While in general it has a clear identity and clear boundaries, sometimes its conception of "us" includes layers of people who do not meet all the requirements for membership. It often sees itself as a social elite, claiming exclusive salvation or at least the fullest blessings. The "old ethnic ideal of a chosen people was inherited from Judaism and conferred upon the voluntary subscribers to the Christian faith."[11]

A high level of commitment is demanded of the sect's followers. Personal perfection is the expected aspiration. Commitment to the sect must be total, whether it be to a leader's commands, to a set of doctrinal beliefs, or to regulation of one's social and moral affairs as the sect directs. A sect has a totalitarian rather than segmental hold over its members.

---

8. Bryan R. Wilson, *Religious Sects*, 7. His early seminal work is "An Analysis of Sect Development." His most recent works include *Magic and the Millennium*, and *Religion in Sociological Perspective* (1982).
9. Wilson, "Analysis of Sect Development," 4, 11–12.
10. Wilson, *Religious Sects*, 29.
11. Ibid., 30–31.

The sect is generally a lay organization. It accepts the priesthood of all believers, at least ideally. A high level of spontaneity and lay involvement occurs in worship and administration. There are usually no professional functionaries, but when they do exist they are not distinguished as a clergy. Unless the sect originated under a charismatic leader, members occupy offices in rotation, by lot, or by seniority. Later, a lay leader is chosen for his or her particular abilities. Once such leaders are trained, the "radical democracy" of the sect breaks down, spontaneity disappears, and the sect moves closer to denominationalism. Elites emerge that may be chosen by the members but tend to become self-recruiting. They may serve to preserve the sect or to move it toward the denomination, depending on whether or not they are specially trained and professional.

The sect's attitude toward the world is one of separation. It sees the maintenance of a separate identity as crucial to its continued existence. It may use isolation: vicinal, linguistic, or by injunction to separateness. Or it may utilize insulation: behavioral rules designed to protect sect values, such as distinctive dress or marriage only within the group. The principle of separation can come into tension with a sect's injunction to evangelize. The sect is threatened by the admission of new members who, according to its standards, have not been fully socialized. It may develop a hostile or indifferent attitude toward the world and the state, and may separate from the world to the degree of adopting an other-worldly orientation. In so doing, it may reject society's values in favor of the sect's spiritual values. It may also expect the imminent culmination of human history.

Finally, the sect is a protest group. The sects studied by Troeltsch and Weber were protests against established churches. Wilson comments that the sect may not be so much a protest against other religious groups as it is one against secular society and perhaps also the state. Its precepts differ from, and at times are in direct conflict with, those of secular society.[12]

These theories have value for a study of early Christianity when used as tools of description and analysis and not as a means of forcing modern categories upon groups in antiquity. A direct application of these theories to *1 Clement* and the *Shepherd* would only tell us how to label the groups behind these works if they existed today.

---

12. Wilson, *Religion in Sociological Perspective*, 93.

But a judicious use of the theories can help us sort through the details in these two works in order to discover how the members of each group looked at themselves, the nature of the organization they called the church and the society around them, and, in light of those beliefs, how they differed from one another.

EVOLUTION IN THE CHRISTIAN CONGREGATIONS OF ROME

Wilson's theories enable us to demonstrate that *1 Clement* represents a congregation that had evolved beyond its original self-definition and attitude toward the world. Clement's congregation developed a more world-embracing attitude as it sought to redefine its identity in a world it no longer considered a threat to its existence. This evolution can best be understood by comparing *1 Clement* to the *Shepherd*, since the nature of the church upheld in the latter work resembles Wilson's notion of the classic form of the sect.

We may now assess *1 Clement* and the *Shepherd* according to Wilson's eight key categories: requirements for membership, level of commitment demanded, exclusiveness, attitude toward unworthy members, attitude toward rival religious groups, attitude toward authority and office in the group, attitude toward the world, and protest orientation.[13]

Membership

At first glance, Clement's congregation looks to be the classic sect. Membership in it, like that in the sect, was based on a claim to personal merit: possession of eternal salvation. Clement considered the members of the church God's "called" (Salutation; 32.4; 65.2), "elect" (1.1), and "chosen" (6.1). God had called them, and the members had turned to God, repented, and gained salvation (7.5, 7). *First Clement* is replete with examples to convince the audience that rebellious Christians must repent and could expect to receive the forgiveness of God and the Christian community. Clement does not suggest a limit to the number of times a Christian may repent.

---

13. The term "sect" is used in the following analysis for the sake of convenience, as a label for a certain set of self-definitions and attitudes toward the world. It is not meant to imply that this term as such is appropriate to a study of early Christianity.

The fear of God gives salvation (21.8), and even though members are justified by their faith (32.4), they must have right hearts (15.1–4) and be obedient to God's laws in order to be "chosen" among the number who will be saved (48.4; 58.2). As shown in chapter 5, Clement uses citizenship as an analogy for membership in the church. The members should be adorned by their "virtuous and honorable citizenship" (2.8), use their citizenship in a worthy manner (3.4), and do good deeds as worthy citizens (21.1). Like the second generation of the classic sect, the children of members must also demonstrate their faith through obedience (1.3). They are to be instructed in humility, in love for God, and in the fear of God that "gives salvation" to the obedient (21.8).

The *Shepherd* also resembles Wilson's sect in its requirements for membership. It bases salvation on repentance by the individual (*Vis.* 1.3.2; 3.7.5). Like *1 Clement*, it calls believers the "chosen" who are saved by faith (*Vis.* 3.8.4). Also like *1 Clement*, it expects the believer to remain obedient in order to be saved (*Vis.* 1.3.4; *Mand.* 7.5). The one who refrained from "every evil lust" would be saved (*Vis.* 3.8.4). But Hermas feared that some of his sins might not be forgivable (*Vis.* 1.2.1). More significantly, Hermas presented as a new revelation the teaching that disobedient believers had one chance to repent. If they sinned again after that repentance, they would not be saved (*Vis.* 2.2.5; *Mand.* 4.3.6). He warned, for example, that those who display a lack of faith in the coming persecution will not be forgiven (*Vis.* 2.2.5). Therefore, he presented a new qualification for membership in his circle: acceptance of the belief that the Christian could remain sinless throughout life, but if he fell, he had only one opportunity to repent. Any Christian who fell into sin, repented, then fell again was by definition excluded from this group. The children of members were expected to adhere to this new teaching. Hermas is told to convert his family, and salvation is promised them if they repent (*Vis.* 1.3.1–2). However, if his children deny their faith during the coming great persecution, they will lose their salvation just like their elders.

That repentance was a basis for membership in both *1 Clement* and the *Shepherd* indicates that both authors viewed their groups as voluntary associations of believers, like the sect. Members of both groups showed in some way their repentance and obedience. Hermas added a new and important doctrine that must be accepted by mem-

167

bers of his group, and that would distinguish the adherents of his group from other Christians.

Level of Commitment

Clement's group also resembles a sect in the level of commitment it demanded. Clement's congregation expected its members to maintain a high level of commitment. They were to obey the laws of the Christian tradition, identified by Clement as the laws of God:

> For you did all things without respect of persons, and walked in the laws of God, obedient to your rulers, and paying all fitting honor to the older among you. On the young, too, you enjoined temperate and seemly thoughts, and to the women you gave instruction that they should do all things with a blameless and seemly and pure conscience, yielding a dutiful affection to their husbands. (1.3)

Members of Clement's congregation thus were expected to follow a strict code of behavior. They were to keep from evil actions (30.3), perform good deeds, and thus be considered worthy of God (21.1). They were also expected to have correct inner attitudes. The young were encouraged to have right thoughts, the women to do all with a "pure conscience" (1.3). An attitude of submission to God's will was necessary (19.1; 35.5). Clement demands this level of commitment from the new leaders in Corinth. He expects them to show their commitment to the group by voluntarily exiling themselves (54.2).

Hermas's group demanded total commitment. Its members were to perform good deeds in support of other members. The rich were to provide for the material needs of the poor, and the poor were to pray for the rich. They were expected not to compromise their faith by sinful actions or through associations with nonmembers. They had to draw apart from unrepentant sinners within the group in order not to be tainted by them (*Mand.* 4.1.9). The members of Hermas's group also were expected to have proper inner thoughts. The ideal member for Hermas has "righteous designs" instead of evil desires (*Vis.* 1.1.8). He expected the members to resist denying their Lord in the coming persecution, even to the point of suffering death (*Sim.* 9.28.2–4). The seriousness of this expectation is emphasized in his assertion that those who deny Christ in the future would forever lose their salvation (*Vis.* 2.3.4).

First Clement and the *Shepherd* both demonstrate the high level of commitment demanded by the sect. For both, commitment must be total and is guided by a clear set of beliefs. Clement placed greater emphasis on obedience to leaders than Hermas. But implicit within the *Shepherd* is the assumption that Hermas's message will be accepted and obeyed. Like the leadership of the classic sect, the leaders in both groups claimed the right to regulate every facet of a member's life.

Exclusiveness

Clement's group retained the exclusiveness of a sect in that its members still considered their membership in the group the most important thing about them. But by the time of *1 Clement* it had lost enough of that exclusiveness to see itself in continuity with other Christian groups and with Old Testament Israel. Clement envisions the church as both "the number of his elect that has been numbered in all the world" (64.1) and local groups (ἐκκλησία) identified with cities such as Rome and Corinth (Salutation). Members are called the "elect" (ἐκλεκτός; 1.1; 46.4; 58.2; 59.2). He characterized the church as a family and called his Corinthian audience "brethren."[14] The congregations in various cities comprised together "the whole brotherhood" (2.4) and Christ's "flock" (16.1; 44.3; 57.2). *First Clement* 8 implies a continuity between Old Testament Israel and the church. Following quotations from Ezekiel and Isaiah, he says, "Thus desiring to give to all his beloved a share in repentance, he established it by his Almighty will" (8.5).

The church for Hermas is the "ecclesia" (ἐκκλησία) of God. Its members are "saints" (ἅγιοι). Like Clement, Hermas addresses his readers as "brethren" (ἀδελφοί), and the "elect" of God (ἐκλεκτοί).[15] They are also called the "slaves of God" (*Mand.* 5.2.1; *Sim.* 1.1). Hermas knew there were Christians in other cities (*Vis.* 2.4.3), but he never referred to an ἐκκλησία abroad. And he left no place for congregations who did not accept the validity of his revelation. Christians who rejected his view, whether in Rome or abroad, would in his mind cease to be a part of the church and would not have been accepted in Hermas's house church.

14. *1 Clem.* 4.7; 13.1; 14.1; 33.1; 45.1; 52.1; 62.1.
15. For *Ecclesia*, see *Vis.* 1.3.4; 2.4.3; 4.1.2; *Sim.* 9.18.2. For saints, see *Vis.* 2.1.3; 2.2.5; 2.4.2; 3.3.3; 3.8.3; 3.8.9; 4.2.5; 4.3.6. For brethren, see *Vis.* 3.1.1; 3.1.4; 4.1.1. For elect, see *Vis.* 1.3.4; 2.1.3; 2.2.5; 2.4.2; 3.5.1; 3.8.3; 4.2.5.

The church for Hermas was not the new Israel. Unlike Clement, who attributed the origin of the church to Christ, Hermas asserted that the church was created before all things, and the world was established for its sake (*Vis.* 2.4.1). In keeping with this view of the church's antiquity, the subject of his initial visions was an elderly woman called Ecclesia. Although he relied on the authority of charismatic revelation and not on that of ancient traditions, this concept of the church's antiquity served to give his group a unique sense of its own importance and permanency.

Hermas compared the church to a tower that God, assisted by angels, was in the process of building (*Vision* 3; *Similitude* 9). The towers in these passages were composed of Christians with varying levels of faith and obedience. But no one would be a part of the tower unless he or she remained obedient throughout life or repented of former sins and proved the genuineness of his or her repentance by not sinning again.

Clement was less exclusive than Hermas. While both believed in specific requirements for membership, Clement considered his congregation part of a larger group. Hermas's new revelation kept him apart from that group. The need to lead a sinless life was of vital importance to Hermas. He and his followers believed that one had to meet this additional criterion to be part of the accepted group. Hermas's group thus had a more exclusive self-identity than Clement's, and more closely resembles the modern notion of a sect.

Unworthy Members

The way a group treats members it considers unworthy is related to a group's exclusivity. Here again Clement's group bears some resemblance to a sect. Clement equated unworthiness with "dissension" (στάσις) or disobedience toward rulers in the church. The new leaders were "rash and self-willed" (1.1). They had "pride and unruliness," and "rush into strife and sedition" (14.1–2). They exalted themselves over Christ's flock although Christ was not on their side (16.1). Since they were opposed to God's will, they were enemies of God (36.6). They may have appeared to desire stability in the church, but Clement considered their wish hypocritical (15.1). Clement seems to have had no specific knowledge of the situation in Corinth, since all of the characterizations he offers could have been based on the simple fact that the new leaders convinced the members to install them in office. Clement believed that the new leaders had perverted the Corinthian congregation by taking control. Clement says that the resulting division had turned many aside and caused many to be discouraged or to doubt their faith (46.9). This specific information was far more important to Clement—whatever their personal character, the new leaders had caused confusion and disorder by disrupting the proper transition of power. Thus, they were unworthy. He asks them to consider the needs of the group and voluntarily leave the church. Such a move would be proof of their repentance, and they would be honored by God and humankind (54.2–4). The thrust of the letter is that if they will not leave voluntarily, the congregation should expel them.

Unworthy members in the *Shepherd* comprise a broader spectrum of people. Some, called "sons of wickedness," lacked a sincere belief (*Vis.* 3.6.1). They include apostates and betrayers of the church who will never repent (*Sim.* 8.6.4). This passage suggests that Hermas knew of Christians who had denied their faith and informed on other Christians, perhaps under threat of punishment by the state. Others—young in their faith, presently backsliders in their behavior, caught up in riches, or only partly righteous—could receive forgiveness (*Vis.* 3.7.1–5). Hermas also was concerned with hypocrites who promoted strange doctrines (*Sim.* 8.6.5) and with evil speakers who were always promoting schisms (*Sim.* 8.7.1). Some Roman Christians might have considered Hermas one of these heretics. He distinguished himself from false teachers simply by appealing to the validity of his revelation. He did not worry about causing schism, probably because he believed his message was true and would be accepted by all.

The sins Hermas found most vexing show us how his group looked at the problems facing the Roman congregations. He was most upset with "those who are concerned with business and do not cleave to the saints" (*Sim.* 8.8.1). Although they once were faithful, they

> became rich and in honor among the heathen; then they put on great haughtiness and became high minded, and abandoned the truth, and did not cleave to the righteous, but lived together with the heathen, and this way pleased them better. (*Sim.* 8.9.1)

Hermas was concerned most not with betrayers of the church or those who denied their faith, but with those who pursued wealth and honor rather than associate with other Christians and pursue a holy life. They had abandoned the truth for the ways of the heathen. Hermas believed that they needed to lose their wealth or, at the least, have only one business in order to be useful to God. Some of the Roman congregations at the turn of the second century witnessed rising socioeconomic status among their members. The social divisions among Roman Christians that would have resulted from this may have contributed to Hermas's consternation.

Hermas presents the responsibility of members in good standing toward the unworthy when he addresses the subject of adultery (μοιχεία). The shepherd in Hermas's visions broadens the definition of adultery:

> "Not only," said he, "is it adultery if a man defiles his flesh, but whoever acts as do the heathen is also guilty of adultery, so that if anyone continues in such practices, and does not repent, depart from him and do not live with him, otherwise you are also a sharer in his sin." (*Mand.* 4.1.9)

Those who follow the ways of the heathen, pursuing wealth and consuming conspicuously, were considered adulterers by Hermas and had to be shunned by the congregation. Hermas threatened those who had knowledge of Christ but continued to sin that God would punish them twice as harshly as he would punish the heathen. While Hermas left the ultimate punishment to God, he expected Christians to withdraw fellowship from unworthy members. Thus, Hermas's group believed that unworthy members should be excluded.

In both *1 Clement* and the *Shepherd,* unworthy members must demonstrate personal repentance before they can be restored. Hermas, in addition, required them to accept his new revelation and reorder their lives accordingly. Clement was concerned more with the contravention of organizational precepts, specifically with the usurpation of authority and the ensuing disorder at Corinth. The *Shepherd* addresses primarily moral errors, with some concern for doctrinal error, but shows little interest in organizational disorder. Both authors believe that unworthy members should be excluded from the group. Clement focuses on the need for order in the congregation and excludes unworthy members only to maintain that order, but Hermas focuses more on the unworthy members themselves and excludes them because their presence in the group simply is not right.

Rival Religious Groups

In its attitude toward rival groups, *1 Clement* shows less similarity to the classic sect than does the *Shepherd*. The Corinthian church is the only contemporary religious group Clement mentions by name. He considered this group as much a part of the church as his own group. He referred to Jews only in the context of the biblical tradition (e.g., 8.3; 29.2).

The groups in Rome that opposed Clement's congregation, though not directly identified, apparently were composed at least in part of former Christians whom Clement compared to Lot's wife, in that they had turned aside "to others" because they were double-minded and doubted God's power (11.1–2). He later added that the report of στάσις at Corinth "has not only reached us, but also those who dissent from us, so that you bring blasphemy on the name of the Lord through your folly, and also are creating danger for yourselves" (47.7). Clement has in mind not the state, but other religious groups that would be most likely to use schism in the congregation as a pretext for attacking Christianity. These dissenters probably were not Christian congregations, since they are accused of bringing "blasphemy on the name of" Christ.

Clement's dissenters may have come from former Christians among the Jewish synagogues of Rome. Disaffected Jewish converts would be more likely to return to Judaism than to turn to any other religion. Clement may have in mind the Roman Jews when he attributes the Neronian persecution to jealousy (see chap. 1).

He also mentions "opponents," but their identity is unclear. He describes them only as "foolish, imprudent, silly, and uninstructed men" who "mock and deride us" in order to exalt themselves (39.1). He refers obliquely to those who "hate us wrongfully" in 60.3.

Hermas makes no mention of religious groups outside the Christian tradition. His religious opponents, who all identify themselves as Christians, include schismatics who may have formed rival groups. He condemns teachers with strange doctrines who corrupt God's servants (*Sim.* 8.6.5), and equates schismatics with law-breakers and the double-minded (*Sim.* 8.7.5; 8.8.5; 8.9.4). These fallen teachers are doubly responsible before God (*Sim.* 9.31.4). Like Clement, Hermas encourages them to repent and put away their schisms.

Both *1 Clement* and the *Shepherd* show no tolerance for divergent religious groups. Both regard schism as sinful. But Clement is more concerned about "those who dissent from us," former Christians who have joined another religion and no longer identify with Christianity. Hermas is concerned not with groups outside the church, but with Christians who behave in inappropriate ways. Thus, his work represents a narrower sectarian response to the world.

Authority and Office in the Group

The typical sect is a lay organization and encourages a high degree of spontaneity and lay involvement. Clement's group had moved away from this aspect of the sect, whereas Hermas's concept of organization resembles it.

The basic responsibility of members in Clement's group was not involvement in ministry, but obedience to the group's rulers. The Corinthians are commended for having once been "obedient" (ὑποτάσσω) to their rulers (1.3). Clement expects Christians to "respect" (αἰδέομαι) their rulers (21.6). They should never question those in authority since God appointed the rulers and gave them the orders they relate to the group. Clement compares the church to the army: everyone down the line carries out orders as if they come from the emperor (37.2–3). Christians, in like manner, are to carry out Christ's "faultless commands" (37.1). Each member is to "be subject" (ὑποτάσσω) to his fellow member, "according to the position granted to him" (38.1). With the new Corinthian leaders in mind, Clement wrote that the one who steps out of his "appointed place" is not pleasing to God, and will suffer the penalty of death:

> Let each one of us, brethren, be well pleasing to God in his own rank, and have a good conscience, not transgressing the appointed rules of his ministry, with all reverence. . . . Those therefore who do anything contrary to that which is agreeable to his will suffer the penalty of death. (42.1, 3)

Clement delegates ministry to an elite, self-appointed group, separate from and not directly answerable to the larger membership, which performed its functions blamelessly and without the assistance of the common members. In chapters 43 and 44, Clement describes the apostolic origin and self-perpetuating nature of church leadership. He introduces the topic by reviewing how Aaron and the Levites were appointed to the Jewish priesthood. God ordered a public ceremony and identified Aaron by the miraculously budding rod. Clement says he did this in order to avoid the "disorder" (ἀκαταστασία) that could arise from the jealousy of the other tribes (43.1–6). In the same way, Christ's apostles knew that there would be "strife" (ἔρις) for the title of bishop (ἐπίσκοπος). So they appointed successors everywhere they went, and left behind the instruction that other "approved men" should succeed them (44.2). Clement concludes from this that it is wrong to remove from office those who were appointed by the apostles or their successors (presumably the ejected presbyters at Corinth included some of both). These leaders took their positions with the consent of the "whole church" and ministered without blame (44.3). Unlike the sect, leadership in Clement's group was self-perpetuating, although the whole membership was expected to ratify the choice.

The assertion of blamelessness is repeated three times in chapter 44:

> We consider therefore that it is not just to remove from their ministry those who . . . have ministered to the flock of Christ without blame. . . . For our sin is not small, if we eject from the episcopate those who have blamelessly and in holiness offered its sacrifices. . . . You have removed some from the ministry which they fulfilled blamelessly. (44.2, 3, 6)[16]

These assertions must have been made in response to claims that the former presbyters could be blamed. Clement seems to imply that blame was a basis for ejection, but he never develops the concept. *First Clement* never discusses the proper way to eject a presbyter. Whether the "blame" leveled against the former leaders was improper moral conduct, the inadequate or dishonest dispatch of their responsibilities, the absence of personal charismatic authority, or something else, Clement never discusses the particulars. The need to maintain order in accordance with his idea of legitimate authority overrode the particulars of the situation. Rather than describe the proper course for the dismissal of leaders, Clement evidences an a priori belief that a presbyter appointed by God would never act in such a way as to make his removal legitimate. That is, since the ejected presbyters were appointed by God, they must have fulfilled their ministry blamelessly. Clement offers no examples of properly

---

16. The translation of this last phrase is debatable. Grant and Graham translate it "[you] have removed some who were conducting themselves well from the ministry they have irreproachably honored" (*First and Second Clement*, 74).

appointed leaders within the church who made themselves unworthy of leadership.

Clement considered still in effect the offices of bishop (ἐπίσκο- πος), presbyter (πρεσβύτερος), and deacon (διάκονος). He mentions apostles only in the past tense. He probably would not have approved of Hermas, since *1 Clement* refers to prophets only in the context of the Old Testament. In chapter 44, addressing the situation in Corinth, he refers to the apostolic appointment of leaders in Corinth and elsewhere. This was done to avoid strife over the "title (ὄνομα) of bishop" (44.1). Thus, the Corinthian leaders are identified here as bishops. This is confirmed in verse 4, where Clement condemns the ejection of blameless men from the episcopate. In verse 5, however, he calls them presbyters. He also refers to them as presbyters in 47.5 and 57.1. Since Clement uses these terms synonymously, it seems likely that his group made no distinction between bishop and presbyter. Clement never refers to a monoepiscopacy, in Rome or elsewhere. Although it probably existed in other cities, apparently it had not yet developed in Rome and Corinth. His two references to deacons occur alongside references to bishops (42.4–5), implying that these two offices are distinct. However, he never explains the differences between the two.

Also unlike the sect, Clement's group had a low degree of congregational involvement. His group was modeled in part on the example of Israel, in which the high priest, the priests, the Levites, and the people all had their responsibilities:

> Thus to the high priest have been appointed his proper services, to the priests their own place assigned, upon the Levites their proper duties imposed; and the layman is bound by the rules for laymen. (40.5)

He condemns the one who performs functions not within his "appointed rules" of ministering (41.1). The focus of his vehemence are lay people such as the new leaders in Corinth who attempted to function like officeholders. But Clement also bases his view of the church on the body analogy used by the apostle Paul (1 Corinthians 12). So he affirms that all members have an area of service. For example, all are charged with helping meet one another's material needs, and all are expected to provide for the educational needs of their families (21.8).

Unlike Clement's, Hermas's attitudes toward office and authority in the congregation resemble those of a sect. He does not locate authority solely in officeholders. He places a high value on congregational involvement. Hermas does not share Clement's uniformly high regard for church leaders. He is told to exhort Roman Christian officeholders to "reform their ways" in accord with his revelation (*Vis.* 2.2.6). Hermas did not reject all leaders, however. He saw the time of the apostles as a golden age, then one to two generations past, when the leaders "always agreed among themselves," listened to each other, and enjoyed peace (*Vis.* 3.5.1). By contrast, Hermas repeatedly chastises the present leadership of the Roman churches. He warns them not to desire the "chief seats," and to stop acting like poisoners (*Vis.* 3.9.7). They needed to correct one another and establish peace among themselves (*Vis.* 3.9.8, 10). Hermas refers to deacons (διάκονος) who have ministered improperly in *Sim.* 9.26.2. Hermas also was aware of false prophets within the church (*Mand.* 11.1). He condemns those who argue over "first place" in the congregation (*Sim.* 8.7.4).

Hermas never specifically commanded obedience to rulers within the church. Rather, he commanded the Christian to obey God. He severely condemned schism and disorder within the group, but pictured it as rebellion not against officeholders but against one's responsibilities within the group. Although Hermas held no office, he is the only human to whom obedience is even implicitly required. The shepherd assures Hermas that his ministry will find favor if he works hard at his task and behaves properly (*Mand.* 12.3.3; *Sim.* 10.4.1). This does not mean that Hermas opposed obedience to officeholders, but that he placed far less emphasis on it than did Clement's group.

Unlike *1 Clement*, but like the classic sect, the *Shepherd* does not legitimize proper authority figures by their appointment to an office. Rather, it legitimizes them by their behavior and actions. Proper leaders, according to Hermas, worked hard, taught with pure motives, and tirelessly served those in need (*Sim.* 9.25.2; 9.27.2–3). Hermas emphasizes not their unique function within the group but their faithfulness to provide for the spiritual and material needs of the congregation. The congregational prophet prophesied only after other members of the group had prayed for the "angel of the prophetic spirit" to rest on him (*Mand.* 11.9).

Like the sect, Hermas's writings do not make a significant distinction between officeholders and other members. He refers to the current officeholders as leaders (προηγούμενος) of the church and those who take the chief seats (*Vis.* 2.2.6; 3.9.7), and as presbyters (πρεσβύτερος; *Vis.* 2.4.2; 2.4.3) who are in charge of the church. In a general reference to church leaders, he uses the terms "apostle," "bishop," "teacher," and "deacon" (*Vis.* 3.5.1). He refers again to apostles and teachers in *Sim.* 9.25.2, and to bishops in *Sim.* 9.27.2–3. These leaders are commended for serving the members "in holiness and reverence" and for avoiding dissension. Godly bishops are identified with hospitable people who open their homes to needy members. Hermas also refers to prophets in the church. Reiling does not believe that prophets were officers in the church, since they did not exercise ongoing authority but prophesied at irregular intervals.[17] But of greater importance is whether Hermas made such a distinction. He clearly considered prophets an important part of the church. In light of his prophetic message and his concern over the quality of the present bishops and presbyters, he may have elevated prophets to a place of honor equal to that of officeholders with more regular duties.

Hermas also reflects the beliefs of a sect in that he placed a high value on lay participation in the ministry. Hermas himself, a man of modest education and servile origin who did not hold office, was chosen to receive God's message to his generation. He was not told to turn the book over to the leaders, as would have been expected of a member of Clement's congregation. Rather, he was to read all of it "to the saints" (*Vis.* 3.8.11). This is called his "ministry" (διακονία) in *Mand.* 12.3.3. Hermas was not the only layman with a ministry responsibility, however. In *Mandate* 11, his sole portrait of a functioning house church, the assembly of the righteous must intercede with God in order for the true prophet to receive God's message. This picture of interdependency shows that Hermas considered lay participation essential, at least by adult males. Together with the absence of descriptions of officeholder functions in the *Shepherd*, this suggests that Hermas and his followers favored spontaneity over fixed order.

Clement and Hermas represent very different attitudes toward authority and office in the church. Both affirm the need for leaders

17. Reiling, *Hermas and Christian Prophecy*, 169.

within the group, but Clement equates leaders with officeholders and sees them as an elite within the congregation. These leaders have specific responsibilities that they alone can fulfill. Although all members have their places of ministry, Clement's use of the Levite analogy shows that the officers in his group are responsible for the leadership and sacerdotal aspects of ministry, unlike the typical sect. The bishops, presbyters, and deacons who lead the group may have overlapping functions, but their functions are quite distinct from those of non-officeholders. Unlike Hermas, Clement never entertains the notion that a layperson could rebuke an officeholder. Unlike those in the sect, the leaders of Clement's congregation are self-perpetuating, not chosen by rotation, lot, or seniority.

World Orientation

Clement's attitude toward the world, like his attitude toward authority in the church, had ceased to resemble that of the leader of a sect. Although Clement's group did not go so far as to see itself as an extension of the larger society, it was able to find many acceptable elements in the larger society.

Clement's congregation retained its distinct identity apart from the world. It considered the people of the world accursed by God, his enemies, and hateful to him (30.8; 36.6; 35.6). They are "aliens to God" like the ancient Ninevites (7.7). Clement also calls them "doers of evil" and "perverse," in contrast to the righteous members of his group (22.6–8; 46.3, 4). But Clement and his followers did not reject the world. Christ's blood had brought the "grace of repentance" to the whole world (7.4). God had chosen from among the nations those who loved him (59.3). Alluding to a number of Old Testament passages, Clement prays that all nations may come to know the true God and God's son Jesus Christ (59.4). He predicts that God will give the heathen to the son as his inheritance (36.4; cf. Ps. 2:8).

To a degree unprecedented in early Christianity, Clement's group was able to identify with the world. This represented a break with its sectarian past. Grant and Graham assert that in its attitude toward the world, *1 Clement* "goes well beyond anything in the New Testament and prepares the way for later Christian ideas."[18] Although

18. Grant and Graham, *First and Second Clement*, 96.

he regarded heathens as sinners and enemies of God, Clement was able to see some good in them. He regretted that jealousy had caused heathen city-states and nations to be overthrown (6.4). He offers the positive example of heathen rulers who have sacrificed themselves for their people (55.1). He asks God to

> Give peace and concord to us and to all who dwell on the earth . . . and grant that we may be obedient to your almighty and glorious name, and to our rulers and governors upon the earth. You, Master, have given the power of sovereignty to them . . . that we may know the glory and honor given to them by you, and be subject to them, in nothing resisting your will. (60.4—61.1; cf. 60.20)

Their authority, although not always administered without "offense," must not be resisted since it is given to them by God (61.1-2). The Christian's obedience to God is coupled with obedience to earthly rulers. Clement also refers to the leaders of the Roman army as "our generals" (37.2).

Clement was interested in the afterlife. He warns his audience of the eternal consequences of wrong actions and the eternal benefits of right actions. He reminds them that God will come in judgment at some unexpected time (23.5; 34.3). All the faithful who had died will be resurrected (26.1) and "made manifest at the visitation of the Kingdom of God" (50.3). Clement introduced the concept of a fixed number of the elect who will be saved (2.4; 58.2; 59.2).[19] He believed that the return of Christ would occur when the fixed number of the elect was reached. F. F. Bruce observes, "This conception may have originated in an attempt to explain the deferment of the Parousia—the question 'Why has the Lord not come yet?' receives the answer: 'Because the number of the elect is not yet complete.' "[20]

Despite this, Clement's group was oriented toward this world. A main focus of *1 Clement* is proper behavior in this life and the consequent earthly blessings. His letter is concerned primarily with actions that will achieve certain earthly results: the replacement of στάσις with concord and peace. And these actions were to be motivated less by promises and threats from the next life than by the desire to live up to past examples of correct earthly behavior (19.1-2). The

19. The Revelation, written about the same time as *1 Clement*, refers in chap. 7 to 144,000 believers. But this passage probably was meant not to indicate a limit to the number of Christians but to highlight a particular group of Christians.

20. F. F. Bruce, "Eschatology in the Apostolic Fathers," 78.

wrongful usurpation of authority in Corinth has led to serious earthly problems which Clement's group wishes to address. The lack of harmony between members kept the Corinthians from continuing in their former good works (1–2). Clement offers examples of how past generations have failed or succeeded to live up to the goals of peace and concord, a spirit of repentance, obedience, and humility (chaps. 4–18). He lists five things as "the gifts of God" in 35.2: "Life in immortality, splendor in righteousness, truth in boldness, faith in confidence, self-control in holiness." The last four apply to this life. While Clement's group had not lost belief or interest in the next life, its arena of action was this world. Its primary concern was to establish and maintain organizational unity.

Hermas, on the other hand, clearly distinguishes the church from the world. His ideas closely resemble those of a sect. The shepherd tells him that

> all of creation fears the Lord, but it does not keep his commandments. Those, therefore, who fear him and observe his commandments have life with God. But those who do not observe his commandments do not have life in him. (*Mand.* 7.5)

All of humanity, unlike the Christians who agree with Hermas, fails to keep God's commandments. This notion stands in contrast to the view of Clement's group, in which rulers carry out their God-given rule according to God's will, and for which Roman soldiers present a positive model of behavior. Hermas sharply contrasts Christians with the heathen (ἔθνος) of the world (e.g., *Vis.* 1.4.2; 2.2.5). Unlike Clement, Hermas finds no redeeming qualities in the heathen. Christians must avoid unnecessary contact with the world, or risk being tainted by it. A principal concern in the *Shepherd* is for Christians who had allowed contact with the world to undermine their level of commitment without actually destroying their faith.

Hermas's rejection of the world leads him to conclude that Christians who had faith but also possessed "the riches of this world" are useless to God: they would deny their faith if persecuted (*Vis.* 3.6.5). He returns to this theme in *Mandate* 5, where he says that ill temper arises from "daily business," food, a friend, or a question of "giving and receiving" (*Mand.* 5.2.2). He condemns extravagant feasts and the desire for women (*Mand.* 6.2.5; cf. *Mand.* 8.3). Some Christians, though not rejecting their faith, had been tainted by business,

the pursuit of wealth, "heathen friendships and many other occupations of this world . . ." (*Mand.* 10.1.4; cf. *Mand.* 12.1.2; 12.2.1).
Others, without rejecting their faith, had become so caught up in
wealth that they avoided Christian brothers whom they feared would
seek material support (*Sim.* 8.8.1). Although they had not lost their
faith and did not follow the sinful deeds of the heathen, they had
become high-minded and had abandoned the truth. According to
Hermas, they inevitably would be corrupted by the heathen and lose
their salvation unless they rejected those friendships (*Sim.* 8.9.1).

Hermas not only condemns the corrupting influence of the
world on members, but also finds a stark contrast between the goals
and values of his group and those of the world. In *Similitude* 1, he
contrasts "this city," Rome, with "your city."[21] Roman Christians live
in a "strange" city, and should not behave like citizens of that city. To
buy fields, build large dwellings, and become involved in various
business transactions is to act like a citizen of "this city." These material pursuits are under the "power of another" whom Hermas calls
"the Lord of this city" (*Sim.* 1.3). This person, clearly the Roman
emperor, is contrasted with God. The emperor's law, which holds
sway in his city, is opposed to God's law. Hermas leaves no room for
compromise: members must decide whether to follow the lord of
this city and his law or God and God's law. He predicts that wealthy
Christians one day would have to make a decision about which law to
obey. Christians who followed the law of this city would be excluded
from God's city: they would lose their salvation. The heathen world
had nothing to offer Hermas. For him, its values and beliefs were
antithetical to those of the church.

Unlike *1 Clement*, the *Shepherd* resembles a sect in its other-worldly
orientation. The true dwelling place for Hermas's group is not in
this world but in the "world to come" (*Vis.* 4.3.5). He questions why
Christians prepare fields and build buildings in "this city." Instead,
they should be looking forward to dwelling one day in their "own
city" (*Sim.* 1.1). If they use their money to help the poor, they will be
purchasing "lands and houses" in their own city (*Sim.* 1.9). The
present world is like winter for the righteous. The world to come is
like summer for Christians, but winter for nonmembers (*Sim.* 3.2;
4.2). But this does not mean that the present world holds only misery

21. This appears to be a proto-Augustinian notion of the "city of God."

for Christians. Hermas promises that whoever follows the commands in his writings will have salvation and also be happy in this life. Whoever disobeys will not be saved and will be unhappy in this life (*Sim.* 10.4.1). Thus, the primary motivation for right actions in the present life is the promise of blessings in the next life.

Hermas's other-worldly orientation arises in part from his conviction that the end of the world was at hand. He says that Christ was born in the "last days of the end of the world" (*Sim.* 9.12.3). His parables of the church as a tower imply that the building is nearly completed. First, he warns his readers to repent quickly if they would be included in the tower (*Vis.* 3.6, 7; *Sim.* 9.32). Then, Christians who need to repent before the tower is finished, in order to be saved, are rejected stones (*Vis.* 3.5.5). Finally, Hermas asks Ecclesia "about the times, if the end were near." She responds that the end will come when the tower is completed, and warns that "it will quickly be built up" (*Vis.* 3.8.9).

His picture of the coming great persecution is directly related to his notions about the end of the world. *Vision* 4 depicts this persecution as a terrible beast. Its head is colored black, red, gold, and white. Hermas is told that these colors represent the present world, the fact that this world must be destroyed "by blood and fire," the members who have been martyred, and the world to come in which the members of his group will dwell (*Vis.* 4.3.2–5). The implication is that this persecution, which Hermas expected within his lifetime, would culminate in the destruction of the world.

Unlike the typical sect, Clement's group is not concerned to maintain a separate identity from the world. In fact, non-Christians share common values with his congregation. He considers church and state compatible. Also unlike the sect, Clement's group was oriented toward this world. Clement was most concerned with how a Christian's actions would affect group order and growth in this world. His group had begun to see the larger society as an imperfect reflection of God's standards and values, which could be modified and used by the group. The *Shepherd* better reflects the beliefs of a sect, since it maintains a far stronger sense of separateness from the world. Hermas's repeated warnings about the corrupting influence of heathen friends and the material lures of this world indicate that he considered the maintenance of a separate identity crucial to his group's survival. Like the sect, the *Shepherd* advocates the use of isolation and insulation to maintain this separation. It gives injunctions to separateness, which served to isolate the group, and sets behavioral rules unique to the group, which helped insulate it. Christians are to forsake "heathen friendships" and associate only with Christians who have accepted Hermas's codes of behavior.

Protest Orientation

Wilson's final category identifies a sect as a group that originated in protest against another religious group or against society at large and continues to define its existence by protest. Clement's group may have originated in protest, but by the time of *1 Clement* it had ceased to define itself as a group in protest and thus no longer resembled a sect. In contrast, Hermas wrote his work as a protest against the type of social compromise with the world *1 Clement* represents.

Based on its obvious acquaintance with a number of Jewish teachings, *1 Clement* may represent a house church which originated in protest against Judaism. Clement comments at length on the sufferings of his group members, but never attributes that suffering to a specific group (chaps. 5–6). He had a perfect opportunity to identify the real enemies of his group, but refused to do so. Thus, although his group may have originated in protest, it no longer used protest as an element of its self-definition. Even persecution (διωγμός), which for later Christians became an experience without comparison, is for Clement similar to the kinds of suffering all people face. He associates persecution with disorder, war, and captivity (3.2). He compares it to estrangement between husbands and wives and to the overthrow of great nations (6.3–4). While persecution remains a potential threat to the group, Clement is not concerned that it might be triggered simply by the wickedness of the state. If it comes, it will be the result of disorder within the group, which "those who dissent from us" may use to accuse the group of civil disobedience (στάσις).

In contrast, Hermas protests against the existing Roman Christian leadership and against the world. He did not set out in his book to organize a church within the church, however. He planned to convince all Christians, including the leadership at Rome, of the truth of his visions. *Similitude* 9, probably written a number of years after the initial *Visions*, suggests that his rebuke was not well received by the leaders. This *Similitude* depicts the punishment of false leaders who had never repented of their sins. This conclusion also is suggested by the Muratorian Canon's rejection of the *Shepherd*'s claim to divine authority. Hermas's message is by nature so uncompromising that a Christian who heard it had either to accept it or reject it. It would not be too surprising if, unable to convince the leaders of his message, Hermas accepted a group of converts to his beliefs as an alternative to the existing Roman congregations.

Hermas also sees the church as directly opposing the state. He foresees a persecution, probably within his lifetime, which would test the faith of Christians as had no other. Unlike Clement, Hermas clearly pictures the Roman state as the source of persecution. The "Lord of this city" could decide at any time to "cast out from his city" (put to death) Christians (*Sim.* 1.3, 4). The reason for persecution also is clear: members did not use the emperor's law but followed the law of God. The state persecuted Christians in order to make them deny their faith so as to avoid suffering. Hermas commends those who were "brought under authority," questioned, but refused to deny their faith (*Sim.* 9.28.4). Unlike Clement, Hermas is not bothered so much by physical suffering under persecution: he believes that suffering, if endured patiently, will result in great blessings. At the top of heaven's hierarchy stand Christians who were martyred and did not deny their faith. Then come those who were persecuted but not killed. Only after these two groups come Christians who obeyed the church's injunctions but were never persecuted (*Sim.* 8.3.6–8). Hermas also predicts that the Christian who denies Christ in the coming persecution will permanently lose salvation (*Vis.* 2.3.4).

Clement's congregation no longer defined itself as a group in protest against others, whether against synagogues, secular society in general, or the government. On the other hand, the *Shepherd* clearly displays the sectarian notion of protest. Hermas opposed the office-holders in the Roman churches. He also opposed the society and the state. In contrast to Clement, he suggests no grounds of commonality with society, nor does he give any hope that, despite past experiences, peaceful relations with the state could be attained. Future persecution directed by the state was anticipated. Any group that grew up around Hermas originated in protest.

CONCLUSION

Based on the criteria generally accepted among sociologists of religion, both *1 Clement* and the *Shepherd* show affinities to the sect ideal type. Both advocate voluntary associations of members, which had to be joined formally by their children. Both demand total commitment to the congregation. *First Clement* is less exclusive than the *Shepherd*, but both draw a distinction between Christians and outsiders. Both are concerned about unworthy members and favor their expulsion, although the focus in *1 Clement* is on the preservation of order rather than on the offending members.

Attitudes in the *Shepherd* resemble those of a sect in ways that *1 Clement*'s do not. Hermas rejects the notion of a clergy set apart. His notion about who could act in an official capacity is more fluid than Clement's. Hermas considers the maintenance of a separate identity crucial to the preservation of the church. He considers isolation and total socialization of new members important. He strongly protests Roman society and government and the practices of many existing Roman house churches.

The congregation behind *1 Clement* had evolved beyond its initial resemblance to a sect. Clement establishes a division between clergy and laity, and reserves the most significant tasks for the former. Leadership is self-perpetuating, and its decisions are subject only to confirmation by the general membership. Although *1 Clement* speaks of eternal promises and rewards, its orientation is essentially toward this world. The congregation behind it shares a number of values with the world, and is not concerned about losing its unique identity. It retains no vestiges of protest.

Christianity in Rome in the first and early second centuries comprised a number of house church congregations spread throughout the city, which probably agreed on many points but also held contradictory views of themselves and society. The examples of *1 Clement* and the *Shepherd* make it clear that the differences were fundamental and did not just involve unique but compatible customs. The *Shepherd* depicts the leaders of the church as unable to agree among themselves (see the discussion in chaps. 1 and 2). Thus, it provides us with insight into *1 Clement*'s concern to establish order and harmony on the basis of obedience to an authority validated by a specific tradition. An imperial freedman like Clement, who had witnessed firsthand the hierarchical structure of Roman government and respected it, would naturally conclude that the churches in Rome needed one and only one source of authority if unity was to be achieved.

This also may provide insight into the origin of the monoepiscopacy in Rome. It is significant that it did not exist prior to mid-second century, by which time a number of other cities of the empire were ruled by a single bishop. Unlike the house churches in other cities, the congregations in Rome still were not united in the early second century. The difficulty that Roman Christian leaders experienced in developing a monoepiscopacy and effective control over all the congregations in Rome is illustrated by the *Shepherd* and underlies *1 Clement's* concern for order. The longer period of struggle may help account for the eventual strength of the Roman hierarchy.

10

SECOND-CENTURY DEVELOPMENTS IN ROMAN CHRISTIANITY

The actions of second-century leaders of the Roman church reflect the ideology first advanced in *1 Clement*. They continued to pursue organizational unity through unity in doctrine and practice. This was no small task. Teachers within and without the Roman church taught doctrines in conflict with traditional Roman Christian beliefs. Some of these leaders, by virtue of their personal popularity, posed a real danger to the authority of the official leaders, who believed that contrary religious practices threatened the unity of the church. In meeting these challenges, the later Roman Christian leaders never contradicted the spirit or teachings of *1 Clement*. They also began, by the end of the second century, to reinforce their authority over a unified church by establishing church ownership of the Christian catacombs and house churches.

CHALLENGES TO THEOLOGY

About five years after the death of Hermas in 130, the teacher Marcion came from Asia Minor to Rome. Marcion rejected the identification of the church with Israel, a concept fundamental to *1 Clement*'s understanding of Christianity. Marcion wished to draw a firm line between the Law and the Gospel, between the Old Testament and the writings of the apostles. His ideas were popular and probably attracted a sizable following in Rome. He was initially well received by Roman church leaders as well, but, by 144, they came to consider him such a serious threat to unity that they expelled him from Rome.

Two other traveling teachers, Cerdo and Valentinus, brought Gnosticism to Rome sometime around 140. Cerdo, who came from Syria, taught that the God of the Old Testament, the creator of the world, is actually a Demiurge. He asserted that the Father of Jesus

Christ is a different and superior God. About the same time, Valentinus brought his version of Gnosticism to Rome. His teachings, also in obvious conflict with the theology of *1 Clement,* were vigorously resisted by the Roman leaders. Nevertheless, Gnosticism found a number of adherents in Rome. The result, as Frend points out, was that even by the end of the second century, no clear-cut separation existed between Gnostics and the orthodox Roman community.[1]

In part as a response to these divergent teachings, sometime during the second century the traditional leaders of the Roman church developed the Roman or Apostolic Symbol, which contributed to the later Apostles' Creed. The Roman Symbol is probably the oldest doctrinal creed, at least in the West. This Symbol, originally a series of questions to baptismal candidates, as a minimum affirmed God as Father and Creator; Jesus as the Son of God, as a man who lived on earth and suffered death, and as the judge to come; the Spirit; and the resurrection of the flesh.[2] This represents a significant step toward doctrinal purity and the attendant organizational unity advocated in *1 Clement.*

CHALLENGES TO PRACTICE

Around mid-second century, the Roman church finally came under the control of a single bishop. *First Clement* supports the principle of a single ruler of the church when, for example, it compares church leaders to the Jewish high priest and advocates apostolic succession. Nevertheless, the church that would later claim primacy over all Christendom was one of the last major churches of the empire to establish a monoepiscopacy. This delay resulted not from the Roman leaders' reluctance to take a position of leadership among the churches, as Clement's remonstrating letter to the Corinthians in 96 and the actions of second-century Roman bishops Anicetus and Victor demonstrate. Rather, continuing differences in theology and practice among the leaders of the Roman congregations and the divisive influence of Marcionites and Gnostics had made it very difficult for any individual bishop to gain universal support. Perhaps the success of so many contrary teachings and practices just prior to

1. W.H.C. Frend, *The Rise of Christianity* (Philadelphia: Fortress, 1984), 213.
2. La Piana, "The Roman Church at the End of the Second Century," 212 n. 8.

mid-century so alarmed the more traditional leaders that they felt the need to unite under a single bishop.

Roman leaders around mid-century attempted to achieve unity in practice. Unity was essential in the celebration of the Eucharist, since it was the most important practice of the Roman church. Justin describes the practice of the Eucharist around 155 in Rome. The bread and wine are first brought to the "president of the brethren," who pronounces thanks on behalf of the brethren and then gives them to the deacons to distribute to those present and to "carry it away to those that are absent." Only those who believe "that the things we teach are true" may participate. Justin goes on to assert that the "president" uses money collected from Roman Christians to aid orphans, widows, the sick, prisoners, and strangers: "In fact to all that are in need he is a protector" (*Apology* 1.65–67). This passage suggests that the Eucharist in the second century was already becoming a method of imposing uniformity on the Roman congregations. The leader of the congregations gives the elements a special blessing, and only those who accept the orthodox Roman teachings may partake. This practice finds a precursor in Clement's comparison of practice in the church to the cultic practices of Israel presided over by the high priest (*1 Clement* 40–41).

The Roman practice of adult baptism also became a way to reinforce uniformity. Justin says that Roman leaders baptized only those "who are persuaded and believe that the things we teach and say are true, and promise that they can live accordingly" (*Apology* 1.65). As we have seen, the list of theological questions asked of candidates for baptism became the Roman Symbol.

Beginning in about 175 with Hegisippus, authors compiled lists of Roman bishops going back through Clement to the apostle Peter. Although the traditional dates are suspect, the names are probably authentic, referring to leaders of one or more Roman house churches. Only with Bishop Anicetus (154–65) can we be fairly confident that the list refers to single rulers of the Roman church.[3] During his time, both Justin Martyr and Valentinus were active in Rome. The

3. Irenaeus's list, from *Adversus haereses* 3, included Peter, Linus, Anenclitus, Clement, Evarestus, Alexander, Xystus, Telesphorus, Hyginus, Pius, Anicetus (154–65), Soter (166–75), Eleutherus (175–89), and Victor (189–99). Paulo Brezzi doubts that Anicetus was the sole Roman bishop (*The Papacy: Its Origin and Historical Evolution*, trans. Henry J. Yannone [Westminster, Md.: Newman Press, 1958], 27).

190

Paschal controversy dominated Anicetus's time in office. Christians from the East, who had migrated to Rome, celebrated Christ's crucifixion on Nisan 14, the date of Passover according to the Jewish calendar. Since this date could fall on any day of the week, the Roman church traditionally celebrated Easter on the Friday through Sunday following Nisan 14. Anicetus attempted to force the Asiatic Christians in Rome to adopt the practice of the Roman church. His efforts met with opposition from Polycarp, the respected bishop of Smyrna. Polycarp went to Rome and attempted to persuade Anicetus to adopt the Asiatic tradition. While he failed at this, he did convince Anicetus not to force Asian Christians in Rome to observe the Roman custom. Considering the number of serious theological differences between Roman congregations at this time, we can understand why Anicetus backed down. He was unwilling to risk a serious rift with the large number of Asian Christians in Rome, most of whom had few theological quarrels with Roman church officers.

But Anicetus and his successors found another way to assert their authority over the practices of Asian Christians in their city. During the second half of the second century, the Roman church established the rite of the *fermentum*, in which the bishop of Rome sent parts of the elements from the episcopal mass to the presbyters of the *tituli* to mix with their supply of elements.[4] Eusebius quotes Irenaeus to the effect that the bishops prior to and including Anicetus and his successor Soter, although they did not observe the Asiatic custom, sent the eucharistic elements on Nisan 14 to those congregations in Rome which did so (*Historia Ecclesiastica* 5.24; 14). Thus, they sought to maintain their authority without risking a split in the church.

Not until the end of the second century does a Latin, in the person of Victor (189–99), finally ascend to the Roman see. Victor was a North African presbyter of Latin stock. The Roman church, born among Greek and Asian slaves and immigrants, still was largely Greek-speaking and in the control of non-Latins. Victor's selection hardly constitutes a dramatic takeover of the church by Latin elements, however. A number of later bishops such as Stephen (254–57), Sixtus II (257–58), and Dionysius (260–69) were Greek. Also, catacomb inscriptions indicate that Latin and Greek continued

4. La Piana, "Roman Church," 217.

to compete for dominance in the Roman church throughout the third century.[5]

La Piana sees the selection of Victor as one of the most important events in the early Roman church, signaling a Latinization of the church.[6] Victor, with his strong belief in the right to impose organizational unity by force, was the ideal choice of a Roman Christian elite which, since the time of Clement, had interpreted Christianity in light of Roman ideology. The fact that he was Latin made little difference; to use La Piana's term, the Roman church had begun the process of Latinization long before Latins came to control it.

Victor felt compelled to resolve the Paschal controversy and eliminate the division in practice that his predecessor had condoned some fifty years earlier. Victor convened several local and regional councils, and insisted that all churches abandon the Asiatic (or Quartodeciman) practice. He was opposed principally by Polycrates, bishop of Ephesus. When the churches of Asia Minor refused to comply with his demand, he resisted the counsel of Irenaeus and excommunicated them. Several presbyters of Asiatic congregations in Rome, notably Blastus and Florinus, also opposed Victor and formed independent churches. Probably most Asian Christians in Rome adopted the Roman practice, at least publicly. The controversy would erupt again in 325 at the Council of Nicaea, which ultimately would endorse Victor's position.[7]

Victor's actions, though far different from those of Anicetus, are in concert with *1 Clement*'s ideology of leadership. Clement implores the Corinthians to expel the leaders who had usurped power. He repeatedly tells Christians to adhere to the practices outlined by their rightful leaders, since this will preserve the unity which he considers so necessary. Victor clearly had a greater sense of the Roman see's authority than did Anicetus, but he also had more compelling reasons to force Roman uniformity in practice. In fifty years, the situation in Rome had changed significantly. The Latin contingent of the Roman church was much stronger, and probably the Asian Christian community was proportionally smaller. In addition,

---

5. Frend, *Rise of Christianity*, 340.
6. La Piana, "Roman Church," 204–5. On Victor, see Brezzi, *Papacy*, 30–32.
7. Cruttwell, *Literary History of Early Christianity*, 2:369–71.

after many decades of division, the Roman church at the end of the second century may have been on the verge of dissolution. Thus, the need to enforce uniform practices among those who accepted "orthodox" theology was more imperative. Bishop Victor's actions represent a simple evolution from the ideology expressed in *1 Clement.*

PROPERTY OWNERSHIP AND AUTHORITY

In the late second century, the Roman church began to assert organizational control over the real property used for public worship and burial. This action was risky, since it conflicted with Roman law. Rome did not recognize Christianity as a *religio licita*, a recognized religion, and so the church had no right to own property. By the second century, many of the twenty pre-Constantinian *tituli*, along with other unknown homes, were host to house churches. Most were homes owned by individual Christians. Extensive remodeling of nearly all of these *tituli*, beginning in the late second century, provides evidence that the Roman church began to acquire ownership of the private homes at this time. In most if not all cases, the Christian owner gave the property to the church. This is the origin of the Roman church's existence as a financial entity.

At about the same time, the Roman church came into possession of burial grounds once owned by individual Christians. The first public Christian catacomb is named for Callistus, the deacon who presided over it and a later bishop of Rome. Around the year 200, the Roman church was given land on the Appian Way, south of Rome. Callistus considerably enlarged this cemetery. During the third and fourth centuries, the other major Christian catacombs came under the control of the Roman bishop. They were administered by the Roman titular churches. Control of the catacombs must have added significantly to the influence of the Roman church, since Roman Christians were very concerned about receiving a proper burial. Many lacked the ability to buy their own places of burial and dreaded the prospect of being dumped into unmarked graves or buried with pagans. This gave Roman Christians a powerful incentive to stay in the good graces of the church hierarchy.

Church ownership of property, while not specifically addressed by *1 Clement,* is in harmony with Clement's notion of the church. Since Clement sees the church as the new Israel, he might have asserted that the church has the same right to own property. Property ownership seems to be in conflict with the *Shepherd of Hermas*, however, which rebukes Christians for accumulating lands and houses. For Hermas, the church is not so much a physical entity on earth as it is an entity whose real nature exists on a spiritual plane.

CONCLUSION

Actions by the leadership of the Roman church in the second century fit with the Roman ideology first espoused in *1 Clement*. Obedience to a hierarchy of church leaders is of paramount importance, since it ensures unity. This obedience must come both in theology and practice. Theological speculation is dangerous by definition, and never preferable to accepting the traditional teachings. Teachers who oppose the official church leaders must be removed from places of influence. Compromise with those who deviate is out of the question. The elite of the Roman churches, represented in *1 Clement*, ultimately gave the Roman church its unique identity as it brought into existence and controlled Rome's monarchical episcopate.

CONCLUSION

Christianity in Rome in the first and early second centuries was not an organizationally and ideologically unified "church." *First Clement* represents not the ideology of the Roman congregations of its day but the ideology of a small group of Roman Christians which could be called the "social elite" of the Roman congregations. In contrast to the Christians represented in the *Shepherd of Hermas*, these Christians no longer defined their group as a "sect." They were optimistic about society and their futures in it. Hermas, whose social status probably was similar to that of most Roman Christians, found this optimism unacceptable and resisted it. The eventual development of the Roman church shows that his resistance failed.

The social climate in which *1 Clement* and the *Shepherd* were written encouraged a lack of unity among the congregations. The congregations behind Clement and Hermas probably had access to the Pauline corpus of writings as well as to the Old Testament and other Jewish and Christian literature. But their use of this literature and their interpretation of it were affected by their particular social situations. The interpretation Clement's group developed laid an important basis for Roman Catholic theology and practice.

Both congregations arose in a highly structured society. Rome's official class distinctions, and the unstated but no less clear levels of status within the congregations, meant that converts to Christianity from the various status levels brought with them very different self-identities and attitudes toward society. Furthermore, some came from Jewish backgrounds by birth or conversion, some came from pagan religions, and many probably were slaves who had witnessed to greater or lesser degrees the workings of Roman institutions. At some point, probably after *1 Clement* and the *Shepherd* were written, free-born pagan Romans began converting in numbers large enough to make an impact. Each of these kinds of people probably congregated with others like themselves. *First Clement* and the *Shepherd* represent two of these homogeneous groups. They were contemporaneous yet expressed very different concerns.

First Clement was concerned ultimately with "concord," which meant in effect organizational unity and the absence of disagreement. In pursuit of this goal, Clement borrowed from Roman ideology. He developed the principle that order and stability required recognizing the husband and father as *paterfamilias* of the Christian family and, by analogy, recognizing the church leader as *paterfamilias* of the congregation, a leader whose authority might not be questioned. The laity, like good subjects of the empire, had to do its part for the church and not question the leaders. Clement found in his positive view of Roman institutions the basis for restructuring the congregation as a hierarchy. The order and discipline that for Clement were hallmarks of the Roman state and army required that the established church hierarchy be unchallenged and allowed to do its work.

The *Shepherd of Hermas* demonstrates that the ideas in *1 Clement* were not representative of all Roman Christianity at that time. Hermas was influenced by Roman society in subtle ways of which he was not consciously aware. But he rejected both Roman society and other Christians who adopted its attitudes and practices, and he defined the church's identity in contradistinction to it. Hermas probably would have gained a following among the slaves, ex-slaves, and freeborn foreigners in the lower classes of Rome. Its members, like Hermas, had probably faced periodic economic deprivation and had little hope that things on earth would change for the better.

The Roman concepts Hermas borrows are redefined in radically new directions. He turned the model of patronage on its head when he taught that those with a lower social status have greater spirituality and so are superior. He was hostile toward the Roman government and expected further persecution from it. He was also hostile toward the kind of thinking represented in *1 Clement*. Christians with an accepting attitude toward the larger society were judged by Hermas to be motivated by the desire for luxury and material comfort.

These conclusions, reached by applying a static model of Roman society to *1 Clement* and the *Shepherd*, are confirmed by a dynamic model of the evolving sect. Sociological analysis suggests that Clement's group, originally similar in self-definition and world orientation to a sect, was becoming an organization that bore little resemblance to a sect and would lay the foundation for the Roman church. Hermas and his followers contested this development in Roman congregations by attempting to recapture what they considered the spirit of the apostolic age.

Clement sought to legitimize his ideas through an appeal to Jewish, Christian, and pagan traditions. *First Clement*'s appeal to tradition disguised the fact that its congregation had altered its self-identity when it embraced Roman ideology to a greater extent than had any Christian group before it. On the other hand, Hermas's authority was based on charisma, and, like the classic sect, the *Shepherd* positions itself in protest against the world and other religious groups.

Clement's group retained vestiges of its sectarian origin but was in the process of becoming something quite different. It still resembled a sect in that, as in the *Shepherd*, membership in the congregation remained voluntary and based on a claim to "personal merit," to use Wilson's term. It retained the sect's demand for total commitment by the members, in which it again was similar to Hermas's ideas. It also retained a sense of its exclusive nature, believed that members judged unworthy must be disciplined, and (to a lesser degree) was concerned about rival religious groups. But it no longer considered these issues central to its concerns, unlike the attitude in the *Shepherd* and of the classic sect described by Wilson. Clement's congregation had ceased to resemble a sect in that it introduced a division between laity and clergy, emphasized official duties over spontaneity, was willing to identify with the larger society, and refused to define itself as a group in protest.

Indeed, the *Shepherd* protests against Christian ideology that embraced the world, such as that represented in *1 Clement*. In this sense it resembles closely Wilson's model of the sect. Assuming that the *Shepherd* represents the thinking of a number of Roman Christians, one can conclude that Clement's group, far from representing the thinking of all Roman Christians, looked to some of them like an abandonment of the received Christian traditions. The *Shepherd* defines the proper Christian as one who rejects both the secular world and those Christians who have not accepted Hermas's teachings. It focuses on basic differences between Christianity and secular society and argues that love for God necessitates hostility toward "the world." Sociological analysis demonstrates the near-polar opposition between Clement and Hermas in orientation toward the world. It is difficult to imagine how the two views could be reconciled. For Clement's view to predominate in Rome, it had to overcome the views of Christians such as Hermas. This need to overcome opposition probably played a part in the development in Clement's group of a strict hierarchical model of church government.

My conclusion that the thinking in *1 Clement* represented only a small segment of the Roman churches is confirmed by a study of the archaeological and literary evidence relating to Flavia Domitilla and the Basilica of San Clemente in Rome. It appears probable that Domitilla had enough interest in Christianity to allow a household association of Christians to form and meet for worship on one of her properties. During her lifetime, a Christian named Clement led a house church somewhere in Rome, probably in the warehouse under the present-day San Clemente church. Several things make it quite plausible that Clement and his group met under Domitilla's patronage in this warehouse: (1) Domitilla, as a member of the Flavian household, could have owned the land upon which this warehouse stood; (2) her interest in Christianity; and (3) the fact that Clement (probably an imperial freedman) had the same *cognomen* as Domitilla's husband, Flavius Clemens. Although this conclusion is only plausible, it becomes more likely when we consider the references to imperial freedmen and Roman aristocratic ideology in *1 Clement*. The totality of this evidence serves to confirm the probability that Clement's group was composed in large part, if not entirely, of imperial slaves and freedmen.

First Clement represents a turning point in the life of the Roman churches. In it, the social elite among the Roman Christians enunciated for the first time their policies for restructuring the church's identity and relationships. No longer would it see itself as a protest against the wealthy and powerful, but instead it would look for ways to bridge the gap between itself and the larger society.

The small group behind *1 Clement* did not immediately impose its views on all other Roman congregations. But the *Shepherd* is evidence that *1 Clement*'s view, in the early second century, still had not crowded out all others. That the late-second-century Muratorian Canon mentions the *Shepherd*, and was unwilling to condemn it outright, suggests that the *Shepherd*'s popularity among second-century Christians at Rome was not insignificant. But the thinking in *1 Clement* eventually did become the thinking of the Roman church. This suggests that, as the charismatic authority in the Roman congregations became routinized, the common Christians came to see their social betters in the church as their spiritual superiors. Average Christians also may have been persuaded by their social betters' higher level of education. The education available to Christian imperial freedmen could have made them an intellectual elite as well as a social elite in the Roman churches.

By the late second century, monoepiscopacy (which is anticipated, though not mentioned, in *1 Clement*) was established in Rome. Apostolic succession and hierarchical government, separation of church membership into clergy and laity, property ownership, and emulation of Roman models, all advocated or anticipated in *1 Clement*, were becoming the norm for the Roman church. It still had to deal with disagreements involving groups of Eastern Christians who had settled in Rome, such as the Paschal controversy. It also had to face disunity caused by persuasive teachers like Valentinus. But it had dealt effectively with homegrown dissension by the mid- to late-second century. For example, while the Muratorian Canon did not reject the *Shepherd*, it silenced the *Shepherd*'s claim to authority by denying it a place in the public reading of Scripture. Clement's group, long after its leader's death, finally succeeded in displacing the thinking of Christians like Hermas and in molding the identity of the entire Roman church and, by extension, all of Christianity.

BIBLIOGRAPHY

Audet, Jean-Paul. "Affinités Littéraires et Doctrinales du Manuel de Discipline." *Revue Biblique* 60 (1953): 41–82.

Aune, David E. *The New Testament in Its Literary Environment.* Library of Early Christianity 8. Philadelphia: Westminster, 1987.

Bacon, Benjamin W. "The Doctrine of Faith in Hebrews, James, and Clement of Rome." *Journal of Biblical Literature* 19 (1900): 12–21.

Barberet, F. "La Formule 'Zen to Theoi' dans le Pasteur d'Hermas." *Recherches de Science Religieuse* 46 (1958): 379–407.

Bardy, Gustave. "Expressions Stoiciennes dans la I Clementis." *Recherches de Science Religieuse* 12 (1922): 73–85.

———. "Le Pasteur D'Hermas et les Livres Hermétiques." *Revue Biblique* 8 (1911): 391–407.

Barnard, L. W. "The Early Roman Church, Judaism, and Jewish-Christianity." *Anglican Theological Review* 49 (1967): 371–84.

———. *Studies in the Apostolic Fathers and Their Background.* New York: Schocken, 1967.

Barnes, Arthur Stapylton. *Christianity at Rome in the Apostolic Age.* London: Methuen, 1938.

Barnes, T. D. *Early Christianity and the Roman Empire.* London: Variorum, 1984.

Bartsch, Hans-Werner. "Röm. 9,5 und 1. Clem. 32,4: Eine notwendige Konjektur im Römerbrief." *Theologische Zeitschrift* 24 (1965): 401–9.

Bauer, Walter. *A Greek-English Lexicon of the New Testament and Other Early Christian Literature.* Trans. William F. Arndt and F. Wilbur Gingrich. 4th ed. Chicago: University of Chicago Press, 1957.

Benko, Steven, and J. J. O'Rourke, eds. *The Catacombs and the Colosseum: The Roman Empire as the Setting of Primitive Christianity.* Valley Forge, Pa.: Judson, 1971.

Berger, Peter. "Sectarianism and Religious Sociation." *The American Journal of Sociology* 64 (1958–59): 41–44.

———. "The Sociological Study of Sectarianism." *Social Research* 21 (1954): 467–85.

Bevan, G. M. *Early Christians of Rome.* New York: Macmillan, 1927.

Beyschlag, Karlmann. "1. Clemens 40–44 und das Kirchenrecht." *Reformatio und Confessio: Festschrift für D. Wilhelm Maurer.* Ed. F. W. Kantzenbach and G. Müller. Berlin: Lutherisches Verlaghaus, 1965.

————. *Clemens Romanus und der Frühkatholizismus.* Tübingen: J.C.B. Mohr, 1966.

————. "Zur Eirene Batheia." *Vigiliae Christianae* 26 (1972): 18–23.

Blake, Marion E. *Roman Construction in Italy From Tiberius Through the Flavians.* Washington, D.C.: Carnegie Institute of Washington, 1959.

Boismard, M. E. "Clement de Rome et l'Evangile de Jean." *Revue Biblique* 55 (1948): 376–87.

Bonner, Campbell, ed. *A Papyrus Codex of the Shepherd of Hermas (Similitudes 2–9) With a Fragment of the Mandates.* Ann Arbor: University of Michigan Press, 1934.

Boyle, Leonard E., ed. *San Clemente Miscellany.* 2 vols. Rome: Collegio San Clemente, 1978.

Brown, Raymond E., and John P. Meier. *Antioch and Rome: New Testament Cradles of Catholic Christianity.* New York: Paulist, 1983.

Bruce, F. F. "Eschatology in the Apostolic Fathers." In *The Heritage of the Early Church: Festschrift to Georges V. Florovsky.* Rome: Pontifical Institute of Oriental Studies, 1973.

————. *New Testament History.* New York: Doubleday, 1971.

Brunner, Gerbert. *Die theologische Mitte des ersten Klemensbriefs: Ein Beitrag zur Hermeneutik frühchristlicher Texte.* Frankfurt Am Main: Josef Knecht, 1972.

Brunt, P. A. *Italian Manpower: 225 B.C.—A.D. 14.* Oxford: Clarendon, 1971.

Bumpus, Harold Bertram. *The Christological Awareness of Clement of Rome and Its Sources.* Cambridge: Cambridge University Press, 1972.

Cantarella, Eva. *Pandora's Daughters: The Role and Status of Women in Greek and Roman Antiquity.* Trans. Maureen B. Fant. Baltimore: Johns Hopkins University Press, 1987.

Carcopino, Jerome. *Daily Life in Ancient Rome.* Ed. Henry T. Rowell. Trans. E. O. Lorimer. New Haven: Yale University Press, 1940.

Carettoni, G., et al. *La Pianta Marmorea de Roma Antica.* Forma Urbis Romae. 2 vols. Rome: Cura Della X Ripartizione del Comune di Roma, 1955.

Case, Shirley Jackson. *The Evolution of Early Christianity: A Genetic Study of First-Century Christianity in Relation to Its Religious Environment.* Chicago: University of Chicago Press, 1914.

Christ, Karl. *The Romans.* Trans. Christopher Holme. Berkeley: University of California Press, 1984.

Coarelli, Filippo. *Guida Archeologia di Roma.* Rome: Arnoldo Mondadori, 1974.

Colborne, W. "A Linguistic Approach to the Problem of Structure and Composition of the *Shepherd of Hermas.*" *Colloquium* 3 (1969): 133–42.

————. "The '*Shepherd*' of *Hermas:* A Case for Multiple Authorship and Some Implications." *Studia Patristica* 10.1. Texte und Untersuchungen 107. Berlin: Academie Verlag, 1970.

Crook, John. *Law and Life of Rome.* Ithaca, N.Y.: Cornell University Press, 1967.

Cruttwell, Charles Thomas. *A Literary History of Early Christianity: Including the Fathers and the Chief Heretical Writers of the Ante-Nicene Period.* New York: AMS, 1971.

D'Ales, Adhémar. "La Discipline Pénitentielle." *Recherches de Science Religieuse* 2 (1911): 105–39.

Daniélou, Jean. "The Fathers and the Scriptures." *Theology* 57 (1954): 83–89.

———. *The Theology of Jewish Christianity.* Trans. John A. Baker. Chicago: Henry Regnery, 1964.

Daube, David. *Roman Law: Linguistic, Social, and Philosophical Aspects.* Edinburgh: University Press, 1969.

Davison, James Edwin. "Spiritual Gifts in the Roman Church: I Clement, Hermas and Justin Martyr." Ph.D. diss., University of Iowa, 1981.

DeRossi, G. B. "I Monumenti Scoperti Sotto la Basilica de San Clemente." *Bulletino di Archeologia Cristiana* (2d series) 1 (1870): 129–53.

DeVisscher, Fernand. *Le Droit des Tombeaux Romains.* Milan: Giuffre Editore, 1963.

Donfried, Karl Paul, ed. *The Romans Debate: Essays on the Origin and Purpose of the Epistle.* Minneapolis: Augsburg, 1977.

Duff, A. M. *Freedmen in the Early Roman Empire.* New York: Barnes & Noble, 1968.

Edmundson, George. *The Church in Rome in the First Century.* London: Longmans, Green & Co., 1913.

Eggenberger, Christian. *Die Quellen der politischen Ethik des 1. Klemensbriefes.* Zurich: Zwingli Verlag, 1951.

Elliott, John H. "A Catholic Gospel: Reflections on 'Early Catholicism' in the New Testament." *Catholic Biblical Quarterly* 31 (1969): 213–23.

———. *A Home for the Homeless: A Social-Scientific Exegesis of 1 Peter, Its Situation and Strategy.* Minneapolis: Fortress, 1990.

Ermini, Letizia Pani. "L'Ipogeo detto dei Flavi in Domitilla I, II." *Revista di Archeologia Cristiana* 45 (1969): 119–73; 48 (1972): 235–69.

Faiure, Alexandre. "Le 'Systeme Normatif' dans la Lettre de Clement de Rome aux Corinthiens." *Revue de Sciences Religieuses* 54 (1980): 129–52.

Feissel, Denis. "Contributions a l'Epigraphie Grecque Chretienne de Rome." *Revista di Archeologia Cristiana* 58 (1982): 353–82.

Ferrua, Antonio. "Il Cubicolo dei Mattei nella Catacombe de S. Domitilla." *Revista di Archeologia Cristiana* 58 (1982): 305–21.

———. "Nomi de Catacombe nell'Iscrizioni in Lucinis." *Rendiconti Atti della Pont. Accademia Romana di Archeologia* 27b (1953): 247–54.

Filson, Floyd V. "The Significance of the Early House Churches." *Journal of Biblical Literature* 58 (1939): 105–12.

Finley, Moses I. *The Ancient Economy.* Berkeley: University of California Press, 1973.

———. *Ancient Slavery and Modern Ideology.* London: Chatto & Windus, 1980.

Finn, T. M. "Social Mobility, Imperial Civil Service and the Spread of Early Christianity." *Studia Patristica* 17 (1982): 31–37.

Frank, Tenney. *An Economic History of Rome.* 2d ed. Baltimore: Johns Hopkins University Press, 1927.

Frend, W.H.C. *The Early Church.* Philadelphia: Fortress, 1984.

———. *Saints and Sinners in the Early Church.* Wilmington, Del.: Michael Glazier, 1985.

Fuchs, Harald. *Die griechischen Friedensgedanken: Augustin und der antike Friedensgedanke.* New York: Garland, 1973.

Fuellenbach, John. *Ecclesiastical Office and the Primacy of Rome: An Evaluation of Recent Theological Discussion of* First Clement. Washington, D.C.: Catholic University of America Press, 1980.

Fuller, F. W. *The Primitive Saints and the See of Rome.* London: Longmans, Green, 1900.

Gager, John G. *Kingdom and Community: The Social World of Early Christianity.* Englewood Cliffs, N.J.: Prentice-Hall, 1975.

Gamble, Harry, Jr. *The Textual History of the Letter to the Romans: A Study in Textual and Literary Criticism.* Grand Rapids: Wm. B. Eerdmans, 1977.

Garnsey, Peter. *Social Status and Legal Privilege in the Roman Empire.* Oxford: Clarendon, 1970.

Gerke, Friedrich. *Die Stellung des ersten Clemensbriefes innerhalb der Entwicklung der altchristlichen Gemeindeverfassung und des Kirchenrechts.* Leipzig: J. C. Hinrichs, 1931.

Glimm, Francis X. *The Letter of St. Clement of Rome to the Corinthians.* The Fathers of the Church. Ed. Ludwid Schopp. Washington, D.C.: Catholic University of America Press, 1962.

Goodspeed, Edgar J. "*First Clement* Called Forth by Hebrews." *Journal of Biblical Literature* 30 (1911): 157–60.

———. *A History of Early Christian Literature.* Rev. R. M. Grant. Chicago: University of Chicago Press, 1966.

Grant, Robert M. *Early Christianity and Society: Seven Studies.* San Francisco: Harper & Row, 1977.

———. "Eusebius, H. E. VIII: Another Suggestion." *Vigiliae Christianae* 22 (1968): 16–18.

Grant, Robert M., and Holt H. Graham. *First and Second Clement.* New York: Thomas Nelson & Sons, 1965.

Grazzi, Luigi. *Il Papa dell'Anno 97 e 3 "Fedeli" di Roma.* Parma: Artegrafica Silva, 1975.

Guidobaldi, Federico. *Il Complesso Archeologico di San Clemente: Risultati degli Scavi Piu Recenti e Riesame dei Resti Architettonici.* San Clemente Miscellany 2. 2 vols. Ed. Leonard E. Boyle. Rome: Collegio San Clemente, 1978.

Hagner, Donald Alfred. *The Use of the Old and New Testaments in Clement of Rome.* Supplements to Novum Testamentum 34. Leiden: E. J. Brill, 1973.

Hall, A. "*1 Clement* as a Document of Transition." *La Ciudad de Dios* 181 (1968): 682–92.

Harnack, Adolf von. "Christianity and Christians at the Court of the Roman Emperors, before the Time of Constantine." *Princeton Review* 2 (1878): 239–80.

————. *Einführung in die Alte Kirchengeschichte: Das Schrieben der römischen Kirche und die korinthische aus der Zeit Domitians (I. Clemensbrief)*. Leipzig: J. C. Hinrichs, 1929.

————. "Der erste Klemensbrief. Eine Studie zur Bestimmung des Charakters des ältesten Heidenchristentums Sitzungsberichte der K." *Pruessischen Academie der Wissenschaften* (1909): 38–63.

————. *The Mission and Expansion of Christianity in the First Three Centuries*. Ed. and trans. James Moffatt. New York: Harper & Row, 1961.

Harris, J. Rendel. "On an Obscure Quotation in the First Epistle of Clement." *Journal of Biblical Literature* 29 (1910): 190–95.

Heintze, Werner. *Der Klemensroman und Seine Griechischen Quellen*. Leipzig: J. C. Hinrichs, 1914.

Hengel, Martin. *Property and Riches in the Early Church: Aspects of a Social History of Early Christianity*. Trans. John Bowden. Philadelphia: Fortress, 1974.

Hermansen, Gustav. *Ostia: Aspects of Roman City Life*. Edmonton, Alberta: University of Alberta Press, 1982.

Hill, Michael. *A Sociology of Religion*. London: Heinemann, 1973.

Hock, Ronald F. *The Social Context of Paul's Ministry: Tentmaking and Apostleship*. Philadelphia: Fortress, 1980.

Hopkins, Keith. *Conquerors and Slaves*. New York: Cambridge University Press, 1978.

Jackson, Elton F. "Status Consistency and Symptoms of Stress." *American Sociological Review* 27 (1962): 469–80.

Jaeger, Werner. *Early Christianity and Greek Paideia*. Cambridge: Harvard University Press, 1961.

Jaubert, Annie. *Clément de Rome: Épitre aux Corinthiens: Introduction, Texte, Traduction, Notes et Index*. Sources Chrétiennes 167. Ed. C. Mondësert. Paris: Les Éditions du Cerf, 1971.

————. "Les Sources de la Conception Militaire de L'Eglise en 1 Clément 37." *Vigiliae Christianae* 18 (1964): 74–84.

————. "Thémes Lévitiques dans la Prima Clementis." *Vigiliae Christianae* 18 (1964): 193–203.

Jewett, Robert. *A Chronology of Paul's Life*. Philadelphia: Fortress, 1979.

————. "Romans as an Ambassadorial Letter." *Interpretation* 36 (1982): 5–20.

Joly, Robert. *Hermas: Le Pasteur. Introduction, Texte Critique, Traduction et Notes*. 2d ed. Paris: Les Éditions du Cerf, 1968.

————. "Hermas et le Pasteur." *Vigiliae Christianae* 21 (1967): 201–18.

Jones, A.H.M. *The Greek City from Alexander to Justinian*. Oxford: Clarendon, 1940.

————. *The Roman Economy: Studies in Ancient Economic and Administrative History*. Ed. P. A. Brunt. Totowa, N.J.: Rowman & Littlefield, 1974.

Jordan, Heinrich. *Topographie der Stadt Rom im Altertum*. 4 vols. Berlin: Weidmannsche Buchhandlung, 1878.

Judge, E. A. "The Early Christians as a Scholastic Community: I and II." *Journal of Religious History* 1 (1960): 4–15; 2 (1961): 125–37.

———. *Rank and Status in the World of the Caesars and St. Paul.* Canterbury: University of Canterbury Press, 1981.

———. *The Social Pattern of the Christian Groups in the First Century.* London: Tyndale, 1960.

Judge, E. A., and G.S.R. Thomas. "The Origin of the Church at Rome: A New Solution?" *The Reformed Theological Review* 25 (1966): 81–94.

Junyent, Edoardo. "Nuove Indagini Sotto la Basilica Primitiva di San Clemente." *Revista di Archeologia Cristiana* 15 (1938): 147–52.

———. "La Primitiva Basilica di S. Clemente e le Costruzioni Antiche Circostanti." *Revista di Archeologia Cristiana* 5 (1928): 231–78.

———. *Il Titolo de San Clemente in Roma.* Rome: Pontificio Istituto de Archeologia Cristiana, 1932.

Kajanto, Iiro. *Onomastic Studies in the Early Christian Inscriptions of Rome and Carthage.* Helsinki: Tilsmann, 1963.

Keck, L. E. "On the Ethos of Early Christians." *Journal of the American Academy of Religion* 42 (1974): 435–52.

Keresztes, Paul. "The Imperial Roman Government and the Christian Church." *Aufstieg und Niedergang der Römischen Welt* II.23.1 (1979): 247–313.

———. "The Jews, the Christians, and Emperor Domitian." *Vigiliae Christianae* 27 (1978): 1–28.

———. "Law and Arbitrariness in the Persecution of the Christians and Justin's First Apology." *Vigiliae Christianae* 18 (1964): 204–14.

Kirsch, Johann Peter. *The Catacombs of Rome.* Trans. Giulio Belvederi. Rome: Societa "Amici Delle Catacombe," 1946.

———. *Die christliche Cultesgebäude im Altertum.* Cologne: J. P. Bachenn, 1893.

———. *Die römischen Titelkirchen im Altertum.* Paderborn: Ferdinand Schöningh, 1918.

Kleist, James A. *The Epistles of St. Clement of Rome and St. Ignatius of Antioch.* Westminster, Md.: Newman, 1961.

Knoch, Otto. *Eigenart und Bedeutung der Eschatologie im theologischen Aufriss des ersten Clemensbriefes.* Bonn: Peter Hanstein, 1964.

Knopf, Rudolf. *Der Erste Clemensbrief: Untersucht und Herausgegeben.* Leipzig: J. C. Hinrichs, 1899.

———. *Die Lehre der Zwölf Apostel; Die Zwei Clemensbriefe.* Tübingen: J.C.B. Mohr, 1920.

Koenig, John. *New Testament Hospitality: Partnership with Strangers as Promise and Mission.* Philadelphia: Fortress, 1985.

Kraabel, A. T. "Jews in Imperial Rome: More Archaeological Evidence from an Oxford Collection." *Journal of Jewish Studies* 30 (1979): 41–58.

Krautheimer, Richard. *Early Christian and Byzantine Architecture.* 4th ed. New York: Viking Penguin, 1986.

Kreissig, Heinz. "Zur Sozialen Zusammensetzung der Frühchristlichen Gemeinden im ersten Jahrhundert u. Z." *Eirene* 6 (1967): 91–100.

Lake, Kirsopp. *The Apostolic Fathers.* 2 vols. Loeb Classical Library. Cambridge: Harvard University Press, 1912.

―――. "The *Shepherd of Hermas* and Christian Life in Rome in the Second Century." *Harvard Theological Review* 4 (1911): 25–46.

Lampe, Peter. *Die stadtrömischen Christen in den ersten beiden Jahrhunderten.* Tübingen: J.C.B. Mohr, 1987. English translation forthcoming from Fortress Press.

Lana, Italo. *La Teorizzazione della Collaborazione degli Intellettuali con il Potere Politico in Quintiliano.* Torino: G. Giappichelli, 1973.

Lanciani, Rudolfo. *The Ruins and Excavations of Ancient Rome.* New York: Houghton Mifflin, 1897.

La Piana, George. "Foreign Groups in Rome During the First Centuries of the Empire." *Harvard Theological Review* 20 (1927): 183–403.

―――. "The Roman Church at the End of the Second Century." *Harvard Theological Review* 18 (1925): 201–77.

Lattimore, Richard. *Themes in Greek and Latin Epitaphs.* Urbana: University of Illinois Press, 1962.

Laub, Franz. *Die Begegnung des frühen Christentums mit der antiken Sklaverei.* Stuttgart: Katholisches Bibelwerk, 1982.

Leon, Harry J. *The Jews of Ancient Rome.* Philadelphia: Jewish Publication Society of America, 1960.

Lietzmann, Hans. *The Beginnings of the Christian Church.* 4 vols. Trans. B. L. Woolf. London: Lutterworth, 1949.

Lightfoot, J. B. *The Apostolic Fathers.* 4 vols. London: Macmillan & Co., 1890.

Lluis-Font, Pedro. "Sources de la Doctrine d'Hermas sur les Deux Esprits." *Revue d'Ascetique et de Mystique* 39 (1953): 83–98.

Lösch, Stephan. *Epistula Claudiana: Der neuentdeckte Brief des Kaisers Claudius vom Jahre 41 n. Chr. und das Urchristentum.* Rottenburg: Adolf Bader, 1930.

Lugli, Giuseppe. *Itinerario di Roma Antica.* Milan: Periodici Scientifica, 1970.

MacMullen, Ramsay. *Christianizing the Roman Empire.* New Haven: Yale University Press, 1984.

―――. *Roman Social Relations: 50 B.C. to A.D. 284.* New Haven: Yale University Press, 1974.

Mâle, Emile. *The Early Churches of Rome.* Trans. David Buxton. Chicago: Quadrangle Books, 1960.

Malherbe, Abraham J. *Social Aspects of Early Christianity.* 2d ed. Philadelphia: Fortress, 1983.

Malina, Bruce J. *Christian Origins and Cultural Anthropology: Practical Models for Biblical Interpretation.* Atlanta: John Knox, 1986.

―――. *The New Testament World: Insights From Cultural Anthropology.* Atlanta: John Knox, 1981.

Mayer, Herbert T. "Clement of Rome and His Use of Scripture." *Concordia Theological Monthly* 42 (1971): 536–40.

Mazzarino, Santo. *L'Impero Romano.* 3 vols. Rome-Bari: Laterza, 1973.

Mazzoleni, Danilo. "Le Catacombe Ebraiche di Roma." *Studi Romani* 23 (1975): 289–302.

Meeks, Wayne A. *The First Urban Christians: The Social World of the Apostle Paul.* New York: Yale University Press, 1983.

————. *The Moral World of the First Christians.* Library of Early Christianity 6. Philadelphia: Westminster, 1986.

Meeks, Wayne A., and Robert L. Wilken. *Jews and Christians in Antioch in the First Four Centuries of the Common Era.* Missoula, Mont.: Scholars Press, 1978.

Meinhold, Peter. "Geschehen und Deutung im Ersten Clemensbrief." *Zeitschrift für Kirchengeschichte* 58 (1939): 82–129.

Meneghelli, Ruggero. *Fede Cristiana e Potere Politico in Clemente Romano.* Bologna: Casa Editrice Patron, 1970.

Merrill, E. T. *Essays in Early Christian History.* London: Macmillan, 1924.

Mikat, Paul. *Die Bedeutung der Begriffe Stasis und Aponoia für das Verstandnis des 1. Clemensbriefes.* Arbeitgemeinschaft für Forschung Des Landes Nordrhein-Westfalen. Geistswissenschaften 155. Cologne: Westdeutscher, 1969.

Milburn, R.L.P. "The Persecution of Domitian." *Church Quarterly* 139 (1945): 154–64.

Moreau, J. L. "Rome and the New Testament—Another Look." *Biblical Research* 10 (1965): 24–43.

Morgan, Lewis H. *Ancient Society.* Cambridge: Harvard University Press, 1964.

Mullooly, Joseph. *Saint Clement, Pope and Martyr, and His Basilica in Rome.* 2d. ed. Rome: G. Barbera, 1873.

Munck, J. "Jewish Christianity in Post-Apostolic Times." *New Testament Studies* 6 (1960): 103–16.

Nash, Ernest. *Pictorial Dictionary of Ancient Rome.* New York: Frederick A. Praeger, 1965.

Nestori, Aldo. Review of *Il Complesso Archeologico di S. Clemente. Risultato degli Scavi Piu Recenti e Riesame dei Resti Architettonici,* by Federico Guidobaldi. *Revista di Archeologia Cristiana* 56 (1980): 187–90.

Nielsen, Charles Merritt. "Clement of Rome and Moralism." *Church History* 31 (1962): 131–50.

Nolan, Louis. *The Basilica of San Clemente in Rome.* Rome: Tipografia Cuggiani, 1910.

Norris, Frederick W. "Ignatius, Polycarp, and *1 Clement*: Walter Bauer Reconsidered." *Vigiliae Christianae* 30 (1976): 23–44.

Oetting, Walter W. *The Church of the Catacombs: The Introduction to the Surging Life of the Early Church from the Apostles to A.D. 250, Based on Firsthand Accounts.* St. Louis: Concordia, 1964.

Osborne, John. *Early Mediaeval Wall-Paintings in the Lower Church of San Clemente, Rome.* New York: Garland, 1984.

Osiek, Carolyn. *Rich and Poor in the* Shepherd of Hermas. Washington, D.C.: Catholic Biblical Association of America, 1983.

————. *What Are They Saying about the Social Setting of the New Testament?* New York: Paulist, 1984.

Paschke, Franz. *Die Beiden griechischen Klementinen-Epitomen und ihre Anhänge.* Berlin: Academie, 1966.

Pergola, Philippe. "Coemeterium Domitillae: le Labyrinthe de la Via Ardeatina." *Dossiers de L'Archeologie* 18 (1976): 86–99.

―――. "La Condamnation des Flaviens 'Chretiens' sous Domitien: Persecution Religieuse ou Repression à Caractere Politique?" *Melanges de l'Ecole Francaise de Rome Antiquite* 90 (1978): 407–23.

―――. "Il Praedium Domitillae sulla Via Ardeatina: Analisi StoricoTopografica delle Testimonianze Pagane Fino alla Meta del III Sec." *Revista di Archeologia Cristiana* 55 (1979): 313–35.

―――. "La Region Dite du Bon Pasteur dans le Cimetiere de Domitilla sur l'Ardeatina: Etude Topographique de son Origine." *Revista di Archeologia Cristiana* 51 (1975): 65–96.

―――. "La Region Dite des Flavii Aurelii dans la Catacombe de Domitille." *Melanges de l'Ecole Francaise de Rome Antiquite* 95 (1983): 183–248.

Pernveden, Lage. *The Concept of the Church in the* Shepherd of Hermas. Lund: C.W.K. Gleerup, 1966.

Peterson, Erik. "Praescriptum des 1 Clemens-briefes." In *Pro Regno, Pro Sanctuario: Festschrift für G. van der Leeuw.* Ed. W. J. Kooiman and J. M. van Veen, 351–57. Nijkerk: Callenbach, 1950.

Peterson, Joan M. "House-Churches in Rome." *Vigiliae Christianae* 23 (1969): 264–72.

Platner, Samuel B. *A Topographical Dictionary of Ancient Rome.* Rev. Thomas Ashby. Rome: Bretschneider, 1965.

Preller, Ludwig. *Die Regionen der Stadt Rom.* Jena: Carl Hochhausen, 1846.

Quinn, J. D. " 'Seven times he wore chains' (*1 Clem* 5:6)." *Journal of Biblical Literature* 97 (1978): 574–76.

Räisänen, Heikki. " 'Werkgerechtigkeit'—eine 'frühkatholishche' Lehre? Überlegungen zum 1. Klemensbrief." *Studia Theologica* 37 (1983): 79–99.

Reiling, J. *Hermas and Christian Prophecy: A Study of the Eleventh Mandate.* Supplements to Novum Testamentum 37. Ed. W. C. van Unnik. Leiden: E. J. Brill, 1973.

Richardson, Cyril C., ed. *The Letter of the Church of Rome to the Church of Corinth.* Early Christian Fathers. Philadelphia: Westminster, 1953.

Riddle, Donald W. "The Messages of the *Shepherd of Hermas*: A Study in Social Control." *The Journal of Religion* 7 (1927): 561–77.

Rohde, Joachim. "Häresie und Schisma im ersten Clemensbrief und in den Ignatius-briefen." *Novum Testamentum* 10 (1968): 217–33.

Rordorf, W. "Die Neronische Christenverfolgung im Spiegel der apokryphen Paulsakten." *New Testament Studies* 28 (1981): 365–74.

Rostovtzeff, M. *The Social and Economic History of the Roman Empire.* Ed. P. M. Fraser. 2d ed. Oxford: Clarendon, 1957.

Saller, Richard P. *Personal Patronage Under the Early Empire.* Cambridge: Cambridge University Press, 1982.

Sanders, E. P., et al., eds. *Jewish and Christian Self-Definition*. 2 vols. Philadelphia: Fortress, 1981.

Sanders, Louis. *L'Hellenisme de Saint Clement de Rome et le Paulinisme*. Lovanii: Universitas Catholica, 1943.

Schermann, D. Theodor. *Griechische Zauberpapyri und das Gemeinde- und Dankgebet im I. Klemensbriefe*. Leipzig: J. C. Hinrichs, 1909.

Schoeps, Hans-Joachim. *Jewish Christianity: Factional Disputes in the Early Church*. Trans. Douglas R. A. Hare. Philadelphia: Fortress, 1969.

Schweizer, B. "Glaube und Werke bei Klemens Romanus." *Theologische Quartalschrift* 85 (1903): 417–37.

Scroggs, Robin. "The Earliest Christian Communities as Sectarian Movement." In *Christianity, Judaism and Other Greco-Roman Cults: Studies for Morton Smith at Sixty*. 5 vols. Studies in Judaism in Late Antiquity 12. Ed. Jacob Neusner, 2:1–23. Leiden: E. J. Brill, 1975.

————. "The Sociological Interpretation of the New Testament: The Present State of Research." *New Testament Studies* 26 (1980): 164–79.

Seitz, Oscar J. F. "The Relationship of the *Shepherd of Hermas* to the Epistle of James." *Journal of Biblical Literature* 63 (1944): 131–40.

Sherwin-White, A. N. *The Letters of Pliny: A Historical and Social Commentary*. Oxford: Clarendon, 1966.

————. *Roman Society and Roman Law in the New Testament*. Oxford: Clarendon, 1963.

————. "Why Were the Early Christians Persecuted?—An Amendment." *Past and Present* 27 (1964): 23–27.

Sjoberg, Gideon. *The Preindustrial City*. New York: Free Press, 1960.

Smallwood, E. Mary. "Domitian's Attitude toward the Jews and Judaism." *Classical Philology* 51 (1956): 1–13.

Smith, J. Z. "The Social Description of Early Christianity." *Religious Studies Review* 1 (1975): 19–25.

Smith, Morton. "The Report about Peter in *1 Clem*. 5:4." *New Testament Studies* 7 (1960): 86–88.

Snyder, Graydon F. *The Shepherd of Hermas*. 6 vols. The Apostolic Fathers: A New Translation and Commentary 6. Ed. Robert M. Grant. Camden, N.J.: Thomas Nelson, 1968.

Stambaugh, John E., and David L. Balch. *The New Testament in Its Social Environment*. Library of Early Christianity 2. Ed. Wayne A. Meeks. Philadelphia: Westminster, 1986.

Stock, St. George. "Hermas and Cebes—A Reply." *Journal of Philology* 28 (1903): 87–93.

Stuiber, A. "Clemens Romanus I." In *Reallexikon für Antike und Christentum*. Ed. Th. Klauser, 3:188–206. Stuttgart: Hiersemann, 1957.

Styger, Paolo. "L'Origine del Cimitero di Domitilla sull'Ardeatina." *Rendiconti Atti della Pont. Accademia Romana di Archeologia* 5 (1926–27): 89–144.

Sundberg, Albert C., Jr. "Canon Muratori: A Fourth-Century List." *Harvard Theological Review* 66 (1973): 1–41.

Syme, Ronald. *Tacitus.* 2 vols. Oxford: Clarendon, 1958.

Taylor, C. "Hermas and Cebes." *Journal of Philology* 27 (1901): 276–319.

Taylor, Lily Ross. "Freedmen and Freeborn in the Epitaphs of Imperial Rome." *American Journal of Philology* 82 (1961): 113–32.

Theissen, Gerd. *The Social Setting of Pauline Christianity: Essays on Corinth.* Trans. John H. Schultz. Philadelphia: Fortress, 1982.

Theron, Daniel J. *Evidence of Tradition: Selected Source Material for the Study of the Early Church.* Grand Rapids: Baker, 1958.

Treat, John Harvey. *The Catacombs of Rome and a History of the Tombs of the Apostles Peter and Paul.* Boston: Old Corner Bookstore, 1907.

Trinci, M. Cecchelli. "Osservazioni sulla Basilica Inferiore di S. Clemente in Roma." *Revista di Archeologia Cristiana* 50 (1974): 93–120.

Troeltsch, Ernst. *The Social Teaching of the Christian Churches.* 2 vols. Trans. Olive Wyon. New York: Harper & Row, 1960.

Tucker, T. G. *Life in the Roman World of Nero and St. Paul.* New York: Macmillan, 1910.

Turner, C. H. "The *Shepherd of Hermas* and the Problem of Its Text." *Journal of Theological Studies* 21 (1920): 193–209.

Van Cauwelaert, R. "L'Intervention de L'Eglise de Rome a Corinthe Vers L'an 96." *Revue D'Histoire Ecclesiastique* 31 (1935): 267–306.

Van Unnik, W. C. "Is *1 Clement* 20 Purely Stoic?" *Vigiliae Christianae* 2 (1950): 181–90.

———. "First-Century A.D. Literary Culture and Early Christian History." *Colloquy* 1 (1970): 1–21.

———. "*1 Clement* 34 and the Sanctus." *Vigiliae Christianae* 5 (1951): 204–48.

———. "Noch Einmal 'Tiefer Friede': Nachschrift zu dem Aufsatz von Herrn Dr. K. Beyschlag." *Vigiliae Christianae* 26 (1972): 24–28.

———. "Le Nombre des e'Lus dans la Première Épitre de Clément." *Revue D'Histoire et de Philosophie Religieuses* 42 (1962): 237–46.

———. " 'Tiefer Friede' (1. Klemens 2,2)." *Vigiliae Christianae* 24 (1970): 261–79.

Wadsworth, Emily L. "The Vault Under San Clemente." *American Academy in Rome: Memoirs* 4 (1924): 56–57.

Ward-Perkins, J. B. *Roman Imperial Architecture.* 2d ed. New York: Penguin, 1981.

Weaver, P.R.C. *"Familia Caesaris": A Social Study of the Emperor's Freedmen and Slaves.* Cambridge: Cambridge University Press, 1972.

———. "Social Mobility in the Early Roman Empire: The Evidence of Imperial Freedmen and Slaves." *Past and Present* 37 (1967): 3–20.

Weber, Max. *Economy and Society.* 2 vols. Trans. and ed. Guenther Roth and Claus Wittich. Berkeley: University of California Press, 1978.

———. " 'Objectivity' in Social Science and Social Policy." In *The Methodology of the Social Sciences.* Trans. and ed. Edward A. Shils and Henry A. Finch, 267–301. New York: Humanities Press, 1949.

————. "Politics as a Vocation." In *From Max Weber: Essays in Sociology.* Trans. and ed. H. H. Gerth and C. Wright Mills, 77–128. New York: Oxford University Press, 1946.

————. *The Protestant Ethic and the Spirit of Capitalism.* Trans. T. Parsons. 1920–21. Reprint. New York: Charles Scribner's Sons, 1958.

————. "The Social Psychology of the World Religions." In *From Max Weber: Essays in Sociology.* Trans. and ed. H. H. Gerth and C. Wright Mills, 267–301. New York: Oxford University Press, 1946.

Weiss, Bardo. "Amt und Eschatologie im I. Clemensbrief." *Theologie und Philosophie* 50 (1975): 70–83.

Werner, Eric. "Post-Biblical Hebraisms in the *Prima Clementis.*" In *Harry Austryn Wolfson Jubilee Volume,* 794–818. Jerusalem: American Academy for Jewish Research, 1965.

Wickert, Ulrich. "Paulus, der Erste Klemens und Stephan von Rom: drei Epochen der frühen Kirche aus ökumenischer Sicht." *Zeitschrift für Kirchengeschichte* 79 (1968): 145–58.

Wiefel, Wolfgang. "The Jewish Community in Ancient Rome and the Origins of Roman Christianity." In *The Romans Debate,* ed. K. P. Donfried, 100–119. Minneapolis: Augsburg, 1977.

Wilken, Robert L. *Aspects of Wisdom in Judaism and Early Christianity.* Notre Dame, Ind.: University of Notre Dame Press, 1975.

————. *The Christians as the Romans Saw Them.* New Haven: Yale University Press, 1984.

————. "Toward a Sociological Interpretation of Early Christian Apologetics." *Church History* 39 (1970): 437–58.

Wilson, Bryan R. "An Analysis of Sect Development." *American Sociological Review* 24 (1959): 3–15.

————. *Magic and the Millennium: A Sociological Study of Religious Movements of Protest among Tribal and Third World Peoples.* London: Heinemann, 1973.

————. *Religion in Sociological Perspective.* New York: Oxford University Press, 1982; London: Heinemann, 1982.

————. *Religious Sects: A Sociological Study.* New York: McGraw-Hill, 1970.

Wilson, John Warwick. "The *First Epistle of Clement:* A Theology of Power." Ph.D. Diss., Duke University, 1976.

Wilson, William Jerome. "The Career of the Prophet Hermas." *Harvard Theological Review* 20 (1927): 21–62.

Wong, D.W.F. "Natural and Divine Order in *1 Clement.*" *Vigiliae Christianae* 31 (1977): 81–87.

Woodhead, A. G. *The Study of Greek Inscriptions.* Cambridge: Cambridge University Press, 1959.

Wrede, William. *Untersuchungen zum ersten Klemensbriefe.* Göttingen: Dieterich'schen University Press, 1981.

Young, F. W. "The Relation of *1 Clement* to the Epistle of James." *Journal of Biblical Literature* 67 (1948): 339–45.

Ziegler, Adolf W. *Neue Studien zum ersten Klemensbrief.* Munich: Manz, 1958.

211

INDEX

Acts of Paul, 80
Apartments, Roman, 4-5, 8, 44, 64, 68, 82-83. *See also* Insula
Apostle, 11, 13, 15, 31, 46, 91-92, 96-97, 102, 107, 124, 145, 151, 153, 175-78, 188-90
Apostolic succession, 151, 189
Aquila, 11, 13-14, 19-21, 41
Associations, voluntary, 31, 36-39, 41, 46, 80-81, 101, 115, 167-68, 186
 funeral, 88
 religious, 37-38, 80-81
Authority ideal types, 145, 149, 151-52, 160, 186. *See also* Weber, Max
 bureaucratic, 146-47
 charismatic, 145-48, 150, 152-55, 157-61, 165, 170, 175, 199
 and gerontocracy, 147
 and patrimonialism, 147
 traditional, 28-29, 71, 122, 125, 145-52, 158-60, 188-91, 194

Barnard, L. W., 22, 91, 155
Basilica, 2, 44-45, 51-52, 54, 71-72, 74-75, 85-86, 198
Bishop, 31, 34, 97, 108, 130, 145, 148, 151, 153, 175-76, 178-79, 187, 189-93
Blameless leaders at Corinth, 31, 94-95, 123-24, 150, 168, 174-76
Bruce, F. F., 180
Bureaucratic authority. *See* Authority ideal types

Callistus, Bishop of Rome, 50, 109, 193
Catacombs, Roman, 2, 11, 39, 48-52, 54, 57, 59-60, 188, 191, 193. *See also* Cemeteries
 catacomb of Domitilla, 48, 50-51, 54
 Christian, 49-50, 57, 188, 193
 and hypogea, 49, 55-59

Cemeteries, Roman, 38, 48-51, 54, 59, 61-62, 193. *See also* Catacombs
 pagan sepulcher, 54
Charismatic authority. *See* Authority ideal types
Chrestus, 12-13
Citizen, 4, 6-7, 11, 13, 17-18, 21, 24, 27, 29-30, 32, 35, 100-101, 103-4, 120, 122, 132, 134-35, 139, 142, 167
Citizenship, 6, 11, 21, 35, 100, 134-35, 139, 142, 167
Classes, Roman social. *See* Status
Claudius, 12, 29-30, 33-34, 65, 75, 93
 edict of, 12, 34
Clemens, Titus Flavius, 25-28, 31-33, 46, 48, 51-53, 60, 62-63, 79, 88, 91, 198
Clement of Alexandria, 97, 157
Clients. *See Familia*
Cognomen. *See* Names, Roman
Concord, 105, 136-38, 142, 180-81

Deacon, 151, 153, 176-79, 190
Denomination, 161-63, 165
Dio Cassius, 26, 28, 60-61
Dionysius of Corinth, 92, 97
Dissension, 15, 135, 137-38, 142, 158, 178, 199
Dominicum 87
Domitian, 25-28, 33, 51, 53-54, 61-62, 69, 71, 75, 82-83, 88
Domus Aurea. See Nero

Edict of Claudius. *See* Claudius
Elliott, John H., 163
Epistle to the Romans, 13-14, 18
Eusebius, 28, 31, 107-8, 191

Familia (Roman household), 2, 15, 30, 64, 116, 121-27, 129, 132, 135, 142, 147, 196

Jewish community in Rome, 3, 9-10, 13, 15-16, 40
Jews, 9-20, 26-27, 35-36, 38-40, 48, 93, 173
Judaism, 10-12, 22, 27-28, 34, 40-41, 45, 47, 49, 54, 56, 160, 164, 173, 184

La Piana, George, 39-40, 143, 192
Legitimacy, 36, 96, 133, 145-46, 148-49, 152, 158, 175, 177
Leon, Harry, 11, 27
Lightfoot, J. B., 29, 33, 86, 92
Pope, Liston, 162
Ludus Magnus, 69-70, 76

Masters, 8, 29-30, 32, 38, 102-3, 105, 108, 117-18, 122-23, 125, 129, 137-38, 147
Merrill, E. T., 32, 94
Mithras religion, 72, 74, 83-87
Monoepiscopacy, 34, 92-93, 108-9, 111, 176, 189, 199
Mullooly, Joseph, 71-72, 74
Muratorian canon, 94, 107, 110, 112, 158, 185, 198-99

Names, Roman
cognomen, 29, 32, 60, 198
praenomen, 29
Nero, 11, 16-18, 30, 39, 64-65, 69, 71, 75, 82, 88, 92-93, 97, 129, 140, 149-50, 159, 173
and his *Domus Aurea*, 64-65, 69-71, 88
New Testament codes of behavior. *See* Household codes
Niebuhr, H. Richard, 161-62

Opus quadratum, 75
Opus reticulatum, 54
Origen, 107
Osiek, Carolyn 22, 106-8, 110-11, 119, 125, 127
Ostia, 77, 80-81

Paschal controversy, 191-92, 199
Patrons. *See Familia*
Patronage, 29, 130-31, 133-34, 142-43, 196, 198
Pernveden, Lage, 156
Persecution, 16-18, 59, 87, 90-92, 97, 112, 140-41, 149, 154, 159, 167-68, 173, 183-85
Phoenix myth, 149
Pliny the Younger, 30, 96, 98, 128

Polycarp, 92, 191
Poor Christians, 119, 133-34, 158
and the pious poor tradition, 125, 134, 143
Presbyters, 44, 93, 95-96, 111, 124, 150-51, 156, 175-76, 178-79, 191-92
Prisca, 19-21
Prophets, 2, 107, 109, 114, 145-46, 148, 155-58, 176-78
false, 155-56, 177
true, 114, 155-58, 178

Regions of Rome, 16, 65, 68
Region III, 70-71
Reiling, J., 22, 107, 113, 115, 155, 178
Religious associations. *See* Associations
Rhoda, 21, 24, 117-18
Rich Christians, 24, 119, 133-34, 158
Roman army, 32, 139-41, 143, 180

San Clemente, 52, 63-65, 68-69, 71, 74-75, 80-81, 85-88, 198
basilicas at San Clemente, 52, 71, 198
and Mithras sanctuary below, 74, 85
and tufa building below (warehouse), 49, 70, 72, 74-77, 79-84, 87- 89, 198
Schism, 90, 135, 137, 171, 173-74, 177
Sects, 16, 18, 25, 40, 92, 98, 111-12, 118, 130, 134, 150, 160-70, 173-79, 181-86, 195-97. *See also* Weber, Max
exclusiveness of, 164, 169
level of commitment of, 164, 166, 168, 181
protest orientation of, 166, 184
and spontaneity, 165, 174, 197
unworthy members in, 166, 170-72, 186
world orientation of, 179, 197
Septuagint, 11, 104, 129
Shepherd of Hermas, 21, 35, 97, 105-6, 121, 152, 194-96
Mandate 1: 22-23, 114, 116-18, 126, 129, 155, 157-58, 177
Mandate 2: 118
Mandate 3: 23-24, 156
Mandate 4: 115, 167-68, 172
Mandate 5: 129, 169, 181
Mandate 6: 116, 181
Mandate 7: 116, 119, 167, 181
Mandate 8: 116, 119, 122, 125, 130, 181
Mandate 10: 117, 129, 182
Mandate 11: 22-23, 114, 155, 157-58, 177-78